A HISTORY OF THE
St. Louis Globe-Democrat

A HISTORY OF THE

St. Louis Globe-Democrat

JIM ALLEE HART

University of Missouri Press • *Columbia*

To

Dr. Frank Luther Mott

Preface

THIS STUDY is primarily a history of one American newspaper. It is impossible, however, to separate the history of a single newspaper from the history of the times during which the newspaper was published. Nor is it possible to separate the history of one newspaper from the development of American journalism. Therefore I have given much attention to the events and the people of the period of the *Globe-Democrat's* development, and have attempted also to show how one paper has contributed to the evolution of the American press.

The compression of 108 years of the *St. Louis Globe-Democrat's* history into a few hundred pages has necessitated the omission of many incidents and facts. Many people who contributed to the development of this newspaper have not been mentioned. However, though my sympathetic admiration for what the *Globe-Democrat* has done through the years should be apparent, no attempt has been made to hide the few skeletons in its closet.

I am deeply grateful to the many individuals who encouraged and helped with the preparation of the manuscript. Dr. William Taft first suggested the subject, and Dr. Frank Luther Mott, to whom the book is dedicated, made the research task exciting by his enthusiasm and wise counsel. Richard H. Amberg, publisher of the *St. Louis Globe-Democrat*, and his staff were extremely kind and helpful in making material available, and Douglas B. Houser graciously furnished information about the Houser family, who were so long a part of the newspaper. Valuable assistance was given, too, by the officials and librarians of the State Historical Society of Missouri, especially Kenneth B. Holmes; the Missouri Historical Society, St. Louis; the Library of the University of Missouri; the Library of Congress; the Filson Club,

Louisville, Kentucky; the St. Louis Mercantile Library; the St. Louis Public Library; and Chubb Library, Ohio University, Athens.

I also wish to thank the following publishers and individuals:

Appleton-Century-Crofts, Inc., for permission to quote from Casper S. Yost's *Principles of Journalism*, Copyright, 1924, D. Appleton and Co.

The Trustees of the Theodore Dreiser Estate and the World Publishing Company for permission to quote from Theodore Dreiser's *A Book about Myself*.

E. P. Dutton & Co., Inc., for granting permission to use material from Ian Anstruther's *Dr. Livingston, I Presume*.

Louisiana State University Press for granting permission to use material from James W. Markham's *Bovard of the Post-Dispatch*.

McGraw-Hill Book Company, Inc., for granting permission to quote from Robert C. Harper's *Lincoln and the Press*.

The Macmillan Company for granting permission to use material from the following: Alfred McClung Lee's *The Daily Newspaper in America*, Allan Nevins, *The Emergence of Modern America*, Frank Luther Mott's *American Journalism*, Dixon Wecter's *The Age of the Great Depression*, Arthur M. Schlesinger's *The Rise of the City*, and Ida M. Tarbell's *The Nationalizing of Business*.

Rutgers University Press for granting permission to quote from Roy P. Bassler, *et al.*, *The Collected Works of Abraham Lincoln*.

Simon & Schuster, Inc., for granting permission to quote from Don C. Seitz's *Joseph Pulitzer, His Life and Letters*.

The Stackpole Company for granting permission to quote from Orrick Johns's *Time of Our Lives*.

The State Historical Society of Wisconsin for granting permission to quote from *Intimate Letters of Carl Schurz*, translated by Joseph Schafer.

University of Pittsburgh Press for granting permission to use material from Cutler J. Andrews' *The North Reports the War*.

Charles Scribner's Sons for granting permission to quote from Charles Lindbergh's *The Spirit of St. Louis* and to use material from Royal Cortissoz's *Life of Whitelaw Reid*.

Professor William E. Smith, Miami University, Oxford, Ohio, for permission to quote from his book, *The Francis Preston Blair Family in Politics*.

Mr. R. M. Stanley for permission to quote from *The Auto-biography of Sir Henry Morton Stanley*.

I appreciate, too, the cooperation of the *St. Louis Globe-Democrat* and the State Historical Society of Missouri in making available photographs from their collections for reproduction in this book.

JIM ALLEE HART

Ohio University
August, 1961

Table of Contents

Chapter I

In the Beginning

IN THE decade before the Civil War the dominant social pattern of Missouri was in the Southern tradition. But in St. Louis, where by 1851 the population had mushroomed to 77,716, the picture was changing. The river-front city teemed with crowds of rough river men; New England business men who favored free labor; soft-spoken Southern business men and plantation owners; German and Irish laborers who had fled the oppression of their native lands; dark-skinned, often lazy slaves; roustabouts on the river levee; merchants, clerks, artisans; and hard-eyed gamblers—on the whole, a polyglot society. The hordes of German immigrants, many of them professional men who had flocked to the city after 1848, were beginning to pose social, economic, and political problems. Thrifty New England business men and manufacturers vied with the easy-going Southerners for the rich trade of the Southwest. City leaders and the socially-dominant Southerners looked with condescension on the more recently arrived Northerners and on the freedom-loving Germans who lived in the southern part of the city. Fires, kindled by divergent social and political beliefs, smoldered under outwardly cordial greetings on the steps of the Courthouse and of the Post Office. St. Louis had become the focal point in the state for the struggle of free labor versus slave labor and for the repeal of the Missouri Compromise.[1]

Into this atmosphere was born the *Missouri Democrat*, a newspaper that Abraham Lincoln was to say was worth more to the North than ten regiments of soldiers,[2] a paper whose publishers and editors were to become recognized nationally as leaders and journalists.

It may have been Francis P. Blair, Jr., familiarly known as

"Frank," who in the spring of 1852 persuaded a group of St. Louis business men that the time had come for the city to have a Free-Soil journal. These men, who believed that the people in the territories should decide whether their states would be admitted as free or slave states to the Union, advanced the money to buy a Ruggles press and other printing equipment.[3] The equipment was installed in the office of the *St. Louis Union*, a newspaper already printing the comments of the aging Thomas Hart Benton, the Free-Soil candidate for representative to the United States Congress. In due course, on July 1, St. Louisans read their first *Daily Missouri Democrat*.[4]

Typical of many papers of that time, it was a seven-column, four-page paper with more than three-fourths of its space devoted to advertisements called "cards." Six columns on the first page were usually filled with these business notices. The editorials appeared on the second page. A half-column of city news items and a half-column of river news shared space with the "cards" on the third page, and sometimes a poem was crowded into a corner of the back page.

Designed primarily to promote the unpopular Free-Soil tenets and Benton's candidacy for Congress, the *Democrat* promised to reanimate the state with "fresh questions, fresh vigor, and fresh men."[5] Blair was the paper's chief editor, but Benton and B. Gratz Brown, Blair's cousin, also wrote editorials. Benton always insisted on seeing his matter in proof, and it fell to the lot of a round-faced German youth in the business office of the *Union*, Daniel M. Houser, to carry the proof slips to Benton's home.[6] Later Houser was to become part owner of the paper.

Frank Blair, the first editor of the *Democrat*, was the son of Francis Preston Blair, who had been prominent in the Washington political scene during Andrew Jackson's presidency. Red-headed, sandy-complexioned, and without an ounce of surplus flesh, Frank, a veteran of the Mexican War, was peppery, energetic, even militant. Ten years earlier, he and his brother Montgomery had established a law office in St. Louis, and both had become leaders in the Free-Soil branch of the Democratic party in 1848.[7] A master of irony and sarcasm, Frank, never so happy as when he was denouncing someone, was soon recognized for his fiery campaign speeches, delivered in his unmusical, but booming voice, and for his hard-hitting editorials which had appeared in the *Signal*, the *Barnburner*, and the *Union*.[8]

From the first, Free-Soil opponents called the *Democrat* a "dirty little sheet."[9] The new paper was attacked in the editorial columns of rival journals—the *Missouri Republican*, leading newspaper in St. Louis; the *St. Louis Intelligencer*; and even the *Union*, in whose shop the *Democrat* was printed. The *Republican* claimed the new paper had a "reckless and total disregard for the truth" and it could not find room in its issues for Benton's speech when the *Democrat* sent over proofs of it.[10]

As was to be expected in that party press era, the *Democrat* editor soon became embroiled in controversies with rival editors. The spirited Blair and Lorenzo Pickering, editor of the *Union*, attacked each other bitterly through the columns of their papers. Then on one dark night as Blair came from a political meeting in the Courthouse, someone shot at him and ran. Blair fired once, ran to the bottom of the steps, and fired again. The *Union* editor was arrested, but for lack of proof no action against him was taken. Almost immediately, however, Pickering left St. Louis. Blair paid a one-dollar fine for participating in a challenge to fight a duel.[11]

By this time, however, the owners of the *Democrat* had made more satisfactory arrangements for the publishing of their paper. Neither Blair nor Brown, both of whom were running for the State Legislature, could devote full time to the *Democrat*. It had soon become apparent that, if the journal were to survive, someone who knew the newspaper business should direct its publication. When the misunderstanding with the *Union* developed, the owners had approached William McKee and William Hill, who ran a job printing shop on Second Street. The two printers were given the *Democrat* for the use of their shop in publishing it.[12] Thus McKee gained his half interest in the paper. After August 1, 1852, Hill and McKee were listed as joint proprietors on the masthead.

The wonder is that McKee had not been chosen to print the

paper in the first place. All St. Louis knew that he was a strong
Free-Soil advocate. Had he not already published two Free-Soil
newspapers in St. Louis? Was he not a New York Irishman? Had
he not learned newspapering on New York journals under Major
Mordecai Noah and James Watson Webb?[13]

William McKee, who was to direct the course of the *Democrat*
for the next quarter of a century, was then thirty-seven years old.
He had come to St. Louis with his bride in 1841. A rather retiring
man outside of his business ventures, he was devoted to his wife
and infant daughter. His eyes, which could be fiery with stub-
bornness or soft with kindness, looked out at St. Louis from a
square heavy face well covered with sideburns and whiskers.
Though determined to grow with the city as a successful and influential newspaperman, he had failed to keep alive three papers
with which he previously had been connected. Now he must have
been gratified to be offered this opportunity to gain prestige and
fortune.

From the first, McKee took the lead. He wrote for the paper
when there was need of it; but he spent most of his time on the
streets, soliciting "cards" and subscriptions.[14] He and Hill called
their paper "the organ of the Democratic Party" and promised
their readers to advocate the principles defined "in the acts and
writings of Jefferson, Jackson, and Benton." But they refused to
obligate themselves to swear on all occasions to the party's "platforms," because frequently these, like some of the party's candidates, were "rotten." According to their "Prospectus" on October 13, 1852, they were in favor of "the several measures which
are often . . . called 'compromise' measures, of river and harbor
improvements, of retrenchment and economy in the Federal expenditure, of a homestead law, of giving limited quantities of the
public domain to settlers for the actual cost of survey, and of a
metallic currency." They were opposed to nullification, banks,
tariffs, and monopolies, and they proposed to support Franklin
Pierce for President of the United States.[15]

Furthermore, McKee and Hill decided that the *Democrat* was
to be more than a mere campaign journal. They promised their
readers that they would expand the paper. Every "requisite to an

interesting and valuable paper" would receive their attention. Commented the *St. Louis Intelligencer* of August 10, 1852:

> How can the *Democrat* help "expanding" when it can't possibly contract to one atom or less? And how true it is that
>
> > Great oaks from little acorns *sometimes* grow
> > Large streams from little fountains *sometimes* flow.
>
> Cherish this little "acorn," Missourians, lest it also become rotten. . . . don't let the ducks and geese trample out this "little fountain."

With such ridicule in established journals, St. Louisans must have been startled on March 12, 1853, to learn that McKee and Hill had bought the *Union* for sixteen thousand dollars and merged the two papers.[16] After that date the *Democrat* was published from the *Union* office on Locust Street. Young Houser stayed on to keep books for the firm, and McKee employed his cousin, William S. McKee, as editor.

This gave McKee more time to devote to the promotion of his paper. He needed it. The path of a Free-Soil publisher in a slave state was not an easy one. Interest rates were high, ranging from 6½ to 10 per cent. That first year money was so short that on paydays McKee would often borrow small sums from the original owners to pay his shop hands.[17]

There must have been times when the *Democrat* owners wondered how long they could keep printing. In December, 1852, the printers of St. Louis formed a union and framed a bill on just prices for labor. McKee and Hill could not pay the rates, and their printers went on strike.[18] Then McKee must have been thankful that he could set type. Periodically, too, the firm advertised for a "roller boy," preferably a German lad.[19]

The *Democrat* was occasionally reduced in size, evidence of the fluctuating supply of newsprint. Of course, McKee and Hill apologized profusely. The paper supply from Cincinnati had not arrived, although they had been notified that it had been shipped. It was difficult to get even the small and inferior sheets that were being used. But the irregularity of boat and wagon freight may not have been as much a handicap for the publishers as was their poor financial credit and the favoritism shown more popular journals.[20]

Be that as it may, the *Democrat* improved. After the merger with the *Union*, it was enlarged to eight columns. The issue dates were changed. Previously published every day except Saturday, it now was issued every day except Sunday. The enlarged paper gave McKee and Hill the opportunity to print more news. One column on the first page was usually devoted to extracts clipped from papers in the East and to the printing of such things as the "Memoirs of General Scott." On the second page with the editorials and the political writings now appeared more city news items, more complete river news, and columns under such headings as "Market News," "Things Theatrical and Musical," and "Steamboat Arrivals."

Seemingly aware of the value of local news, *Democrat* editors improved the reader interest of their paper with a variety of items. Typical of this day-by-day reporting was the "City Items" column of April 8, 1853:

> Mr. Powers, chief engineer on the Olive Street Plank Road, was attacked on that road some fifteen miles out on Wednesday. . . .
>
> We were much pleased and greatly astonished in the half-hour visit we made yesterday to Professor Thibault and Mr. J. Z. Halli at Odd Fellows Hall. . . . about a microscope that magnified fleas.
>
> For School Directors of the Fifth Ward, Mr. William S. McKee received 783 votes. . . .
>
> Our brother of the *News* saw some watermelons at a fruiterers on Fourth Street which were brought from Cuba. Our mouth didn't water. We are like the fox. We don't care about such things anyway.
>
> Peach trees are in bloom around the city. The frost does not seem to have done much injury except in very exposed spots.
>
> We saw two splendid specimens of iron ore on Chestnut Street yesterday from the Pilot Knob. Their weight was estimated at 6,000 and 9,000 pounds, yielding 70 per cent. They are for the World's Fair.

John Smith, for indulging in the luxury of beating one of the sovereigns, was fined $100 yesterday.

John Russell, who was arrested in consequence of an eccentric fancy for horse flesh, was fined $50 as a common vagrant.

True bills have been found against the three soldiers (now in jail), who murdered the Delaware Indians, by the United States Circuit Court Grand Jury.

Mrs. Trowbridge, the wife of Trowbridge, convicted of embezzlement, has returned from Jefferson City. . . .

Among the contributions to the Washington Monument Fund at the Third Ward Polls was a $2-bill on a broken bank.

The slave, John Anderson, who is charged with attempting to violate the person of a lady on the Florissant Plank Road, gave bail in $2,000 before Justice Sharp.

We hear that a new Association is forming here to be called "The Ancient Order of Bricks." We have not learned the requisite qualifications to become a member.

But McKee and Hill did not lose sight of the fact that politics was the chief purpose of the paper. Editorially, the *Democrat* supported any Benton suggestion, concentrating on internal improvements, territorial organization, and a transcontinental railroad through St. Louis. The paper frequently carried the substance of Benton's speeches, and its editorials praised them with such statements as: "The speech will speak for itself, and we are truly sorry that readers of the Bogus Whig *Republican* will have no chance to see it."[21] The *Missouri Republican* did not publish Democratic utterances.

Within a year the influence of the *Democrat* began to spread to the German element of St. Louis. Many of its editorials were being translated and published in the *Anzieger des Westens*, the leading German paper.[22] The *Democrat* editor praised the German paper for its support of Benton:

We ourselves claim no merit for our steadfast support of Mr. Benton yet the *Anzieger's* course in this respect is worthy and commendable. . . .[23]

Although most of the editorials of 1853 were concerned with state and national questions, the paper did not neglect city politics. John How, who had lent McKee and Hill money to buy the *Union,* was elected mayor. The *Democrat* backed How's program to pave streets instead of macadamizing them, the paving to be paid for by property owners; to complete harbor improvements; to construct new wharves; to build a municipal hall; to plan streets needed to extend the city limits; to improve the city workhouse; and to provide for the insane.[24]

St. Louis was growing fast and the *Democrat* was growing with it. McKee and Hill also published the *Weekly Democrat* at a subscription price of a dollar a year, according to the masthead. The subscription price of the daily paper was listed at five dollars a year. The publishers stated that subscriptions must be paid in advance, but the paid circulation probably did not reach a thousand.

The firm's job printing office brought in some revenue, but advertising was probably the source of the biggest income for McKee and Hill. One insertion of one "square," eight single-column lines or less, sold for fifty cents. Reduced prices, according to the firm's announcements, were offered to advertisers who ran "cards" more than one time or which were longer than eight lines. Sometimes as many as 120 advertisements were printed on the front page alone. Income from advertising, if it was collected, must have amounted to approximately two hundred dollars an issue.

But all of this was not enough, with newsprint at about twelve cents a pound,[25] and the proprietors must have grown discouraged over the large debt and the constant criticism of the *Democrat's* unpopular political policies. When William S. McKee, the editor, died in April, 1854, Hill sold his half-interest in the newspaper and printing establishment for a small sum to Frank Blair and his cousin, Gratz Brown.[26] At that time, then, McKee owned a half-interest, Blair owned one-third, and Brown, one-sixth.

Brown, who was later elected governor of Missouri, had moved to St. Louis in 1849 to practice law with the Blairs. He was first a loyal Whig, but influenced by his cousins he early changed his political affiliations and became an ardent Free-Soiler and a fighting Benton supporter. Mainly through Frank Blair's influence, he was nominated for and elected to the Missouri Legislature in 1852.[27]

A thin, rather small man with a wealth of red hair and beard, Brown was not yet twenty-six years old when he was named editor of the *Democrat*.[28] However, he was already recognized in St. Louis for his scathing editorials in the *Democrat* and in the earlier Free-Soil journals. Like Blair, he was outspoken. "Slanders," he once wrote, "should never be allowed to pass unnoticed . . . for at some future date they will rise up invested with the dignity of antiquity," and because of the passage of time be free from the possibility of complete refutation. They should be "whacked upon the head at once and forever."[29]

The new editor carried out this policy in his newspaper duties. He wrote well. His "forceful, witty, and caustic" editorials, which were "cursed by pro-slavery men, commended by Free-Soilers, and read by all," were frequently quoted by other journals.[30]

This, then, was the *Missouri Democrat* in 1854. In the paper's first two years, its ownership had shifted three times, and three editors had directed its political writings. McKee allowed his editors much freedom in their writing, instructing them to adhere strictly to the truth and not to garble facts.[31] Although the paper was still in a precarious financial position, its course was set. In its first eight years, it was to gain prestige for its leadership in promoting antislavery sentiments.

Chapter II

The Path to Emancipation

IN 1854, the year Brown was named editor of the *Democrat*, the political confusion that preceded the Civil War was nowhere more apparent than in St. Louis. The Whigs and the Democrats, the two leading political parties, were breaking up. The Free-Soilers, called the Benton Democrats in Missouri, had already split away from the Democratic party. With each election this cleavage became greater. The old Whig party was also dying, splitting into the Know-Nothings, sometimes called the American party, and into the Anti-Know-Nothings, sometimes called the Free Democrats.[1] Because neither the Benton Democrats nor the Anti-Know-Nothings were strong enough to elect their candidates, the two minority groups sometimes merged for the purpose of electing some one person to a particular office. Frank Blair, acknowledged leader of the Benton Democrats, usually instigated these mergers; Brown's editorials screamed their approval.

In Missouri at that time, city elections were held in April, state elections in August, and national elections in November. The twenty-one newspapers in St. Louis would hardly finish either crowing over or explaining away the results of one campaign before they started bombarding their readers with propaganda about another. Each election was heralded by mass meetings and torchlight parades, often highlighted by riots, shootings, and drunken disorder. As the spokesman for a fighting minority group, the *Democrat* waded into each election with no holds barred.

It was inevitable that the slavery question would become the dominant issue of the period. Leading St. Louis business men from the New England and Middle States believed slavery to be a moral wrong. Many visitors and newcomers who flocked into the city were horrified and incensed at the appalling conditions of Lynch's slave pens and at the inhumane slave auctions on the steps of the courthouse.[2] Business men from the North and the South were beginning to realize that slavery was a detriment to the commercial interests of the city. Added to these groups were the thousands of industrious, thrifty, freedom-loving Germans and Irishmen who were forced to compete with slave labor for pitifully low wages.

Brown plunged into this political and social confusion with editorials that shook the proslave groups. Each issue brought the paper nearer to the time when McKee, Brown, and Blair would split with Benton and declare openly for emancipation.

In 1854, however, the *Democrat* was still an ardent advocate of Bentonism. On January 10 of that year, the paper printed on its masthead its political policy—the advocacy of the Democracy of Jefferson, Jackson, and Benton; the nomination of candidates in the primary election; the election of Benton to the United States Senate; a central route for a railroad from the Mississippi River to the Pacific Ocean; and the immediate organization of the Nebraska Territory.

Not a word about slavery was included in this policy statement. Benton believed that, left alone, slavery would gradually disappear. For this reason he opposed the agitation of this issue.[3] Moreover, because St. Louis was still dominated by proslavery elements, and because the *Democrat* was not yet strong enough to exist without Benton's support, its editorials were confined largely to praising Benton and to attacking his opponents, known as "Antis" or "Nullifiers."

In particular the *Democrat* pleaded for a railroad route through St. Louis. Editor Brown praised Benton for his "Central Route" speeches. "He works for the road," Brown wrote, "and has got it on its legs and is carrying it along; and every man in Missouri who is against him is against the road and is traitor to the state of Missouri."[4] *Democrat* editorials often advocated more liberal aid for the Pacific Railroad Company.[5]

But typical of the journalism of that era, as much space was de-

voted to haranguing the opposition as to praising Benton. By
irony, by sarcasm, by slander, Brown and Blair attacked the Antis, Senator David R. Atchison, and the *Republican*, the newspaper which was to be the *Democrat's* most vociferous opponent
for seventy years. The Antis and Nullifiers were in despair,
Brown reported, because of Colonel Benton's opposition to the
Pierce administration. Furthermore, the Antis had become "ultra"
in their advocacy of the Southern view of the Nebraska question.[6]

Senator Atchison was attacked for his opposition to the Central Railroad Route and for his advocacy of the Douglas River
and Harbor Bill, which the *Democrat* termed an "unconstitu-
tional, unjust, and lamely devised scheme." The Senator had,
Brown wrote, "heinously betrayed his Missouri constituency."[7]
Even more acrimoniously, he labeled Atchison a "coarse and vul-
gar ruffian," who "had the impudence to issue an address . . .
written for him by some hireling" in order to execute "treason
to the Democratic Party, to the state of Missouri, and to the
Union."[8]

If Brown minced no words in his attacks on the opposition, he
became increasingly bitter in his criticism of the *Republican*.
Brown reported that this journal, "once an ardent advocate of the
Central Route," now favored the Memphis or Southern Route
and was doing "everything in its power to create opposition to
the Central Route."[9] Calling the paper a common hireling, he accused its editor of lying and of trying, among other things, to
split the *Anzieger* and the *Democrat*. "These are the arts of the
'pimp' skilled in the ignoble artifices by which innocence is un-
dermined and betrayed to gratify the passions of the vicious and
unprincipled."[10]

Even though McKee had promised *Democrat* readers that his
new editor would not alter the paper's political character,[11] it
must have been evident to St. Louisans that Brown and McKee
were making every effort to gain *avant-garde* readers. Brown instituted several changes in the paper. He adopted a current practice of many newpapers of prefacing his editorial columns with
news items labeled "The News,"[12] which were edited for propa-

ganda purposes. Typical was an item of April 16, 1854, which began: "The echo of the triumphant shout of the St. Louis Democracy after the charter election is at length coming back to us from all parts of the Union."

The new editor also arranged for correspondents to cover political activities in out-state Missouri areas and in southern Illinois towns. A column headed "Missouri News and Politics," which was printed two or three times a week, first appeared on April 17, 1854, and was composed chiefly of political news items grouped by counties or by senatorial districts. On April 20, a column headed "Illinois News and Politics" began appearing twice a week. In July the paper was enlarged to nine columns.

In 1855 both Brown and Blair were running for re-election to the Missouri Legislature. As was to be expected, the *Democrat* became the center of their political activities. Brown used his editorial columns to further party-line splits by stressing the unification of dissatisfied people in all parties. The Democratic Party, he wrote, was "dead-dead-dead" unless the administration was thrown overboard, and the existence of the Whig Party was an "exploded fallacy."[13] Through May, June, and July, a steady stream of editorials praised Benton and attacked the opposition.

During the five years that Brown was editor, a majority of the *Democrat* editorials bore the mark of his verbose but vitriolic style. How many near duels with his political foes there must have been! For example, in 1855, Colonel Stewart, taking exception to some of Brown's abusive utterances, replied with equally harsh words; and Brown "felt constrained to send a challenge." They were to use horse pistols at ten paces, but Stewart dramatically withdrew his remarks after Brown had already arrived at the dueling grounds.[14]

The editor, however, was not so fortunate with Thomas C. Reynolds, United States District Attorney. Three times in as many years the two men were involved in a sharp controversy over what had been written in newspaper articles. Twice the challenge passed before the two men finally dueled in 1856.[15]

The first of Brown's offending editorials arraigned Reynolds, perhaps rightfully, for "persecuting" settlers in Southwest Mis-

souri for cutting timber on government land by charging them
with high treason. Brown wrote that Reynolds and others like
him belonged "to the small class of hermaphroditic politicians
who . . . styled themselves antis, and who, in their blind opposition to Benton, are willing to go to the length of subverting by
the revival of obsolete laws."[16] He further accused Reynolds of
having anti-Catholic articles published in the German *Anzieger*
and of having these translated and published in the *Republican*.
Reynolds challenged, but the duel was called off.

Then in the midst of the city elections of 1855, the *Democrat*
carried an account of Brown's speech in the General Assembly
of the Missouri Legislature in which the editor had defended the
Northern Methodists who had been accused of being Free-
Soilers. This helped provoke the second Brown-Reynolds controversy. Brown said that "more than beer was being brewed" in
the Salvator Brewing Company, recently organized by that
"mongrel partnership" of Reynolds and Editor Henry Boernstein of the *Anzieger*. Brown labeled the two men "the Beer and
Mischief Brewers" and said that they were scheming to deliver
St. Louis government to proslavery groups.[17] Once more Reynolds challenged, and once more the duel was called off.

The controversy that did end in a duel came in July, 1856,
some time after Brown had brought the slavery question into the
open. Reynolds had made a political speech at Mehl's Store in St.
Louis County, and Brown accused him of placing the Germans
and the Irish on a level with Negroes in this speech. He attacked
Reynolds for saying that, if Congress could exclude slaves, it
could exclude the foreign-born citizens. With this remark, Brown
contended, Reynolds had insulted the laboring Germans and
Irish.[18] Reynolds responded through a letter in the *St. Louis Pilot*
in which he called Brown's accusations "an unmitigated LIE,
worthy of a sheet whose proclivity to willful and deliberate false-
hoods" was "only exceeded by the notorious poltroonery of its
editor in defending them."[19]

To this Brown answered that he was too busy in the "conduct"
of his journal "to fritter time and temper in ridiculous controversies."[20] But when in a letter printed in the *Republican* Reynolds

called Brown an "unquestionable coward," Brown challenged. The duel was fought on a sandbar in the Missouri River on August 27. Reynolds was not hurt, but Brown was severely wounded in his knee.[21] McKee must have been relieved when he learned after the duel that his fighting editor was able to carry on with his duties.

In the meantime Brown's clashes had little effect on his crusading pen. The religious and racial issues involved in the August election of 1854 were particularly bloody. Severe rioting broke out in the streets. Eleven were killed, and twenty-two were injured. As was to be expected, there were charges and countercharges. Brown at first accused the *Republican* of causing these riots. Later he termed them Know-Nothing riots and accused Reynolds and Boernstein of being responsible for the "August reign of terror" in St. Louis.[22]

In addition, the editor had begun to agitate the slavery question. As a member of the Missouri Legislature and as editor of the *Democrat*, Brown had ample opportunity to foment the controversy. He used both positions to an advantage when, in 1854, he was appointed chairman of a legislative committee to conduct investigations of the University and of its president, the Reverend James Shannon. Here Brown found more grist for his slavery mill. He frequently derided Shannon in the *Democrat* pages, basing his attacks on Shannon's attempt to thrust proslavery ideas on students. "Great God!" Brown wrote, "That such a scoundrel should be permitted to occupy that sacred desk! To remain at the head of our educational interests, inculcating upon youthful minds of the country such treasonable and outrageous sentiments."[23]

One day in the spring of 1855, a dirty, ragged, and hungry young man with piercing eyes walked into the counting room of the *Democrat*. He wanted, he said in the clipped voice of a New Englander, to write for the paper because it was a Free-Soil journal, and he believed that slaves should be free. He had been in the South, where he had talked to many mistreated slaves. In fact he had walked nearly all the way to St. Louis from Mobile. McKee and Brown must have been overjoyed at finding another zealous opponent of slavery who could write, because they forthwith employed the young stranger.[24] Thus did James Redpath, the first of many *Democrat* writers to become nationally famous, start writing for the paper.

In the year that the *Democrat* was founded, the nineteen-year-old Redpath had begun working for Horace Greeley on the *New York Tribune*. An energetic reformer even then, he had seethed with indignation over the mistreatment of slaves. His zeal for their cause had taken him on a tour of the South which had ended at the *Democrat* office.[25] A few weeks after he came to St. Louis, McKee and Brown sent him to Kansas to cover the bloody events there.

The first Redpath letter appeared in the *Democrat* on July 28. A full column in length, it was strongly antislavery. The correspondent reported on a bill before the Kansas Territorial Legislature to free colored persons and on speeches made by Shannon and Atchison. Signed "J. R.," Redpath's letters, often brilliant, were sometimes emotional, sometimes humorous, and frequently packed with factual details. Typical was his description of the Kansas Territorial Legislature chamber—"a dingy schoolroom with five windows on one side and four on the other."[26]

On September 4, Redpath's letter appeared on the front page of the *Democrat* with the editorial comment that the "admirable sketches of men and things in Kansas" by the paper's Kansas correspondent were being copied by the press throughout the country. Years later Charles Robinson was to write that it was doubtful whether "Kansas could have been saved from the grasp of invaders but for the shot poured into Atchison, Stringfellow, and Company" by the *Democrat* and its correspondent, James Redpath, "the fearless, indomitable friend of the oppressed of all colors."[27]

Redpath remained with the *Democrat* only a few months before he left to further his efforts for slavery in other ways. By 1859 he had become interested in Haiti as a place to colonize the Negroes of the South. As Commissioner of Emigration for the Haitian Republic and as Haitian Consul at Philadelphia, he was instrumental in sending several thousand ex-slaves to that island country. He also served as a Civil War correspondent and, after the war, as Superintendent of Education in Charleston, South Carolina, where he organized a school system for Negroes. But perhaps he became best known as an editor of the *North American Review* and as the founder of the Boston Lyceum Bureau, an organization that later bore his name. His clients included Ralph Waldo Emerson, Julia Ward Howe, Mark Twain, and Petroleum V. Nasby.[28] However, before leaving the employ of the *Democrat*, Redpath recommended as his replacement Albert D. Richardson, who later became a well-known Civil War correspondent for the *New York Tribune*.[29]

In the meantime, in spite of the added prestige that the Redpath letters gave to the *Democrat*, Brown and McKee hesitated to declare the paper openly for abolition. In fact, Brown wrote that "abolitionist thinkers" should be suppressed. Such people were extremists who were responsible for weakening the ties holding the country together, and Massachusetts abolitionists were as intolerant as their forbears. Brown warned them that force would be met with force.[30]

The opposition of the *Democrat* to slavery was based chiefly on the labor problem which its owners and editor believed was being created by slavery. Brown, Blair, and McKee were not so much against slavery as a moral evil as against its extension into the territories on an economic basis. In order to stress the labor problem, Brown addressed his editorials to the merchants, steamboat men, and business men of St. Louis. He pointed out the adverse effect of Know-Nothing policies on the population and growth of the city and on business interests. Sales of suburban property had fallen off 40 per cent at least. Of the fifty companies chartered in 1854, less than ten had gone into operation. He warned that the decline in population, caused by free laborers going elsewhere, could be reflected in the value of real estate, manufacturing, and sale of merchandise. He pointed out that in 1850, in free states, men in agriculture made $330.00 per man, but in slave states white men made only $173.00, and slaves only $85.00.[31]

One day in 1856 when Captain Nathaniel Lyon, who was stationed in the Kansas Territory, was passing through St. Louis, he dropped by the *Democrat* office to renew his subscription to the paper. McKee and Brown were gratified, they told the captain, to find in the Army, usually considered conservative, an officer who would support the radical views of the *Democrat*. To this, Lyon replied: "Every possible means should be exhausted before another slave state is admitted to the Union."[32]

Brown, Blair, and McKee must have explored dozens of ways of promoting their radical views. In 1856 they "left no stone unturned" in attempting to have Benton elected governor on a Democratic Anti-Know-Nothing platform.[33] The *Democrat* carried notices of Bentonite meetings and reports of the national and state conventions. In preparation for the city elections, Blair and Brown sponsored a large meeting of "Equal-Rights" advocates that went on record as being opposed to the introduction of national and state political problems into municipal elections. At an Anti-Know-Nothing convention in March, ward delegates passed a resolution opposing "Black Republicanism."[34]

Yet Blair and Brown indorsed John How for mayor, and How had been accused, rightfully, of being a Republican. When How won the election, the *Democrat* called it a Free-Soil victory. "Great Victory! John How and the Whole Ticket Elected by 2,500 Majority! Bring out the Sun! ! Run up the Flag for the Union for that of fanaticism and intolerance trails in the dust ! ! !"[35]

Moreover, at the first convention of Republicans in Pittsburgh in February, 1856, the *Democrat* was the only Missouri paper which had a representative to cover it. James Redpath, the former Kansas correspondent, sent back special dispatches.[36] Although *Democrat* personnel joined the Republican party that year, they denied that the *Democrat* was Republican-minded. Blair denied his Republican membership by saying that he had always been a Jackson and a Benton Democrat and that he intended to remain so. He was opposed, he said, to the repeal of the Missouri Compromise, and he condemned squatter sovereignty, insisting that he had no intention of surrendering his Democratic principles or of assuming any other name than that of a Democrat.[37]

Nevertheless, Blair, who was running for representative to Congress, wanted Benton to declare openly for Republicanism. Benton refused, and the *Democrat* was forced to take a more conservative stand. Blair wrote to his brother:

> The *Democrat* put up the names of the nominees the day of their nomination. . . . because it was a question of meat & Bread with it, & a question of the existence or non-existence of the Benton Democracy in the State.[38]

Blair must have analyzed correctly the action of the paper in listing Buchanan as its nominee for president instead of John C. Frémont, whom Blair favored and for whom he probably voted. Benton opposed Frémont, his son-in-law, because he thought that Frémont could command only a small vote and that running him would aggravate the sectional feelings.[39]

Brown stepped up the paper's campaign against the extension of slavery in July, 1856. Editorials were filled with references to Blair's speeches on the issue. Then on August 2, the day before the state election, St. Louisans were shocked to find the slate of candidates in the *Democrat* appearing under the heading, "Black Republican Ticket." In St. Louis at this time "Black Republicanism" was synonymous with Abolitionism, an intensely hated term. To be sure, only the papers distributed in the city carried this heading. Papers printed later and sent into the state did not have it. McKee and Brown denied vehemently that they were responsible. It was the work of a prankster, they claimed, and a dastardly fraud. Other papers were asked to publish a note which claimed that a proofreader had made the error during the absence of the compositors.[40] Be that as it may, the laboring German and Irish could read the paper before they voted, and voters of the rural areas would not read it. It may have gained votes.

Blair was elected, and the *Democrat* staff rejoiced, scoffing at the criticism that foreigners had voted on borrowed credentials.[41] They continued to advocate Benton for governor and Buchanan for president. But their support seemed lukewarm; the paper was conspicuous for the little space devoted to Buchanan.

Benton's defeat in the November elections paved the way for

the *Democrat's* open declaration for emancipation. It became evident early in 1857 that the Bentonites as a party were splitting into two factions—the conservatives under Benton, who were strong in the rural areas, and the Blair-Brown faction, strong in St. Louis, who were to declare openly during the year for emancipation.[42] Brown and McKee, devoted to the economic betterment of Missouri and the nation, aligned themselves and the *Democrat* with Blair.

Sensing that Blair and Brown were turning the *Democrat* into an antislavery paper, Benton wrote to a wealthy St. Louisan to secure control of the journal. "Change its name and character—for no useful paper can be made of it. . . . It is given up to the slavery subject, agitating state emancipation against my established and known policy."[43]

But McKee, Brown, and Blair must have determined to break with Benton. Instead of Benton's friend gaining control of the *Democrat*, George W. Fishback purchased an interest.[44] Fishback, who had joined the *Democrat* staff in 1855 and had been in charge of the commercial columns, also had strong antislavery convictions. Knowing Fishback's political views, Blair sold half of his interest to him, which meant, of course, that McKee still owned the controlling interest. The other one-half interest was divided equally among Blair, Brown, and Fishback.

The son of a prominent Ohio judge, Fishback was a graduate of Farmer's College in Ohio, where he had studied law. But, he did not care for the "monotony of a lawyer's life," and in 1854, when he was twenty-six, he emigrated to St. Louis, where he first wrote for the *Evening News* and then for the *St. Louis Intelligencer*. By the time he joined the *Democrat* the following year, St. Louisans had learned to recognize his writings by the rich humor in which he frequently indulged.[45]

Democrat readers learned of the Fishback purchase on January 22, 1857. McKee assured them that the political position of the paper would make no change, and that the *Democrat* would maintain "with unshaken fidelity the course which it has so long followed."

Nevertheless, Brown brought up the question of emancipation

in the next day's issue. In an editorial headed "The Emancipation of Slaves in Missouri," he pointed out that emancipation was now an open question. Five days later he and Blair revealed their plan for gradual emancipation by colonization. They suggested that Missouri's colored people be shipped to Liberia and that slaveholders be fully compensated.

> Our party in Missouri has been conservative in every age, and yet it could not prevent the repeal of the Missouri Compromise, the Kansas outrages, and the disunion agitation last summer. We have held the balance evenly . . . but the weight of the nigger was thrown in by our enemies, and the disturbed equilibrium we were unable to restore. . . . We have wearied of it, and (speaking for ourselves) we now trust our fortunes and our fate to this great cause of Emancipation.[46]

Once the controversy was out in the open, it was as if the floodgates had been opened. Emancipation was not a subject that *Democrat* writers intended to ignore. In February, when a resolution was introduced into the General Assembly declaring emancipation of slaves in Missouri to be impractical, Brown was ready. This bill, he said, was merely an attempt to prop up an institution which was already doomed. It only "renewed agitation of the slavery question and forced the emancipation issue upon the people." Moreover, it was "an attempt to gag" the freedoms of speech and the press. Gradual emancipation, he insisted, was neither "impractical, unwise or unjust," and the only way of ascertaining this fact was the full and free discussion of the entire system.[47]

An editorial on March 7, 1857, denied that the *Democrat* was agitating the Negro question.

> Agitate the Negro question? No! Let us agitate the rights of white men—of free men—of those who live by the sweat of the brow and whose hands and heads are rearing here the proud metropolis of the Great West.

The municipal elections that year gave the *Democrat* an opportunity to exploit its new policy. The paper energetically supported John M. Wimer for mayor. On April 2, the "Emancipation Ticket" was headed with a cut of a blacksmith's hammer, playing on the idea that Wimer had risen from a blacksmith to the judicial bench. A Wimer rally, at which banners proclaimed "White men for our city and our city for white men," and "Africa for the Negroes" was called successful.[48]

The story of Wimer's victory was headed "The Emancipation Ticket Triumphant." Because out-state papers had hailed Wimer's victory, Brown predicted a tide of immigration to Missouri such as the state had never before experienced. He pointed out that in his inaugural address Wimer had said that skilled and intelligent labor of free white men was more productive than compelled labor of slaves.[49]

By 1858 the *Democrat* office had become headquarters for the antislavery movement in Missouri led by Blair, who that year called his party the Free Democrats. The Central Committee frequently met in McKee's office to plan campaign strategy. Brown and Blair spoke at ward meetings, and Brown delivered the main address at the Jackson Day Meeting. His speech set the keynote for the year's campaign—that slavery was unjust to free labor.[50]

On the day following Brown's speech, Blair brought the struggle in Missouri to the attention of the nation with his famous colonization speech in Congress.[51] He proposed inquiring into the purchase of land on which colored people who were already free might be colonized. He believed that all Negroes had the right to be free and that further immigration of free people from Africa as slaves should be prohibited.[52]

Naturally the *Democrat* supported Blair's proposal. Brown used his editorial columns to apply Blair's proposal to Missouri. The state, he wrote, should be for the white men, the tropics were the field for Negro colonization, and Panama was especially fitted for this. He recommended the extinction of slavery in the entire region of the central grain-growing states as one of the first steps in the "Free Labor Movement." He pointed out that the slave system was "virtually dead in Missouri." Farm machinery, he believed, would crowd out slave labor: as agricultural mechanization increased, social and political prestige would pass away from the slave system, which itself was "doomed to pass away."

He blamed slavery for the hard times in Missouri because it had driven away Northern capital which could have been invested in Missouri farms, mineral resources, and factories.[53]

That same year, 1858, Blair was running for re-election to Congress and Brown for re-election to the Missouri Legislature. But for the first time since the birth of the *Democrat* neither was elected. Missourians were not yet ready to accept the emancipation idea, and Brown's acrimonious editorials had been too vehement. Particularly bitter had been his attacks on the *Republican*, which had introduced the Benton-Blair split of the year before into the campaign. Typical was an editorial of July 21:

> Mr. Barret [Blair's opponent] says that he supported Benton by voting against him, that he upholds Buchanan by a profound silence in regard to the Lecompton policy, and we suppose on the same principle he will assert that he sustained his own party through poking his nose into a Know-Nothing lodge. Funny to say the least!

For his views on the Kansas slavery question, Barret was called "Missouri Dick, *alias* Misery Dick, *alias* Know-Nothing Dick," and "Lecompton Dick."[54]

Brown and Blair were bitter about their defeat. Blair and the *Democrat* immediately charged ballot-box stuffing, basing their claims on irregularities in four wards. They maintained that anti-Bentonites voted two or three times on dead men's registration papers.[55] Blair contested Barret's seat in Congress and won, but he resigned immediately and after a speaking tour in the East returned to St. Louis to prepare for the 1860 elections.[56]

There he was shocked at the chaotic political situation. He wrote to his brother:

> I found everything here in confusion on my return. I was compelled to devote myself night and day to the task of infusing confidence into the leaders and making reconciliation among them. . . . Gratz Brown is a very bad manager and whenever I go away gets things into confusion—he assumes the dictator and makes everybody mad with him. I have been compelled to talk plainly to him and hurt his feelings. . . . We must arrange to get him out of the way and set up another editor. His young wife has occupied his time

too much and makes him inefficient instead of inspiring him with the ambition to push ahead.[57]

Apparently Blair's influence was strong enough with McKee and Fishback to remove Brown as editor. Brown's letter of resignation printed in the *Democrat*, April 11, 1859, however, listed business reasons for his resignation.

> Business reasons constrain me to resign the place of editor of this journal. It were needless to add that it is with extreme reluctance that I dissolve a connection which has lasted so long and to which the best years of my life have been devoted.
>
> The *Missouri Democrat* has been the pioneer of the cause of divine Freedom in the State of Missouri, and to that cause my heart is wedded with a devotion that death alone can annul. . . .

Business reasons may have influenced Brown's resignation, because he sold his interest to Fishback and became president of the street railway company in St. Louis. If, however, Blair's allegations about Brown were true, and if he was forced to resign, he became the second man that the *Democrat* had discarded as useless. First, Benton was dropped because he was too conservative, and now, Brown, because he was too dictatorial. There were to be others who would outlive their usefulness to the journal.

Brown, however, had been a great force in his five years as editor. His work on the *Democrat* undoubtedly influenced many people in their political activities and certainly helped to channel the direction of the journal's future course.

Chapter III

Other Views and News of St. Louis

L IFE in St. Louis in the 1850's was not made up entirely of political oratory, torchlight parades, elections, and riots. By 1860 the population of the "Gateway to the West" had soared to 160,773. More than 50,000 were foreign born, and only about 2,000 were slaves. In its first eight years the *Democrat* appealed to this heterogeneous reading public by reflecting more and more their economic, social, and cultural interests.

Notwithstanding the black smoke that hung like a mushroom over the city in the autumn and winter and the livestock that frequently roamed the streets, St. Louis was a very pleasant city. It sprawled along the river front for nearly seven miles and pushed westward at one point nearly three miles. Its well-filled stores, markets and warehouses; its hotels and attractive, comfortable residences; its theaters, churches, schools and colleges; even its sidewalks—all were made of brick.[1]

Most of its people were thrifty, many of them rapidly accumulating wealth. Few were very poor, but none were allowed to go unclothed or unfed. On warm summer evenings families sat on their stone doorsteps enjoying the cool river breeze, watching the carriages rumble along, and discussing the events of the day. By 1860 some two to three thousand people subscribed to the daily *Democrat* and fourteen thousand read the *Weekly Democrat*.[2] Aside from its political writings, the "dirty little sheet" always provided many conversational topics because it recorded the many events that made up the life of the bustling, expanding city.

For the large foreign-born elements eager for news of their native lands, McKee and Fishback provided news about Europe and European personalities, which they reprinted from Eastern

25

26 ST. LOUIS GLOBE-DEMOCRAT

newspapers that were eight to ten days old when they arrived and from foreign journals that came by boat directly to St. Louis. Of course, some of the foreign news items in the *Democrat* concerned political developments, such as the story of foreign intervention in Mexico, reprinted from the *New York Times* and the story ridiculing kings and calling British subjects "citizens of England," reprinted from the *London Times*.[3] But most foreign news concerned prominent persons or sensational events such as the report from Europe that Mrs. Otto Goldschmidt (Jenny Lind) had given birth to twins and had announced her retirement from the stage.[4] Then there was the story that the House of Lords in England had rejected the bill to legalize the marriage of a widower to his deceased wife's sister.[5]

The interest of readers in public affairs aside from political developments was reflected in the printing of court reports and the minutes of meetings of the city council, the school board, and such organizations as the St. Louis Chamber of Commerce, the sewer committee, and the Mercantile Library Association. The *Democrat* also printed its share of public notices such as the city assessment notices, sheriff's orders, lists of real estate to be sold for taxes, and lists of unclaimed letters at the post office. Periodically, the journal warned its readers of deadlines for paying taxes if they wanted to take advantage of the 2 per cent deductions.[6]

Life in St. Louis was not always tranquil, however, for it was scarcely a crime-free city. In 1853, for example, Coroner Brown reported 201 inquests: 15 deaths resulted from murder, 35 from accidents, 17 from debility, 10 from apoplexy, 54 from drowning, 22 from fits, 4 from explosion of powder, 3 from sunstrokes, 3 from burns, and 15 from unknown causes.[7] A jailbreak occurred three weeks before the *Democrat* reported it on August 28, 1860. Unfortunately, the story said, Jailer Roderman had not revealed the event at the time for fear that he would lose the election.

There were also stories of assaults, maiming of horses, child-whipping, drunkenness, and petty thievery. These often were reported humorously, as was this item of February 13, 1859:

Thomas Y. Harmon insisted on leading his pony over the sidewalk of Franklin Avenue, and finally conducted the animal into the Astor Saloon, near Fifth Street. Mr. Harmon was then taken into custody and required to furnish bail.

On August 24, 1859, readers were amused with a report that Mr. French, an attaché of the *Democrat,* was robbed of his clothing and money while he was ill and sleeping in his hotel room:

> Although Mr. French is a "Wide-Awake," he did not on this occasion sleep with "one eye open." If Mr. Burglar will call again, he will introduce him to an animal who has not the pleuro-pneumonia, viz: a thoroughbred Colt.

The greatest catastrophes of the period resulted from fires and floods. Headlines in the *Democrat* were usually one-column labels in slightly larger type than that of the story. But catastrophes and elections occasionally were heralded with three-deck, single-column headlines, decorated with exclamation points. On May 28, 1857, for example *Democrat* readers saw this:

> Terrible Explosion!
> Two Stores Blown to Atoms!!
> Several Persons Killed and Wounded!!!

In June, 1858, the Mississippi River flooded. Water reached Second Street "and in some places encroached upon Broadway. The 'Big Mound' at Mound Street was filled with sightseers, watching ferry boats going to Brooklyn, Illinois, to rescue persons marooned in their homes."[8] This flood must have caused McKee and Fishback considerable anxiety, because the *Democrat* office was located between Second and Third streets.

St. Louis has always been plagued by destructive thunderstorms and tornadoes. The *Democrat* reported such an event on April 26, 1854, in a journalistic style typical of the period.

> Yesterday afternoon the town was visited with a thunderstorm which raged with great violence for an hour. The elements were on a regular bust—rain, hail, lightning, and thunder warring in a melee like so many fiends. The hailstones were quite a phenomenon, some of them being as large as eggs and falling with such force as to do serious damage. Two hundred dollars worth of glass was broken in the splendid windows of the Union Presbyterian Church alone from which we infer that any number of panes was

shattered in the windows exposed to the pelting of the
storm . . . in fact, the windows along the sides of the street
on which the hail stones slanted present an appearance as if
riddled with muskets. Mr. Sellick's house on Walnut Street
was blown down and its fall crushed the adjoining stable
owned by Mr. Blair.

The brutality of riverboatmen in the fifties was common
knowledge to St. Louisans. One day a young *Democrat* reporter
became incensed when he saw a slave laborer being cruelly mistreated by a riverboatman, and in his report of the affair he criticized the man. Subsequently, this man assaulted the young reporter, but publicity of the event in the *Democrat* was said to
have been instrumental in "cleaning up" the river front.[9]

This young reporter was Joseph B. McCullagh, who was to
become the paper's most outstanding editor. Familiarly known as
"Mac," he was seventeen when, in 1859, he started working for
the *Democrat*. A short, chubby lad, born in Ireland of Scotch
parents, he had immigrated to New York in 1842 when he was
only eleven. There he had entered the office of *Freeman's Journal*
as a printer's apprentice. In 1858 he had moved to St. Louis, where
he began working as a typesetter on McAnally's *Christian Advocate*. Intense, lonely, but ambitious, he attended at night a short-
hand school which had been started by William T. Harris, then
superintendent of public instruction in St. Louis. Soon "Mac"
knew more stenography than did his instructor. In the fall of
1859, he moved to the *Democrat* as a typesetter.

One day soon after McCullagh joined the paper McKee and
Fishback were shorthanded and sent him out to gather city news.
"Mac" returned with so many items that they had to be set in
five-point type, smaller than the regular body type.[10] A typical
example, printed on January 12, 1860, reveals McCullagh's ability
to gather news and to write it.

> Minor City Items: The hail and snow brought out the
> "salters" yesterday on the Fifth Street Railroad, and com-
> pelled the Olive Street line to almost suspend operations in
> the afternoon. Most of the cars were drawn by four horses,
> and the accommodations therefore were not so numerous.

... The ice in the river did not appear to thicken yesterday, as was expected, but probably today the ferry boat riders will get big bumps for their money. . . . The latest dodge for the cold weather is a dog blanket, covering the body of the canine excepting head and legs. We saw one yesterday thus clothed in the P. O. . . . Pat Ford, who cruelly gouged out the eye of a horse on the corner of Carr and Twenty-second Street, was yesterday held to bail to appear before the Criminal Court for trial, on a charge of misdemeanor—the crime is punishable by imprisonment in the county jail for sixty days, and a fine of $300. . . . An empty hay wagon, with a long pole protruding from one side far beyond the wheels, was going along the Fifth Street railway track yesterday, when the pole rubbed against the car and frightened the passengers inside. It is a wonder that no damage was done. . . . The motion for security for the costs in the Carztang-Shaw breach of promise case, has been laid over till Saturday, before the trial is ended. The Clerk is desirous of having some responsibility determined in advance. Law is a ticklish thing and the clerks know it as well as anybody. . . . . A case of slander was before the Court of Common Pleas yesterday, wherein Mr. Miller sued Mr. Boisaubin for calling him a cheat and a swindler. The defendant takes the affirmation and undertakes to prove that his charge is true. The affair grows out of an old partnership transaction, Miller having sold out the goods while Boisaubin was absent. The trial has not been concluded yet. . . . Yesterday, the new sheriff, Thos. E. Courtenay, assumed the duties of the office made vacant by the death of Michael S. Cerre.

McKee and Fishback knew a good reporter when they saw him, and McCullagh remained with the *Democrat* as a writer, not a typesetter.

As early as 1854 McKee had announced to his readers that he intended to make his journal the best commercial paper in the Mississippi Valley. It was to be "second to none."[11] Commercial news at the time was confined principally to market quotations obtained from exchange papers in New York, Boston, Cincinnati, Pittsburgh, and New Orleans. Then when Fishback joined the staff, he devoted much of his news-gathering and writing efforts to the commercial interests of St. Louis. By that time telegraph service with the East had been established, and he could get cur-

rent quotations directly from the large markets. Sometimes he
had to report that roads were too bad for farmers to bring their
produce to market, and therefore he had no St. Louis prices to
quote.[12] But on January 1, 1859, he could write that mules and
good horses were selling for "fair prices," and he urged owners
to bring their stock to market because demand and prices would
be better after the holiday.

Streets, roads, and waterways were always of interest to *Democrat* readers. The paper joined the Baden merchants and farmers
along the Bellefontaine and Halls Ferry roads in protesting the
action of County Judge Lanham, who had vetoed the appropri-
ations to rebuild the roads which were impassable.[13] On August
24, 1858, Fishback reported that the city of Carondolet had
"granted Martin Reater a license to quarry rock on Van Buren
Street between Stein and Lehimer streets for an annual fee of
twenty dollars." The city engineer was to supervise the work,
and the contractee was to buy the rock to macadamize the streets.
Later that year the *Democrat* reported that "snags took their toll
of river steamers as all Western rivers were at their lowest stages
in a number of years." At least fifteen boats, Fishback wrote,
were snagged on the Mississippi, Ohio, Missouri, Illinois, and
Alabama rivers.[14]

The opening of new business firms also made good copy for
the *Democrat*. On January 2, 1859, Fishback noted three of
these: Goodin, Hopkins, and Hinters, general commission business at 62 Second Street; J. H. Clarke and Brothers, wholesale
candy manufacturing business at 166 Market Street; and R. P.
Ober and Company, commission merchants and grocers at 117
North Second Street. The McCune Packet Company, he reported, was constructing a "splendid new steamer for the mail line
run between St. Louis and Hannibal at a cost of $6,000."[15]

With its epidemics of cholera and its high death rate from
tuberculosis, St. Louis was not the most healthful city in the
country. Yet the city had an ample number of dental surgeons,
physicians, surgeons, accouchers, and apothecaries, and McDowell's Medical College trained many doctors. After the 1849 cholera epidemic which decimated the city, a sewer committee was

formed, and the *Democrat* kept its readers informed of the work
of these men by publishing the minutes of their meetings. McKee
and Fishback also printed a series of articles by Dr. J. D. Durkin
on consumption and its treatment.[16]

Many St. Louis doctors used the pages of the *Democrat* to
advertise their medicines, which they claimed had fabulous powers for curing almost anything. The Liver Invigorator, prepared
by Dr. Sanford, was "a scientific medical discovery" that worked
"cures almost too great to believe." More than one bottle was
seldom needed to cure any liver complaint from the worst jaun-
dice to a common headache.[17] Other medicines which were advertised as working miraculous cures included Ayer's Cherry
Pectoral, Holloway's Ointment, Smith's Tonic Syrup, Brann's
Tonic Pills, Easterly's Ague Killer, Dr. Harper's Female Cordial, and Dr. Easterly's Vegetable Pain Killer. Charles Landon's
Cordial Gin was reported to be good for the "be-drugged and
poisoned citizens of Missouri."[18]

Although wealthy St. Louis families usually sent their sons to
Eastern universities and their daughters to "female academies" in
Kentucky and Virginia, St. Louis had excellent public and private schools. The *Democrat* always reported the minutes of the
meetings of the school board, Editor William S. McKee being a
member at the time of his death.[19] By 1860 school news was being
given a prominent position on the front page. A typical story
reported on public school examinations in subjects including
mental arithmetic, reading, spelling, drawing, orthography, English grammar and analysis, and history. Parents attended the examinations, and star pupils were named.[20] The paper called attention to the opening of the high school and of the Normal, where
teachers were trained, and parents were reminded that pupils
were required to attend the school established in the district in
which they lived.[21]

St. Louisans also could send their children to Washington
University, and St. Louis workers could attend O'Fallon Poly-
technic Institute "to specialize in mechanic and chemical arts."
There, for a dollar a year, an apprentice or a person under eighteen could obtain library and reading room privileges. For jour-

neymen, mechanics, and clerks, the cost was three dollars.[22] Private schools advertising in the *Democrat* included Mr. Hayden's Writing Academy, Jones Commercial College, Mr. and Mrs. Smith's Seminary, and the English and French School conducted by Miss Long and Miss Mayday Gilbert. By 1860 schools outside of St. Louis were using the *Democrat* pages to attract students. Among these were a Select Family School for Young Ladies in Springfield, Massachusetts, Rush Medical College in Chicago, and Terre Haute Female College in Terre Haute, Indiana.

McKee tried to make the *Democrat* to some extent a literary journal. As early as 1854 he advised his readers that a column or two on the first page would be devoted daily "to literary and miscellaneous matter,"[23] such as poetry, fiction, biography, and short humorous paragraphs. These were usually reprinted from the New York and Boston papers. As the paper was enlarged, first to nine columns and then to ten, more literary items were printed. By 1857 the Saturday issues were carrying eight to ten additional columns of such reading matter for the "hardworking men who have no time for reading during the week." Brown called this a "new feature of journalism" which had "met with much favor" from his readers.[24] Then, late in 1858, McKee and Fishback once more started publication of a Sunday *Democrat* which contained "an original story from one column and a half to two columns."[25]

Dickens and Artemus Ward were favorite authors. In May, 1854, for example, Dickens' "latest novel," *Hard Times*, ran serially. St. Louisans also read in the *Democrat* about Dr. O. W. Holmes's lecture on Wordsworth and "An English Criticism of Edgar Allen Poe."[26] Local literary aspirants also wrote for the *Democrat*, although it is highly doubtful that they received any money for their efforts. Once readers were treated to the poem, "Fading Hopes," by Miss "A. L."

> Stars that shine and fall
> Flowers that drop in the springing
> These alas are types of all
> To which our hearts are clinging.

Who would see or prize
    Joys that end in aching?
Who could yield to ties
    That every hour are breaking?

Far better, 'twere to be
    With darkness around us lying
Than have these joys we see
    Forever from us flying.

Our brightest hopes still fade
    The fondest are the fleetest
And all our joys were made
    To leave us when the sweetest.[27]

But the *Democrat* "poet editor" believed that Miss "A. L." wrote these lines in a "querulous and unhealthy tone." Admitting that he was "something of a transcendentalist," he "dashed" off a poem which he said was "an answer to the spirit, more than to the letter." It began:

Remember, sad songstress, that planets and stars
    With glory unfading still shine in their spheres
You still may behold the red forehead of Mars,
    And the hunter Orion, unwithered by years.

Six stanzas and five planets later, it ended:

The joys that we cherish in youth's golden prime
    Like the earth-rooted amaranth blooming in Heaven
Will flourish with fruitage afar in that clime
    Where stand round the throne the elect and the SEVEN.

About once a month the *Democrat* published four or five book reviews. Each book was treated in a short paragraph which may have been written from the publisher's advertisements. Reviewed on September 13, 1860, for example, were *The Woman in White* by Wilkie Collins, *Italy in Transition* by William Arthur, and *Chapter on Wives* by Mrs. Ellis.

The paper also kept its readers informed on current amusements. The principal theaters in St. Louis during this time, according to advertisements in the *Democrat*, were the St. Louis Theater, Woods Theater, People's Theater, and the St. Louis

Museum. Minstrels, circuses, and burlesque operas were frequently held in these establishments. Shakespearean productions
were important enough to rate reviews. A critic said of Edwin
Booth that the "performance last night at the People's Theater,
by this young actor, was one of those decided hits upon the stage
which we experience at long intervals."[28] Of a performance of
"Macbeth," a *Democrat* reviewer wrote:

> The popularity attaching to the production of this trag-
> edy with its admirable appointments is sustained by undi-
> minished numbers. The box list is filled, we may say almost
> in advance and the parquette is crowded. In the character
> of Macbeth, Mr. Brooke truly won golden opinion from all
> sorts of men as the mighty plaudits testify.
>   With practice the choruses led by Miss Julia Bennett, as
> Hecate, and Tom Booth, have become even more effective
> than on the first and second nights and are perfection in
> their way. Nothing has even been brought out in St. Louis
> that can compare with it in any way, and those who perhaps
> have little idea of what may be done with *Macbeth* in the
> way of scenery, etc., should not miss so great and original
> a pleasure.[29]

St. Louis was a socially-minded city. Visits of important people called for great celebrations, which received full coverage in
the *Democrat*. Readers learned on June 13, 1854, of the long parade which honored former President Millard Fillmore when he
came to the city the day before. Fillmore declined a public dinner in his honor, but when Governor Matterson and other dignitaries of Illinois visited the city on March 2, 1854, they were honored with an elaborate banquet at the Varieties Theater. Guests
ate four kinds of fish, ten kinds of roast, four boiled meats, two
baked meats, and six game dishes along with salads and desserts.
Brass bands played and Mayor How gave the welcoming address.
Among the fourteen toasts were these: "The Press—without a
censor, a liberator; with him, an enslaver," and "Illinois and Missouri—bread and iron for a continent."[30]

    Every holiday was an excuse for masquerades, dress balls, and
gracious dinners. Scarcely an issue of the *Democrat* failed to print
announcements of three to five such entertainments. The Mer-

cantile Library Hall was used for meetings, society balls, mas-
querades, and sometimes banquets. But perhaps it was used most
often for lectures. There St. Louisans listened to the Reverend
Patrick John Ryan lecture on "Galileo and the Roman Inquisi-
tion," George William Curtis on "Gold and Gilt of Young
America," George Vanderhoff on "Tragedy and Comedy in
Dickens' Novels," Dr. Thomas Hall on "How Intellectual and
Moral Philosophy Are Connected with Historical and Physical
Science and Theology," and Bayard Taylor on "Man and Cli-
mate."[31]

How different was the *Democrat* of 1860 from the little sheet
that the St. Louis business men had started publishing in July,
1852! Not a little of the political influence of the paper in its
early years may have resulted from this ability of McKee and his
small staff to produce a journal of great reader interest in areas
other than political. Just as he had pushed his paper's editorial
policies toward Republicanism as fast as the public of a slave-
holding state would allow, so, too, had he broadened its news policies and coverage as quickly as improved communications and
"shoestring" financing would permit.

Now it was a four-page paper of blanket size with ten columns to the page. "Ears" had been added to the front page. These
were upward extensions of the first and last columns, the left
"ear" containing the names of the editor and of the proprietors
and the subscription rates, the right "ear" giving the advertising
rates and regulations. In addition, column headings had been increased to include "Commercial," "Telegraphic," "Court Reports," "Hotel Registrants," "Meteorological Observations," and
"Steamboat Arrivals." These, of course, varied in length from day
to day, but added to the increased political, general, and literary
coverage, they formed a journal with wide reader interest.

From 50 to 75 per cent of each issue of the paper, even after
its enlargement, was devoted to advertising. But McKee was now
attracting a wide variety of larger advertisements from the leading business establishments of the city. Small cuts of steamboats,
trains, oysters, pen points, and artificial limbs often enlivened the
"cards" on the front page.

Among the leading advertisers were Charles Beardslee and
Brothers, importers and dealers in clothes, who sold cassimeres,
vestings, beaver, blankets, tailors' trimmings; F. Dings and Company, dealers in hosiery, gloves, combs, table and pocket cutlery,
and fancy and variety goods; T. M. Taylor and Company, which
sold brandies in wood or glass, old sherries, Madeira and Port
wines in wood and glass, German claret and champagne wines,
whisky, rum, and London Porter and Scotch ale; Pinaud and
Jungst, who sold fashionable hairdresses and premium wigs. Grocers advertised sugar at 3¼ to 4¼ cents, Rio coffee at 10 cents,
and flour at $3.60 a barrel. They listed nails, lard in kegs and bar-
rels, figs, Timothy seed, and washboards in large lots, but quoted
no prices. Clothing merchants of the time were selling moleskin
hats, cloth caps, black opera caps, and fine caps with plush bands
for traveling. A big item in the "Firearms" column was Sharp's
patent breech-loading and self-priming rifle, which could be
loaded on horseback at a smart gallop. Of interest to the women
readers of the *Democrat* were Dupuy's "Kiss Me Quick" per-
fume, the catamenial bandage or menstrual protector, and Singer
sewing machines.

But what publishing problems this increased coverage and
larger paper brought to the owners! McKee had been forced to
raise his subscription rates. In 1859 the *Daily* sold for ten dollars
a year, the *Weekly* for two dollars, and the *Tri-Weekly*, which
was being published as early as 1855, sold for six dollars. McKee
and Fishback also initiated several devices for increasing their circulation. In 1857, for example, they ran a contest in which the
person who sent in the largest number of subscriptions in a given
time would receive a 160-acre farm in Missouri. Second prize was
an 80-acre farm; third prize, 40 acres; and fourth prize, a valuable
lot in any city in the state.[32]

The proprietors also started a practice, used by many papers
in that time, of publishing a campaign special. Called the *Campaign Democrat*, it was offered for a short period at greatly reduced prices. In 1860 a *Campaign Daily* subscription that began
in July and lasted through the November elections cost $2.50.
The *Campaign Tri-Weekly* was offered for $6.00 for "clubs" of

five copies, $12.00 for ten, and $24.00 for twenty. The *Campaign Weekly* sold for thirty cents to clubs of ten or more.[33]

Advertising, of course, remained a source of considerable income for the paper. McKee and Fishback believed in advertising. "A business man might as well stop his daily paper as his advertising," a *Democrat* editorial said.[34] One insertion of one "square," eight single-column lines or less, sold for fifty cents. An extra charge was made for illustrations, and advertisements inserted in the editorial columns were priced at ten cents a word. Notices of fairs, soirees, concerts, "any public entertainments where charges were made for admittance," or any private enterprise "calculated and intended to promote individual interest" were inserted only when they were paid for in advance. As every issue in 1859 carried from one to two columns of such notices, McKee and Fishback must have collected a fair sum from them.

In addition, the job and printing office which the proprietors operated in conjunction with the *Democrat* was a rather lucrative enterprise. As early as 1854 McKee advertised that "we are now prepared to execute all types of job printing at reasonable rates with neatness and dispatch." He claimed that his office was equipped with "the latest styles of new and fashionable type of every description necessary for the prompt execution of Book and Plain and Fancy Job Printing."[35] He was able to contract for much of the city, county, and state printing. During the first three months of 1859, for example, his firm printed forms and circulars for the city assessor's office in the amount of $193.50.[36] The *Missouri Democrat* newspaper, book, and job printing office also printed pamphlets of speeches by Blair and Brown, and later the proceedings of the General Assembly.

With the increase in business, McKee was able to keep up his yearly payments on the debt he had contracted when he purchased the *Union*, so that on April 29, 1859, he could tell his readers that the *Democrat* was out of debt. The last installment of the sixteen thousand dollars had been paid.

Still, the years of struggle had not been easy. McKee not only had trouble keeping an ample supply of newsprint, but he had distribution problems. In 1854 he told his readers that any failure or delay in receiving the *Democrat* was "the fault of mails and the postmaster."[37] This announcement came after he had received complaints from the postmaster at Newhope, Missouri, only sixty miles away. The *Weekly Democrat*, it seemed, was not seen there for months at a time, although other St. Louis papers arrived regularly.[38]

To further his contention that his distribution problems were a result of political partisanship in the post office, McKee reported editorially that a Mr. Jacoby, who had been connected with the newspaper department of the post office and who was noted for his industry and fidelity, had been forced to resign because of ill-natured and groundless charges made by the *Republican*. Times had come to a fine pass, the editorial said, when the *Republican* could exercise the function of an executive or remove at pleasure officers in the public service.[39]

Other troubles had also beset the *Democrat*. The intense heat of the summer softened the press rollers and the ink would not distribute properly, a common printing difficulty of the time. Furthermore, in spite of his drives to increase his circulation, and in spite of his increased news coverage, McKee had not been able to equal the circulation of the *Republican*, his greatest competitor.

Still, McKee and Fishback had paid off the big debt and they had increased the prestige of the paper. They must have known that if they could weather the next few years, they could give the *Republican* much greater competition. There would come a time when the *Democrat* would be the leading paper in St. Louis.

Chapter IV

A Republican Stronghold

WHEN B. Gratz Brown left the *Democrat* in April, 1859, McKee and Fishback did not have to seek outside the paper's staff for an editor with Republican convictions. They promoted their assistant editor, Peter L. Foy,[1] who was already well-known in Missouri newspaper circles.

Foy had come to the *Democrat* in 1856 from Cape Girardeau, where he had published *The Expositor*, a paper he had bought in 1854. Devoted to Benton, he had been the Senator's "faithful friend" in the celebrated gubernatorial canvass of 1856. But when Benton was not elected, Foy had stopped the publication of his paper and had moved to St. Louis.[2] McKee, realizing Foy's journalistic abilities, and knowing his strong antislavery views, employed him as an editorial writer and political reporter.

"A tireless reader and a profound thinker," Foy soon won acclaim for his vigorous writing.[3] McKee and Fishback had sent him to Jefferson City to report the legislative proceedings and to Washington to cover congressional activities.[4] But by the time that he was named editor, he had become best known for his *Democrat* editorials on the unfair competition of black labor with white labor. A series of these had greatly interested Lincoln. Under such headings as "The Claims of White Labor," "Free White Labor," "Free and Slave Labor," "The White Labor Question," and "Negroes Filling White Men's Jobs," Foy's editorials were characterized by his use of the word "Nigger." The frequency of this word in *Democrat* editorials increased after Brown's resignation.

Brown had moved the *Democrat* from Bentonism to Free Democracy, and as a strong advocate of gradual emancipation and an admirer of Frank Blair, Foy was to lead the paper into Repub-

licanism. Already recognized as having exercised a great influence
during its first eight years, the *Democrat* under Foy's editorship
was to become known as the leading Republican paper of the
West.[5]

A few days before Brown's resignation, the Free Democrats,
led by Blair, had been successful in re-electing O. D. Filley as
mayor. With the municipal canvass out of the way, Foy was free
to concentrate from the first on the coming presidential campaign
and on further agitation for emancipation. He began by printing
a letter to the Whig Committee written by Edward Bates, a Missouri Old Line Whig and a possible presidential candidate. He
did this, he said, so that the *Democrat* readers could know Bates's
position on protection as the chief end of government and could
think over Bates's comments against the agitation of the slavery
question.[6]

At first, however, Foy was reluctant to commit the *Democrat*
to a particular candidate. He would wait, he said, until all candidates had announced. The *Democrat* then would support the
man who best personified the paper's principles.[7] But four days
later the editor did suggest that Bates would be a suitable nominee
of the Republican party. At the same time he pointed out that
Bates had been indefinite in his letter on the slavery question but
that he had, in actuality, opposed the repeal of the Missouri Compromise, opposed the Douglas territorial theory, and maintained
the constitutionality of Free-Soil enactments for the territories.[8]
It was not, however, until October that the *Democrat* announced
for Bates "beyond cavil or doubt," because a Missouri emancipa-
tionist would be a pledge of the "speedy release of the State from
the incubus of Slavery."[9]

In a series of editorials Foy traced the tendency of the National Democrats toward proslavery. He saw better times ahead
and predicted that the Republicans would unite in thought and
feeling and carry the 1860 elections. He attacked the system of
slavery and discussed the struggle between white-men mechanics
and the owners-of-slaves mechanics. The *Democrat*, he said, was
opposed to Stephen Douglas because the Illinois senator had
lapsed into the "slough of niggerism," Foy's favorite term for

proslavery. The Dred Scott Case did not aid the Buchanan-Douglas platform because that decision was limited to the declaration that a Negro was not a United States citizen and the rest of the decision had no authority.[10]

Foy warned that all who wished to see sectionalism suppressed should cooperate with the Republican party. Then on July 15, the *Democrat* "bloomed for Republicanism." Foy wrote:

> The Republican party is in reality the palladium of the Union and of the rights of the States. It has emasculated the abolition party. . . . Were the Republican organization dissolved, the National Democracy would experience no resistance in the propagation of slavery. . . . Looking below the surface, it becomes apparent that the Republican Party is the true conservator of the Union and of Constitutional liberty.

If Republicanism failed, he said, disunion would result because a fiercely abolitionist party would come in. Therefore those who were indulging in petulant criticism should use their influence in behalf of the Republican party.

For the rest of the year Foy was engaged in selling Republicanism to *Democrat* readers. The paper consistently backed Blair, who was acquiring a national reputation for his understanding of border state problems, by publishing his speeches in full and advocating editorially his platform of free white labor, Negro colonization, anticorruption in the government, and a central railroad to the West.[11]

Foy seemed to ignore the minor issues; he concentrated in his editorials on the big question of slavery. When the John Brown raid occurred, he placed the blame on Brown, saying that none but bad men would "avail themselves of the recent occurrences to aggravate sectional animosities." He thought that Brown and his men should suffer the most "disgraceful death which the humanity of the offended laws" could inflict.[12] Venomously and sarcastically, Foy attacked the efforts of the *Missouri Republican* to confuse the issue.

> We earnestly advise our neighbor. . . . to go in for Nigger exclusively. For the last month it has been full of nigger.

Yesterday it had three columns . . . about old Brown and nigger. Nigger is a dish which it serves up with great and constant variety—nigger baked, nigger boiled, nigger hashed, nigger giblets, nigger head with woolly sauce, nigger, nigger, nigger, nigger to the end of its disgusting bill of fare. . . .[13]

The prominence of the *Democrat* staff in directing the Republican party in Missouri became evident early in 1860. Frank Blair and B. Gratz Brown, who were contributing letters to the paper, were selected as delegates at large to the National Republican Convention in Chicago. Editor Foy was chosen as a delegate from the First District in St. Louis.[14]

The wide coverage that the *Democrat* gave to political events of that year is indicated by the daily dispatches and letters, signed "McC," from Jefferson City during the General Assembly; by the special dispatches, signed "Pike," from the Illinois Republican Convention; and from the National Republican Convention. "McC" stood for Joseph McCullagh, whose accurate reporting of speeches made before the Missouri Legislature led to a better paying job on the *Cincinnati Gazette*.[15] The "Pike" letters and the convention reports were probably written by Henry Villard.[16]

The *Democrat's* advocacy of Bates for president seemed to have been nothing more than a gesture. The Missourian's name was placed before the convention by Blair, but when the voting started, Bates almost immediately gave his support to Abraham Lincoln because he considered Lincoln a "sound, safe, national man."[17] The *Democrat* declared editorially that Lincoln's nomination was "hardly a disappointment but rather an agreeable surprise," and that the Republican platform was faultless.[18]

A month before, the *Democrat* writers had begun to attack the opposition. They anticipated trouble in Charleston, where the National Democratic Convention was to meet. "Next Monday the great witenagemot of the National Democracy meets in the capital of Niggerdom," Foy wrote. "There will be but one question before it—whether Stephen Arnold Douglas shall or shall not be nominated."[19] He was jubilant when the Charleston convention adjourned to meet later in Baltimore. The National Democratic party, he said, had proved "utterly incapable of managing its own leaders." In addition, he called the Charleston meeting "the worst form of Nigger agitation" that the country had ever seen and he was certain that whatever portion of the Democratic party was left intact by the "Plug Uglies of Baltimore" would be wiped out by the people in the November election.[20]

Brown, Blair, and Foy returned from the Republican Convention to work personally for the election of Lincoln. Daily editorials extolled the Republican candidate and derided the Democratic efforts to elect Douglas.[21] The paper ran an interview with Lincoln, who was called the "man of the people" and the "living symbol of the Union and fraternity of the States."[22] As early as August, Blair and the *Democrat* predicted a Lincoln victory.

To aid and abet the success of the Republican party, McKee and Fishback published their *Campaign Democrat*.[23] They announced that the paper would labor for the progress and triumph of the Republican cause; that it would promote the best interests of the masses and the progress and prosperity of the country; and that it would contain a complete history of the presidential campaign, the platforms of the several parties, and the full reports of the most important meetings and speeches. They hoped, in the end, to announce "the triumphant choice of a Republican president."[24]

Blair officially opened the presidential campaign in Missouri at a rally in St. Charles, which was announced and fully reported in the *Democrat*. By late August, Blair was scheduled to speak at seventeen meetings in behalf of the Republican candidate.[25] That the *Democrat* was the mouthpiece of the Republican party is indicated by the editor's note following this list of meetings. Foy asked all Republican papers to run Blair's speaking engagements. Moreover the Central Steering Committee of the Republican party frequently met at the *Democrat* office.[26]

As election day neared, the *Democrat* announced that Lincoln's election seemed certain, but it feared fraud at the polls. To prevent this, Blair organized the Wide Awakes, a group which

was to play a mounting role in the turbulent times of the following year. The paper carried frequent announcements of Wide
Awake meetings and listed the Wide Awake Vigilance Committees, which were to guard the voting places.[27] Daniel M. Houser,
now the *Democrat* bookkeeper,[28] was a member of the Sixth
Ward Vigilance Committee.

On the eve of the election the *Democrat* pages were filled with
short paragraphs urging the readers to vote for Lincoln. Foy
pointed out that every vote for Douglas, Bell, or Breckinridge
was a vote for the extension and perpetuation of slavery. Every
vote for Lincoln was a vote for the perpetuation of the Union,
for a country where slavery would not exist.[29]

Hardly had the complete returns of the election been recorded
before McKee and Fishback announced their political stand for
the coming year. The great Republican party had redeemed the
country, and the *Democrat* would march abreast with the grand
movement. It would cordially and unfalteringly support the administration of Abraham Lincoln.[30]

But even while reporting the election returns from over the
country, McKee's paper began a campaign against secession. It
carried reports of which states were for and which were against
secession, running one and a half columns on a secession meeting
in Georgia. A correspondent, signing his dispatches "Encore,"
ranged as far south as New Orleans to report on such meetings.
Editorials blamed the cotton lords of the border states for runaway slaves, and Editor Foy pointed out that financial losses
caused by the disunion movement already amounted to $659,-
120,000. Furthermore, he said that the Constitution did not give
the several states the right to secede.[31]

At the same time the paper was condemning in its editorials
the new governor of Missouri, Claiborne F. Jackson. In his first
message to the General Assembly, Governor Jackson had recommended the calling of a state convention "to adopt measures for
vindicating the sovereignty of the state and the protection of its
institutions." Calling this a disunion speech, the editor urged all
Union men to watch the traitorous designs of their governor and

to be prepared to meet all attempts to place Missouri in a false position.[32]

When the bill calling for this convention was passed, *Democrat* writers campaigned for convention delegates who were known to be Union men. Editorially the paper declared that the "Union must not be staked in any party game. It must not be put in the balance against any party platform. . . . The eligibility of the candidates must not be treated by any party associations."[33] The *Democrat* was fighting to keep St. Louis and, if possible, Missouri from seceeding.

Blair urged that the city stay in the Union in the only possible way, by electing a ticket of Unconditional Union men without regard to party. He wrote in a letter to the people:

> I am for the Union all over. . . . I go for the Union so strongly that I will vote for any political opponent I have on earth for the convention, if he is for the Union unconditionally, and I will vote for no man who is not for the Union. . . .[34]

When the election was over and the State Convention met at Jefferson City, its proceedings were reported to the paper by special dispatches, signed "G. W. F."[35] The editors were pleased when the Convention moved to St. Louis, where the climate was more favorable toward Unionism. A series of letters addressed to members of the Convention appeared on the front page of the *Democrat*, beginning March 1. Signed "Common Sense," they were in the style of Editor Foy. He advised the members to vote for remaining in the Union. Secession, he contended, would stop emigration to Missouri. He also believed that the members would not be justified in granting the Georgia Commissioner, Luther J. Glenn, permission to address them. Glenn, he said, was trying "to advise the people to devote their whole energy to the protection of the few thousand Negro owners" to the "utter neglect and utter contempt of interests of thousands of our own people who own no Negroes." Niggerism was not the sole policy of the state. The "divinity of slavery" should be dropped.[36]

These may have been the last editorials that Foy wrote as chief editor. Lincoln, to reward the *Democrat* for its support of him, had appointed Foy postmaster of St. Louis.[37] The editor left the paper late in March to assume his new duties. Later he was to edit a rival journal.[38]

McKee and Fishback promoted A. H. Lewis to succeed Foy, but he died in September, 1862.[39] By this time the *Democrat* proprietors were looking for someone to add prestige to their paper. They offered the editorship to Whitelaw Reid at a good salary and, according to Reid, with the promise of a speedy increase. But Reid turned their offer down.[40]

Then McKee and Fishback approached John F. Hume with an offer to make him the paper's leading political writer. A lawyer from New England who had come to St. Louis several years earlier, Hume had contributed many antislavery articles to the *Democrat*. He accepted the offer of the proprietors with the understanding that there would be no let-up on emancipation.[41]

However, when Foy left the *Democrat* in 1861, Blair and the paper were fighting hard merely to keep Missouri in the Union. In fact it was this crusade for Unionism that brought two mob attacks to the doors of the *Democrat* offices. Mobbing of newspapers was not unusual in the pre-Civil War days, but McKee saw his paper attacked twice within less than six weeks.

The first attack followed the municipal elections. During March the *Democrat* had daily extolled John How, the candidate for mayor on the "Unconditional Ticket," and viciously berated Daniel G. Taylor, his opponent. How was defeated. But on election day drunken mobs terrorized the city. That night a dozen ruffians gathered in front of the *Democrat* office, threatening in vile language to smash the presses. Inside, McKee and his staff stood ready to defend themselves. After a few minutes, however, the demonstrators moved off to vent their ire on other Union men, and the *Democrat* escaped unscathed.

McKee and his staff were uncowed by this threat of violence. The next day the paper commented:

> To us it seems that those who wish to stay in St. Louis and in the Union at the same time, will have no alternative but an appeal to arms in defense of their position. . . . The ruffianism which the authorities have heretofore kept down

seems to feel that it is free from restraint already, as the conduct of a band of rowdies, who appeared in front of this office last night, sufficiently proves.[42]

Actually it was the use of arms that caused the second mob attack on the *Democrat* office. Rumors had circulated early in February that Southern sympathizers planned to seize the United States Arsenal at St. Louis.[43] In April, in an attempt to deter secessionists from attacking, the editor published a story on the Arsenal, claiming that eight or nine hundred men were stationed there.[44] This, however, did not prevent Governor Jackson from ordering General D. M. Frost to encamp with seven hundred state guardsmen in Lindell Grove. This bivouac area was called Camp Jackson.[45]

Blair and Captain Nathaniel Lyon, commander of the Arsenal, believed that Frost meant to attack the Arsenal and capture the arms and ammunition for the secessionists. To prevent this, Lyon ordered his men to march on Camp Jackson on the afternoon of May 10. Frost surrendered without fighting, but in the process of moving the prisoners to the Arsenal, spectators, Union men, and prisoners became involved in a fight. Twenty people were killed. Resentment over this brought out angry, armed mobs that roamed the streets for two days and nights,[46] and the *Democrat* building was mobbed a second time.

The rioters blamed Blair for the bloodshed, because his Wide Awakes had marched with Lyon's troops, and the "dirty" *Democrat*, because it was the headquarters for the Black Republicans and had promoted Unionism. So on the night following the bloody encounter on the streets of St. Louis, a mob of proslavery sympathizers, bent on revenge, attacked McKee's paper.

Most of the *Democrat's* staff were members of Blair's Wide Awakes and were still at the Arsenal when dusk settled over the terror-stricken city. McKee, almost alone in his office, knew that the mob was certain to come, but again he was determined to stand his ground. Then at dusk seven or eight policemen and a handful of Union sympathizers, some of whom the publisher had never seen before, appeared at the office to help him. They stretched, a thin column, across Locust Street and waited. The policemen had only their clubs; McKee and his Union friends were armed with revolvers.

They could hear the screaming mob long before it rounded the corner. According to F. J. Fry, who was in the thin line of Unionists, several thousand drunken men, well-armed with bricks and stones, "came down on the double quick." Terrifying yells rent the air, but the little band of defenders did not waver. They ordered the rioters to halt. The policemen waved their clubs, and the Union men drew their pistols. Still the mob came, hurling rocks before them. Then suddenly within a few feet of McKee and his friends, they turned and fled. Not a shot was fired.[47]

This terrifying experience did not deter McKee from expressing editorially his Union beliefs, nor keep him from praising Blair for his part in the fall of Camp Jackson. *Democrat* writers called Frost a Jackson man, and Jackson was termed a traitor. They warned secessionists that if any harm came to Blair "summary punishment, without 'benefit of clergy,' " would be inflicted.[48]

Yet in less than six months Blair and the *Democrat* were at odds. The difficulty arose over the question of emancipation. McKee and Fishback were by now campaigning for immediate emancipation, while Blair was still hoping for gradual compensated emancipation.

General Frémont, who had assumed the duties of Commander of the Army Department of the West, had issued a proclamation ordering all persons who were taken with arms in their hands within the Union lines to be tried by court martial, and, if found guilty of bearing arms against the government, shot. All property of persons in arms against the government was to be confiscated and their slaves, if any, were to be freed.[49] The *Democrat* rejoiced over Frémont's ordinance, declaring that the General could have done nothing else.[50]

And so when Blair criticized Frémont the paper turned sharply against its long-time partisan and part-owner. Lincoln ordered an investigation of Frémont, which the *Democrat* believed had been instigated by Blair. The paper became so abusive of Blair that he later said:

> I was at the time owner of a considerable interest in the
> *Democrat* newspaper, without having shared in its profits
> . . . and found myself soundly abused every morning on
> type, which was my own property, by men who, less than
> a week before, shared fully in the opinions which they at-
> tacked me for holding.[51]

After the investigating committee left St. Louis, Frémont had
Blair arrested for insubordination. The *Democrat* editors acknowledged that Blair's arrest was embarrassing, but they regarded it as "the privilege of all true men in this perilous crisis to
stand firmly and fearlessly by General Frémont."[52] Throughout
the war, the *Democrat* continued to praise Frémont and attack
Blair.

The Blair-Frémont controversy marked the beginning of a
split of the Republican party into two factions, Conservatives
and Radicals. Blair led the Conservatives, who favored gradual
emancipation; Brown, backed by the *Democrat*, headed the Radicals, who favored immediate emancipation. Believing that abolition would shorten the war, Hume, the new editor, campaigned
ceaselessly for emancipation.[53]

The question was, he said, how best to emancipate Missouri
from slavery.[54] In 1862 he vigorously supported the work of the
State Convention when it disenfranchised rebels and disloyalists.
But he ridiculed the Convention for refusing to provide financial
aid to carry out emancipation.[55] The colonization plan, advocated
by the *Democrat* only two years before, was no longer a substi-
tute for emancipation.

In 1863 Hume applauded the work of the Radical Convention.
He praised the appointment of the Committee of Seventy to meet
with Lincoln in Washington to present Radical grievances.
Nearly every issue of the *Democrat* lauded Charles D. Drake, the
committee spokesman, who had taken over the leadership of the
Radical party when B. Gratz Brown was named United States
Senator.[56]

The campaigns of 1864 gave the paper further opportunities
for disseminating Radical propaganda. James S. Thomas, a Radical, was elected mayor in April by a majority of more than three

thousand votes.[57] Thomas C. Fletcher, a Radical whom the *Democrat* favored, was elected governor in November.[58] In spite of the paper's earlier criticism of Lincoln, it had campaigned for him; after his election, the *Democrat* could claim the distinction of being the only slave-state journal supporting Lincoln in 1860 and 1864.[59] McKee justifiably was proud of the part his paper had played in keeping the Republican administration in office.

As early as July, 1863, the *Democrat* and the Radical party began agitation for a new state constitution that would free slaves.[60] Subsequently, the Constitutional Convention met in St. Louis in January, 1865. The *Democrat* ran its proceedings on the front page, and Hume's editorials praised each ordinance. When the Convention passed the one that freed all slaves in Missouri immediately, the *Democrat* was jubilant. Colonels, majors, and captains in glittering array "watched the death of slavery in Missouri." Crowds gathered in the streets, flags were run up on public buildings, and hilarity and festivity reigned.[61]

The question of suffrage, however, was not so easily settled by the Convention. Delegates argued for days while the *Democrat* editorially proclaimed Drake's radical ideas—that it was unnecessary to bar Negroes from office because none would be elected anyway, that rebels should not be allowed to vote, and that the disloyal should not participate in the administration of public affairs.[62]

Hume added fuel to the fire by saying that the paper's subscription list was an indication of who the loyal people throughout the state were.[63] Drake, the acknowledged author of the Constitution, wrote a series of articles for the paper, explaining and justifying his ideas. He warned all true Radicals against a "forgive and forget" doctrine. Even the surrender of Lee and the death of Lincoln were used to further arguments for the adoption of the new constitution. "Let the subjugated states be dealt with as they deserve. We have finally conquered the rebellion. Now let us punish the traitors."[64]

When St. Louis voted overwhelmingly against the adoption of the new constitution and it seemed that the Radicals had failed, Hume was distressed and charged fraud. He believed that certain election officials had allowed large numbers of returned rebels to vote.[65] But the final tabulation of the election returns showed that the constitution had been ratified. Then did the *Democrat* really rejoice, because this victory, as Hume said, was of no ordinary significance.[66]

The Radicals, with the *Democrat* as spokesman and *Democrat* writers as leaders, now had control of the city and state government. Missouri slaves had been freed. The new constitution had been adopted. By insinuation, threat, and command, the paper had advocated extreme political measures and had played a major role in placing the Radicals in power. Indeed, the *Democrat* had become nationally recognized as a Republican stronghold.

Chapter V

Reporting the Civil War

The increased and increasing demand for news and the
incessant response of the revolving cylinders speedily wears
the freshness from our type.

The Missouri Democrat, July 9, 1864

THE proprietors of the *Democrat* could complain about their
worn type with pride; the paper reported the Civil War as
actively and copiously as it promoted the policies of the Republican party. Between the fall of Camp Jackson and the columns
of coverage given to the surrender of General Robert E. Lee, the
Democrat appeared to "grow up" as a newspaper. In spite of the
high cost of newsprint and labor and the confusion and hazards
of wartime reporting, McKee and Fishback supplied their readers
with more and more news.

St. Louis was so much a part of the struggle that it was only
natural for the proprietors to devote news and editorial space to
the rebellion and to St. Louis men fighting in the conflict. War
news, at first relegated to the third page of the paper, was soon
moved to the front page. Dispatches came by foot messenger, by
train, by pony express, and by telegraph. Reports from special
correspondents, and writers who also contributed to other papers,
letters from soldiers, copy from the Western Associated Press,
and newspapers from the East—all furnished the *Democrat* with
news from the battle areas.

So much war news was available and public interest was so
keen that often as much as a fourth of the *Democrat* was devoted
to dispatches from the fighting fronts. In addition, there was
always news of bushwhacking and guerilla fighting in Missouri,
which would swell the copy until sometimes as many as twelve

52

of the paper's thirty-six columns were filled with echoes of the
war.

So great did the demand for information become that McKee
and Fishback began publication of the "Evening Edition," a tabloid, four-page, four-column paper. First published on September 24, 1861, it contained "the latest local, telegraphic, and mail
news" received up until three o'clock in the afternoon. Nearly
50 per cent was devoted to advertising, but, except for the latest
market quotations and a short paragraph on river news, the rest
of the paper was made up of war dispatches and letters.[1] Occasionally the evening edition was rushed to the streets with the
inside pages blank. In the latter part of the war, a one-sheet insert,
called a "supplement," was used in regular editions. Sometimes a
second edition with "last night's dispatches" was also published.[2]
In the evening, the latest reports were posted on the office windows, and after supper townspeople would gather on the sidewalk to read and discuss them.[3]

Frequently battle news arrived late, and the editors had to
apologize for such things as storms interfering with the telegraph.
As many as five or six dispatches from the same battle front
would arrive at the same time and be printed in the same issue.
Over four columns were devoted in one issue to the Battle of
Pittsburgh, and dispatches from the Battle of Pea Ridge occupied
nine columns.[4] Multiple-deck headlines, sometimes twenty-five
lines long, came into prominence, too. The closer the end of the
war came, the longer and blacker the headlines became. Each
line usually indicated the contents of a different dispatch, but the
items of the story were not run necessarily in the order in which
they were listed in the headlines. In the *Democrat*, unlike many
of the papers of the time, the latest dispatch was often run first.[5]
Leads tended to be direct, but frequently they were very long,
as in the story of the hanging of a bushwhacker.

> The convicted and sentenced bushwhacker, John Nichols,
> was duly executed at Jefferson City, at three o'clock Friday
> afternoon, in accordance with the verdict of the military
> commission which examined his case, and whose findings
> and sentence were submitted and approved by the presi-
> dent.[6]

Occasionally, too, the *Democrat* published war maps. Two columns wide and eight inches deep, one of these showed the positions at Island No. 10, a hotly-contested vantage point in the middle of the Mississippi. Another showed the operations at Charleston at the time of the attack on Fort Wagner.[7]

Besides the editorials on war situations, other types of war news included lists of prisoners sent to St. Louis prisons, weekly reports of deaths in St. Louis hospitals and camps, troop movements, military funerals, and stories of conditions in hospitals and prisons. Even news from rebel newspapers was frequently printed.[8]

Correspondents, signing themselves with such names as "Busby," "St. Louis," "Union," "Macon," and "Bright 'Un," wrote letters to the *Democrat* editors. These were filled as much with rumors and reports of camp conditions as with news of fighting. "Everything is quiet here," wrote a correspondent from Rolla. "There is some sickness, and a few deaths occur in various camps. There is much anxiety expressed relative to forward movement."[9] From Busby at Springfield came the news that rains made the place sickly with a death a day from camp typhus fever. Seven wagons of wounded men were reported on the way to camp.[10] A description of the Baxter Springs Massacre came from a personal letter of General J. G. Blunt, which a *Democrat* correspondent had transcribed. It ended:

> I was fortunate in escaping, as in my efforts to halt and rally the men I frequently got in the rear and became considerably mixed up with the rebels, who did not fail to pay me their compliments. Revolver bullets flew around my head thick as hail—but not a scratch. I believe I am not to be killed by a rebel bullet.[11]

William McKee's brother, Henry McKee, and J. B. McCullagh were both war reporters. The nineteen-year-old McCullagh, who by this time had joined the staff of the *Cincinnati Commercial*, also reported for the *Democrat*.[12] At the beginning of the war he was a member of Frémont's bodyguards. Later he wrote from Fort Donelson, Shiloh, and Vicksburg, where he was with Admiral Foote.[13] Others who reported the war for the *Democrat* as well as for other journals included G. O. Beaman, Lucian Barnes,

William A. Fayel, Henry C. Kelly, Januarius A. McGahan, and Truman A. Post.[14] Of course, this sharing of correspondents made coverage of the war less expensive for McKee and Fishback.

Oddly enough, as early as February, 1861, the *Democrat* was printing rumors of secret reinforcements of Fort Sumter, but the editors considered this as a "very improbable piece of news." In fact a Southern victory was so unthinkable that a *Democrat* writer joked: "We will bet South Carolina a hat that . . . if she attacks Fort Sumter, she will hear from her in a style to which she is not accustomed."[15] A week later, however, the *Democrat* was carrying letters from wives of soldiers at Fort Sumter about bad conditions there.[16] Then came the first tragic dispatches with news of the fall of the fort, and the editors announced that war had come.[17] When the *Republican* advised to keep cool and await developments the *Democrat* was indignant.

> What! Keep cool when the hand of the assassin is upon your throat? Keep cool! When your house is on fire, and your family threatened with destruction! Keep cool! When the enemy of the country is at your gate, and has already lighted the torch of incendiary war.[18]

During the summer and fall of 1861 news of fighting along the Missouri River and in the southwestern section of the state dominated the paper. Following the capture of Camp Jackson, confused reports told of fighting in nearby Potosi, St. Charles County, Rolla, Mexico, and Boonville.[19] In a running account of the Boonville battle a *Democrat* correspondent, probably Lucian Barnes, said that the engagement was short.[20] The flight of the secessionists began at eight o'clock in the morning, he wrote, and the battle was over by eleven.[21] One of the paper's editorial writers believed this defeat of General Jackson, who led the secessionists at Boonville, had turned the tide in favor of the Union men. "Jackson is routed; his generals have fled the field; his troops are dispersed. The warlike resources of secession are about exhausted."[22]

But the *Democrat's* elation over this victory was short-lived, because bitter scrimmages were reported at Sturgeon and Canton, in Pettis County, on the Mississippi River, and in Northeast Mis-

souri. Later, of course, the paper could announce that General
Grant had the rebels running at Ironton and could call the Battle
of Springfield a "glorious victory." On September 23 a correspondent from there wrote that General McCullagh, the Southern commander at Wilson Creek, and his force of about four
thousand troops were "confidently believed to have left the state,
going south." But in that battle Captain Nathaniel Lyon, whom
the *Democrat* had consistently praised, was killed, and St. Louis
mourned.[23]

Meanwhile in St. Louis, where rumors were hard to separate
from facts, feelings were running high. A *Democrat* writer complained that "with everybody a walking arsenal," nobody was
safe. He believed that if nobody carried arms there would be
little provocation to use them.[24] A few weeks later the paper proposed that every Missouri man not known to be an unconditional Union man be compelled "by military police to surrender
every rifle and shotgun in his possession."[25]

Then in June, General Frémont, whom the *Democrat* had secretly, if not openly, favored for president in 1856, was ordered
to St. Louis to take over supreme command of the Western Department. The paper predicted that his achievements would be
as spectacular as those that the New York journals were envisag-
ing for General McClellan.[26] With the general in charge there
would be no more red tape or delay.[27] McKee and Fishback accepted Frémont wholeheartedly and appeared blind to the irregularities of his contracts. They blamed Washington, not the general, for losses in the West.[28] His emancipation proclamation
endeared him even more to the *Democrat*, because in it he did
exactly what the paper had been advocating.[29]

Ultimately this led to the McKee-Blair split. The *Democrat*
ridiculed Blair for criticizing Frémont, classifying the general's
opponents into three groups: jealous politicians who wanted to
crush him, contractors whom he had thwarted, and unthinking
people who followed the first two classes.[30] The paper asked its
readers to give Frémont a fair chance because, since his arrival in
St. Louis, no man could have done more. The fortifications which
he had thrown up around the city were a master stroke of policy.

With them the city could be defended by a small force against a hundred thousand men and the Grand Army of the West could now be employed for conquering rather than defending.

> Whether General Frémont will prove himself a great captain, or not, remains to be seen. He is brave and his march against the enemies of the Union will be followed by the prayers of its friends. He may fail. The best men sometimes fail in the best of causes. . . . That man is great indeed who attains noble end by noble means—and he is really great if he fails in his noble efforts. He is great, whether he reign like Aurelius, or bleed like Socrates.[31]

To McKee and his staff, Frémont was always great. Even when he was removed from his duties and returned to St. Louis, the paper promoted a big reception and torchlight parade in his honor.[32]

After the retreat of General Claiborne Jackson's forces, and after water commerce was restored between St. Louis and counties on the Tennessee and Cumberland rivers,[33] news of fighting in Missouri was confined to guerilla warfare.[34] Both Union and Southern sympathizers resorted to bushwhacking, plundering, and marauding. Along the Kansas border, General Jim Lane led the Union sympathizers in raids which could be tracked by "fires needlessly kindled and blood needlessly shed."[35] But according to the *Democrat* such action was necessary to sustain the Union because of the destruction of homes of Union men by "secesh guerillas." In southwestern Missouri, Union men had had everything destroyed, even their wagons.[36] Even though rebel armies had been driven from the state, said the paper, military authorities still had the serious duty of suppressing the bloody bushwhacking.[37]

General Henry W. Halleck's order, printed in the *Democrat* on March 13, 1862, to try as murderers and robbers any guerillas captured seemed to have little effect. The bushwhacking became so bad that the order went out to capturing parties to shoot guerillas found lurking or ambushing with arms in their hands. The paper declared that the order was very proper, and Colonel Huston was commended for shooting eight bushwhackers near Lexington.[38]

Still nearly every issue of the *Democrat* contained lurid tales of guerilla outrages. On September 4, 1863, the editors reported that bushwhackers in several parts of the state had made strenuous efforts to prevent delegates from attending the Radical Union Convention in Jefferson City. Delegations from Barry, Lawrence, and other counties in the Southwest had turned back because of guerilla threats. Two of their members were reported killed. Some delegates had endangered their lives by riding through districts "full of bushwhackers from 50 to over 100 miles before a safe conveyance could be reached." The paper especially commended the delegates from one county who had armed themselves and hidden in a wagon of wheat driven by a Negro "who represented himself as on the way to the mill." Finally General Schofield had to go to the "Border District,"[39] where Unionists under Jim Lane of Kansas and Quantrill's "secesh" raiders had kept the countryside in a turmoil for weeks.[40] Even as late as March, 1865, the *Democrat* was reporting guerilla warfare in the state.

Censorship and proscription probably bothered the *Democrat* less than other St. Louis newspapers because of its political views and because of its increased power and prestige. In fact it was the suspension of the *St. Louis Evening News* for publishing articles censuring Frémont that led the proprietors to decide to publish the "Evening Edition." There was need, McKee and Fishback said, for an evening paper to supply the demand for the latest intelligence.[41]

On June 15, 1861, the editor of the *State Journal* was arrested and his private papers seized, and under General Frémont's order on August 14 the *Bulletin* and the *Missourian*, which were printed at the *State Journal* establishment on Pine Street, were suppressed because they had been publishing the South's side of accounts of affairs as well as improbable and absurd rumors. In September the *St. Louis Morning Herald* was suppressed because it had turned "secesh" and had "failed to fulfill a city printing contract."[42] Frémont also banned the sale in Missouri of the *New York News*,

Day Book, Journal of Commerce, Freeman's Journal, and *Brooklyn Eagle.* The Reverend David R. McAnally, editor of the *Christian Advocate,* was arrested in October, 1861, and again in April, 1862.[43]

In January, 1862, General Halleck ordered all newspapers, except those in St. Louis, to send a copy of each issue for inspection.[44] Then in February, Halleck's Order Number 48 was issued. "Any officer who publishes without authority, information respecting the movement of troops, even of battles won, or any official papers," was to be arrested and court-martialed. The whole edition of the newspaper printing such information was subject to seizure. Even the highly partisan *Democrat* proprietors did not like this. They believed that the order was highly restrictive of the press, but they supposed it was necessary and they would comply with it. They were also dubious about Halleck's order restricting newsmen at the front. Such restrictions were not desirable, because the public was anxious for news which would counteract rumors.[45]

Nevertheless, they accused the *Republican* of giving important information to the enemy by printing extracts from a private letter by a naval officer.[46] Regarding censorship of war news, Editor Hume believed that "a reasonable code of rules for the government of newspaper correspondents would be complied with and that, however stringent these rules might be, if compatible with honorable journalism, they would be lived up to in letter and spirit."[47] As he pointed out, "army correspondents employed by the press" were writing an impartial and worthy history of the war. Their errors came from the hurry and confusion of sending hastily written accounts that were derived from "false reports of military officers." Furthermore, he believed that a "healthy criticism of palpable defects in military management" was legitimate because the true function of the war correspondents was just as much embraced in the emphatic demarcation of abuses—the mistreatment of soldiers, habitual intemperance, and brutal neglect of the decencies of life—as in the description of battles. Even the healthy discussion of military strategy might sometimes check the recklessness of generals, provided such accounts did not reveal information that would benefit the enemy.

As might be expected, a newspaper with this attitude did not escape unscathed. Early in July, 1863, the *Democrat* printed a letter from Lincoln to General Schofield which contained instructions on how to handle the political unrest in St. Louis. Schofield was upset because he believed that the letter's contents made it personal. The General first sent for Fishback, who denied responsibility for publication of the letter. McKee had ordered it printed. So Schofield sent a verbal request by Fishback for McKee to report to his headquarters with an explanation of where he obtained the letter. McKee, however, was determined not to reveal his source and ignored this request. Then Schofield sent the publisher a written request. This McKee ignored also, and after several days he was arrested and brought before the Provost Marshal. But McKee was not frightened by this. He still refused to say where he had obtained a copy of the letter. Schofield, perhaps afraid of McKee's power, released him on a verbal parole when he promised to report again in ten days.[48]

Radical Republican leaders were upset, and both Henry T. Blow and James O. Broadhead communicated with Lincoln on the inadvisability of McKee's arrest.[49] Lincoln, however, was not greatly disturbed about the publication of the letter and asked Schofield to settle the problem and spare him the trouble McKee's arrest would cause.[50]

The *Democrat*, which had called the arrest a foolish and unwarranted proceeding,[51] published the ending of the episode:

> Wm. McKee, proprietor of the *Missouri Democrat*, having made satisfactory explanation and apology for failure to obey the summons to appear at headquarters of the commanding general to make explanation of a military offense committed by him, will in consideration of the facts stated by him in regard to the source from which he obtained the President's letter, and the expressed willingness of the President to overlook the offense committed in the publication of the said letter be excused from giving further testimony in the matter, and will be released from his parole to report at department headquarters.[52]

Actually McKee never did reveal the source of the letter, but it generally was believed to have been Charles D. Drake.

Within a short time after the fall of Camp Jackson, both city items and editorials in the *Democrat* began to reflect the troubled times in St. Louis, where hatreds flared. General Frémont's martial law did not allow even city police to carry concealed weapons. He closed saloons for a time, and places of amusement were not permitted to be open after ten-thirty on Sunday nights. By May 22, 1861, all vehicles entering or leaving the city either by rail, water, or road were searched. At all ferries, steamboats, depots, and roads military personnel were stationed to check passes and baggage. Boatmen, who were under military control, were required to take oaths of allegiance; pilots and engineers were continuously having to take new oaths. The homes of people even rumored to be rebel sympathizers were searched.[53]

In this effort to stop traffic with the Southern Confederacy, the Union sympathizers suffered, too. The commerce of St. Louis, especially in the first months of the war, came to a halt: manufacturers ceased to operate unless they were engaged in the production of war material; the steamboat business was paralyzed; building ceased.[54] Trains ran behind schedule. Dr. Boernstein was forced to close his opera house because of "unjust measures by the police commissioners." The St. Louis Theater, "in consideration of the times," lowered its admission price to "seventy-five cents for a lady and gentleman." The O'Callan Land and Oil Company postponed plans for a five-story building.[55] On May 21, 1861, a *Democrat* editorial complained that commerce and trade was annihilated, credit trembled in the balance, confidence in the future was destroyed, and bankruptcy was staring St. Louisans in the face.

The trading situation eased somewhat after the Cumberland and Mississippi rivers were opened on March 3, 1862, and still more at the opening of the Mississippi to New Orleans on July 24, 1863. The weekly review of the St. Louis market on August 25, 1862, showed high prices and a scarcity of products. Hemp was available every day, but prices were quoted at "generally stiffer for all grades." The lead, flour, barley and rye markets were dull. Cotton and corn offerings were small and the prices were up. Wheat was lower, but there was difficulty in getting choice grades. The Army contracted for beef and hay in St. Louis, and bacon was reported in good demand and higher in price. Mess pork was selling for $9.00 to $9.50 and prime at $7.50 with holders asking an advance of fifty cents to a dollar a barrel. The price of whisky was so exorbitant that it was "above the notion of buyers." Rice was scarce and expensive. The market for horses was brisk because the government wanted to buy 1,300 cavalry horses, at a price set previously at $95 per head.

The *Democrat* pages revealed still another wartime problem in St. Louis. The city was overrun with destitute refugees from the battle areas and crowded with wounded soldiers and prisoners for whom there were no adequate quarters. McDowell's Medical College and even Lynch's slave pens were commandeered for military prisons. Soldiers moved continually through the city, crowding it even more.[56]

Several relief organizations were formed. The most famous of these was called the Western Sanitary Commission, headed by James F. Yeatman and financed by contributions from the Chamber of Commerce and private donations. Yeatman was so successful in fitting up hospitals, military prisons, soldiers' homes, and orphanages for soldiers' children, and serving meals and quartering half-clad refugees that he was asked to take his work into the battlefields. When Yeatman left St. Louis in March, 1863, to go into the field, McKee was one of the thirty-six St. Louis men who honored him with a dinner.[57]

Other organizations whose work was reported in the *Democrat* included the Frémont Relief Society, organized by Mrs. Jessie Benton Frémont, and the Ladies Union Aid Society.[58] Mrs. McKee served on the executive committee of the latter organization when with a fair it raised $554,591 for the Western Sanitary Commission.[59] This organization in one month made and contributed to hospitals and camps one thousand items, ranging from pin-cushions to shirts.[60]

The refugee problem became so acute in December, 1861, that General Halleck levied a total fine of $10,000 on sixty-four St.

Louisans who were known Rebel sympathizers.[61] Because most of these people had no cash, the "secesh levies" were collected by confiscating the furniture and other valuable possessions of these people. Confiscated items were sold at auctions at Morgan's Warehouse to raise the amount of the fine. Large crowds attended the sales, where valuable objects could be bought for ridiculously low sums. Once, a piano which was said to have been bought for $1,000, sold for $330.[62] The *Democrat* frequently recorded such "secesh levies" among its daily notations of the arrival of prominent prisoners of war and attempted breaks from military prisons. One such read:

> While the United States Police were executing a 'secesh levy' at a wealthy resident's home a few days ago, a sprightly daughter of the family about seven years of age, gleefully introduced herself to them as thoroughly for the Union. Her father and sisters, she said, were for 'secesh,' but she was for the Union, and no mistake—her mother was, too.[63]

Again in August, 1862, Rebel sympathizers in St. Louis were assessed $500,000 to clothe and arm the Union enrolled militia.[64] But "in the madness which ruled" by this time, the United States Police would take anyone's word for who a Rebel sympathizer was, and property of Union men was seized. Protests were so loud that even the partisan *Democrat* took up the complaint. A letter from a member of the Assessment Board in the paper on June 13, 1863, explained what then happened. A clergyman, an active Union man and a friend of Lincoln, addressed a petition to Governor Hamilton R. Gamble, who endorsed it and forwarded it to Lincoln. In turn, Lincoln wrote on the back, "Stop this whole thing by telegraph." Thus were such assessments eliminated.

Even advertising in the *Democrat* reflected the hard times and the war. Clothing stores listed military outfits as well as civilian clothing. Durant and Company ran a notice to members of the Missouri State Convention that rich spring silks, shawls, and mantles for their wives and daughters were available at "a great closing out sale."

Space devoted to advertising had dropped to under 50 per

cent by 1862, and by the end of the war sometimes only three columns of the front page were used for advertising. Double column and page-long, column-wide advertisements came into use. McKee and Fishback often used a full column for advertising their job and bookprinting business. In use by this time, too, were short "reader" advertisements interspersed in "City Items." Lost and found, for rent, for sale, and wanted advertisements were numerous.

The week before Christmas in 1864 the *Democrat* began to emphasize holiday gifts, Christmas presents, and Christmas goods. French merinos, Irish poplin, and Ottoman cloth were available in stores. Gift bargains could be purchased in silks, watches, gold-headed canes, Roman scarfs, and lap robes. Men were urged to buy an overcoat and "avoid the draft." Keevil dress hats sold for four dollars. Indigo jeans and Lea and Perrin's Celebrated Worcester Sauce appeared to be popular items.

Regardless of the hard times, however, St. Louisans never seemed to lack for entertainment. For the sports lovers the *Democrat* printed wrestling, racing, and baseball news. On January 13, 1864, the paper carried a story on the Heenan-King prize-fight. Racing was particularly popular; a race at the Abbey Park Course in 1863 had a purse of a thousand dollars. A one-column story on the races at LaClede Race Track, in addition to giving the times of the races, was colorfully written.[65] Baseball news was usually covered in long paragraphs under "City Items." Various baseball clubs met on fine days at Gamble's Addition. The Cyclone and Commercial Clubs made arrangements to play at LaFayette Park. "A royal game of baseball between the Empire and Union Clubs" on January 1, 1863, was reported, giving box scores.

Although McKee and Fishback had declared themselves out of debt in 1859, they were in grave financial difficulties again in 1861. On May 18, they mortgaged all their equipment and their subscription list and good will for $8,000. The equipment at this time included one Hoe double-cylinder power press, three Hoe power presses, two hand presses, one card press, one steam engine and boiler, as well as galleys of type, job type, and job office equipment. The $8,000 was borrowed in eight notes of $1,000 each, payable in twelve months. Twenty men let them have the money. Among these were John How, Peter L. Foy, and Frank P. Blair, Jr.[66]

Johnson and Sawyer, St. Louis agents for an Ohio paper manufacturer that had been selling the *Democrat* paper, now refused to sell on credit to McKee and Fishback, and also threatened to bring a suit which would bankrupt them.[67] Hume, even before he became editor, was instrumental in arranging for McKee to buy paper on credit. He was working as a lawyer for Louis Snyder, a large paper-maker of Hamilton, Ohio, and he arranged for a conference between Snyder and McKee. This resulted in Snyder's agreeing to furnish the *Democrat* with paper on a partial credit basis.[68]

Blair, who said later that he had saved the firm from bankruptcy, was convinced that McKee may have acquired money by selling out to the Frémont faction. In a speech in 1862, he said:

> A very notorious individual holding the closest intimacy with General Frémont, and a dispenser of much patronage under him, was observed for three or four consecutive nights at the *Democrat* office, in close conference with McKee. It is probable that to the persuasive arguments of this person, McKee's opinions of Frémont's incapacities and corruption, yielded. . . . I believe that no one here doubted that the concern had been purchased, the only question was as to the price paid. . . .[69]

Whatever the financial difficulties may have been in 1861, McKee and Fishback claimed that the *Democrat* had a larger circulation than the *Republican*. In their affidavit to the Post Office, they swore that their total daily circulation was 13,340; their city circulation, 5,507; and their *Weekly* circulation, 15,360. These figures, they insisted, indicated that the *Democrat* had a larger circulation than that of any other newspaper in the city.[70] Moreover, they challenged the *Republican* to publish its circulation figures, and when the paper made no reply, they charged that the *Republican* had made two false affidavits to the Post Office when it claimed for its daily and city circulations over 9,000 and over 7,275 respectively. They offered to bet fifty dollars on each of three propositions: that the *Democrat's* city circulation was larger than that of the *Republican,* that its total daily circulation was larger, and that the *Weekly* circulation was larger than that of the *Republican Weekly.*[71]

The demand for news during this period of strife, so great that never before had the *Democrat* been forced so often to buy new type,[72] undoubtedly helped increase the newspaper's circulation. But the paper's circulation was also promoted by keeping on the road a traveling agent to sell subscriptions. As early as 1861, twenty-four *Democrat* news agents were listed in "City Items." The paper could also be bought at railroad depots and from newsboys on the streets. People living inside the city limits could have it delivered to their homes.[73]

In spite of increased circulations, however, McKee and Fishback were forced to reduce the size of their paper to nine columns by the end of 1860, the size it remained until 1872. But the price of their journal was increased. In January, 1863, the daily was raised to twelve dollars a year; the *Tri-Weekly* to six dollars; and the *Weekly,* previously lowered to one dollar, was raised again to two dollars. Carriers delivered the paper for twenty-five cents a week, and the price to news dealers was quoted at three cents a copy.

Production and personnel costs rose sharply. The price of war coverage came high, even though the *Democrat* shared with other papers the cost of the salaries of its correspondents. Printing paper, which could be bought for ten cents a pound in 1860, cost thirty cents in 1864.[74] That year, too, *Democrat* printers went on strike. The proprietors advertised for twenty compositors at fifty cents per one thousand ems and for ten good job hands for steady work at twenty dollars per week. Seven days later the price was raised to fifty-five cents per one thousand ems for compositors, and the firm wanted twelve men instead of ten to set type.[75]

Nevertheless, the *Democrat's* profits increased. In 1862 McKee and Fishback announced the purchase of a four-cylinder Hoe press,[76] and on May 8, 1865, the firm proudly announced that its morning paper was published from its new building on the corner of Pine and Fourth Street. This could hardly have been accomplished without a considerable improvement in the firm's financial standing.

In the meantime there had been a change in proprietors. McKee and Fishback on August 25, 1862, used editorial space to welcome a new partner to their firm, which then became known as McKee, Fishback and Company. The change came in the midst of the Blair-Frémont controversy. A few days earlier Blair had been in McKee's office in a heated discussion over the editorial and political policies of the paper. McKee and Fishback refused to temper the paper's attitude toward immediate emancipation. Blair became so upset that he dashed angrily out. In the counting room, he cried out to Houser, who was by this time bookkeeper and cashier of the firm: "Dan, if you want my share of the paper, I'll give it to you."[77]

Blair, however, did not exactly give his one-sixth interest to Daniel M. Houser. The young bookkeeper, then only twenty-seven years old, paid four thousand dollars for it. But Blair allowed him from one to four years to pay the entire sum, which was to draw 6 per cent interest.[78]

During the Civil War period, then, the proprietors and leading writers of the *Democrat* had directed a faction of the Republican party into the Radical party. They had given their readers a reasonably full coverage of the war. The paper had broadened its reader appeal to include a wider variety of news. Its circulation was up, and it had good equipment installed in a new building. McKee, Fishback, and Houser could look back with pride on their accomplishments and look forward with confidence to the reconstruction years.

Chapter VI

Lincoln and the *Democrat*

If the reader has seen lithographs of Mr. Lincoln, which were scattered over the country during the Presidential Canvass, he has a pretty fair idea "of what-for-looking man" he is. I think it would puzzle him to pass himself for a handsome man, anywhere. In person, I should think him a little over six feet high; then, a little stooping; long in his lower limbs, but with a well-rounded thigh. Whilst standing and conversing, he occasionally straightens himself up to his full height, when his eye kindles and his face lights up with intellect and intelligence, and proclaims him, in the unmistakable expressions of the human face divine, no mere ordinary man. His perceptive organs are large, giving to his forehead in a profile view, a receding cast. His complexion is dark. His eye is rapid in its glances, and he is no doubt a quick and accurate discerner of character.

THUS did a *Democrat* writer describe Abraham Lincoln in an interview with the President printed January 8, 1861. The close relationship between Abraham Lincoln and the *Democrat*, which for a century has been a prized highlight in the paper's history, began several years before this interview. One day in April, 1857, Frank Blair, his red hair and beard bristling with excitement, invaded Lincoln's office in Springfield, Illinois.[1] It is easy to picture the scene. Blair's nervous energy kept him moving about the overheated little room while the long-jawed, clean-shaven Lincoln lolled relaxed in his chair. Blair's arms flailed the air as he talked in his strident voice. Lincoln, almost motionless, listened thoughtfully, although laugh wrinkles creased the corners of his eyes. He knew that the ambitious Blair held the *Missouri Democrat* in his hands, and that the *Democrat*, in spite of Blair's apparent "rule-or-ruin complex," unquestionably could aid the cause of the Republican party. It seemed to Blair that this

68

laconic Illinois lawyer was destined for finer things than mere state politics. Here was a man who could easily become a national leader and, as such, could surely further the Blair causes.

Exactly what was said in that conference between Blair and Lincoln is not known, but out of it grew two important developments. First, Blair pledged to Lincoln that the *Democrat* would "bloom for Republicanism" in 1860. Second, Lincoln shortly afterward drew up an agreement, signed by him and nine other Illinois Republicans, to furnish five hundred dollars for the promotion of the *Democrat* in Illinois.[2]

But there had been earlier ties with Lincoln. The alliance had really started during the Free-Soil days of the *Democrat*, when Blair and Lincoln had been in close agreement on the non-extension of slavery into the territories. As early as 1856 the editor of the *Illinois Journal*, a paper with which Lincoln was closely associated, met Blair and commented favorably on his political activities in Missouri. It was about this time, too, that John Hay, who was then reading law in Lincoln's office, became a correspondent for the *Democrat*, and John G. Nicolay, one of Lincoln's political lieutenants, began taking subscriptions for it. Lincoln was later to take both men with him to Washington as his secretaries.[3]

By the time Lincoln wrote out the agreement regarding the *Democrat*, he was already using the St. Louis newspaper to further his antislavery ideas, particularly in southern Illinois where the paper was gaining readers. But Lincoln was not always happy with its vacillating policies. He thought it "passing strange" in 1858, for example, that Blair's paper praised and encouraged Stephen Douglas on the day after Douglas's paper had crowed over Blair's defeat for a Congressional seat.[4]

In 1861 Lincoln said that the two main papers in St. Louis, the *Democrat*, which supported the Republican party, and the *Republican*, which supported the Democratic party, reminded him of a fight he once witnessed in the courthouse yard in Springfield, Illinois. Two men, he recalled, were engaged in a rough and tumble bout. It was such a vicious battle that the spectators could not tell who was winning. Finally the battlers were separated, but even then the crowd could not decide which man had won because "they made the astonishing discovery that each combatant had on the other's coat."[5]

Be that as it may, Blair apparently had no difficulty in persuading McKee to support Lincoln. The *Democrat* proprietor must have foreseen the advantages. If this Illinois lawyer was anything like the man Blair pictured, the paper could easily become a very influential journal merely by being one of Lincoln's first advocates. Besides, the financial agreement which Lincoln had signed must have been a very persuasive factor.

So it was that the *Democrat* strenuously supported Lincoln in his senatorial campaign of 1858. Not only were the Lincoln-Douglas debates fully reported, but Blair himself also participated. He rode with Lincoln in the parades at Springfield and Freeport, where, according to the paper, their reception was "cordial and magnificent."[6] Hay, as the *Democrat's* correspondent, traveled with Lincoln and sent graphic and extended reports of each debate. Almost daily, editorials complimented Lincoln, applauding his stand on the status of the Negro and his success in "clearing away the mists of prejudice from the shining front of Republicanism."[7] Nicolay also attended and took subscriptions for the paper.

McKee and B. Gratz Brown accompanied Blair on the special train to Alton to hear the debate there. Blair introduced them to Lincoln. McKee was pleased with what he saw and heard. Thin and a little stooped, Lincoln occasionally straightened himself to his full height while he spoke. His logical, comprehensive, temperate speech filled with racy humor was very convincing.[8]

After the senatorial canvass, the *Democrat* continued its support of Lincoln. Hay remained a correspondent for the paper, his letters coming from Lincoln's office in Springfield. Frequently these were directly inspired by Lincoln, and according to tradition, some were written by him. More likely, he dictated them by suggesting "say this" or "say that." Lincoln probably was cultivating the *Democrat* because St. Louis was a much larger and more important city than Chicago and because his connection with a metropolitan newspaper in a border state could prove an important factor in his 1860 campaign.[9]

Moreover, Lincoln was a careful reader of the *Democrat*, sometimes scribbling notes on the margin of a copy. On the day before he was nominated for president, he sent Edward L. Baker, editor of the *Springfield Journal*, to Chicago with a marked copy of the issue of May 17, 1860. In it was an account of a speech by William H. Seward. Lincoln had marked three passages, and on the margin he had pencilled a note to Judge Donald Davis: "I agree with Seward in his 'Irrepressible Conflict,' but I do not endorse his 'higher law' doctrine. Make no commitment that will bind me."[10]

In the days following his election, Lincoln also used the *Democrat* for announcements. For example, in a confidential letter, he instructed Edward Bates to "let a little editorial appear in the *Democrat* in about these words":

> We have the permission of both Mr. Lincoln and Mr. Bates to say that the latter will be offered, and will accept a place in the new cabinet, subject, of course, to the action of the Senate. It is not definitely settled which department will be assigned to Mr. Bates.[11]

In return for the support of the *Democrat*, Lincoln, as previously noted, appointed its editor, Peter L. Foy, to what he considered "the best office in my gift within Missouri"—the postmaster of St. Louis. Furthermore, as President, he listened to the pleas of Blair and the *Democrat* in April, 1861, and authorized the enrollment of loyal St. Louis citizens into military units. Captain Nathaniel Lyon, he said, was to proclaim martial law if such act was deemed necessary by Oliver D. Filley, John How, James O. Broadhead, Samuel T. Glover, I. Witzig, and Francis P. Blair, Jr.[12] These were the men who, within six months, were to lend McKee the money to keep his paper alive.

From the election in November, 1860, to the Blair-Frémont controversy in September, 1861, the *Democrat* supported Lincoln with editorials and stories. Blair urged readers to give the new President a chance and to be patient. In January, 1861, Hume interviewed Lincoln in his home in Springfield. His account of this visit, which lasted "perhaps three-quarters of an hour," was widely copied in Northern papers. Hume discovered that the President-elect "chose his words and framed his sentences with deliberation, and with discretion becoming his high position." It was during this interview that Lincoln said that he personally "would be willing, for the sake of the Union, to divide the territory we now own" by the Mason-Dixon line if "it would save the Union and restore harmony." But he thought acquisition of new territory would reopen the question, which, in this light, must be considered and "in some way provided against." On the subject of a compromise, he said: "It was sometimes better for a man to pay a debt he did not owe, or to lose a demand which was a just one, than to go to law about it," but then in compromising our difficulties, he would "regret to see victors put in the attitude of the vanquished, and the vanquished in the place of the victors." He would not contribute to any such compromise as that.[13]

Hume told Democrat readers that he was impressed very favorably with Lincoln's "unsophisticated frankness, his directness, the clear good sense which pervades what he says." The basis of Lincoln's moral character was, Hume believed, "his strong sense of justice and his invincible firmness in adhering to what he believes is right and just." Mr. Lincoln's conversation, Hume thought, showed that he duly appreciated "the difficulties which threaten his incoming administration" and that "he regarded himself as grossly misrepresented and misunderstood at the South."

The Democrat kept its readers informed of Lincoln's trip to Washington and reported his inauguration. Blair went to the capital for this event; the paper's special Washington correspondent reported that no man of Blair's age in the capital had exerted more influence. As leader of the Republican party in Missouri, his efforts in the late struggle, "crowned as they were by successes," were understood and appreciated fully.[14] In St. Louis, McKee was beginning to experience with pleasure the prestige and influence which came with knowing personally a president and with having successfully supported a winner. To be sure, there were important St. Louisans who would not speak to him, and his paper was again having financial difficulties, but McKee was confident that from the strife then existent in St. Louis, he would emerge an important figure in the city.

He saw to it that Lincoln's inaugural address was printed for *Democrat* readers. Editorially the paper supported and commended the sincerity of this speech. It met "the highest expectations of the country, both in point of statesmanship and patriotism." Its effect on the public mind could not be "other than salutary in the highest degree."[15]

When in April, 1861, it appeared that the new governor of Missouri, the proslavery Claiborne F. Jackson, would call out the pro-Southern State Militia, the paper began to urge Lincoln to call out the Union militia. Hume, then signing his articles "H," wrote a long editorial in which he vindicated the President's right to call out the Union troops. Hume used his legal training in explaining that the Constitution gave Lincoln this power.

But in spite of the support that the *Democrat* gave Lincoln in the early days of his administration, it did not hesitate to differ with the President. The first big break with him came over the Frémont-Blair controversy, in which the paper supported Frémont. The strained relations developed initially when the President believed that Frémont was premature in issuing his emancipation proclamation. Lincoln approved Frémont's placing Missouri under martial law, but he asked Frémont to withdraw the emancipation clause. Lincoln then annulled the proclamation in a public order.[16]

The *Democrat* had applauded Frémont when he issued this proclamation and had sided with him against the President and Blair. Editorially it justified Frémont's action in spite of the President's disapproval, on the ground that the General could not be held responsible for runaway slaves. The paper was elated over the support that the Northern press gave to Frémont and pointed out that Lincoln should have allowed Congress to pass on the document.[17] Then, when at Blair's insistence Lincoln sent a committee to investigate Frémont, the *Democrat* once more sided against Lincoln. The arrest of Blair, which followed, strained relations still further. The *Democrat* was too far committed to Frémont to favor anyone who opposed him, whether he was a part-owner, as was Blair, or President of the United States.

However, the paper favored Lincoln's plan, advanced in a message to Congress in March, 1862, for the United States government to cooperate with any state which would adopt gradual emancipation, by paying owners for their slaves.[18] But Missouri did not take advantage of this plan, and the paper's fervor for it cooled when Congress, in January, 1863, failed to appropriate funds to pay "loyal slave-holders."[19] Later the *Democrat* expressed regret at Missouri's failure to cooperate with the gradual emancipation plan, because as a result the state was fifteen million dollars poorer.[20] By this time, however, Lincoln's final proclamation, issued in January, 1863, freeing slaves, without compensation, in all military territories except those occupied by Union Armies, had been sharply attacked by some Northern factions. The *Democrat* supported the President. Editor Hume criticized Northern politicians who claimed to support the administration but who opposed the proclamation. He also commended Lincoln's struggles and appreciated, he said, the President's "difficulties in overcoming his Northern enemies in regard to his proclamation policy."[21]

Furthermore, the *Democrat* sided with the President and against Horace Greeley over the Confiscation Act, which provided that slaves captured or abandoned were to be treated as captives of war and set free.[22] Hume explained in great detail how Greeley and other Northerners were exerting pressure on Lincoln. Because some Union officers were claiming that they had no knowledge of the Confiscation Act, Greeley was urging the President to issue an emancipation proclamation over his signature. According to Hume, Lincoln had parried Greeley's demands by saying that he was first and foremost for the Union. To the *Democrat* editor this was as if "you were asked if you drank tea, and you should answer that you greatly preferred coffee."[23]

The President had said, Hume further reported, "that if abolishing slavery would save the Union, he would abolish it; if sparing slavery would save the Union, he would spare it." But he pointed out also that the President was not a "law-making power." The law was made by Congress, and it was the President's duty to enforce it. If his subordinates shirked the execution of a congressional law it was the President's duty to correct their delinquencies. Hume, however, added that he believed the President would "execute thoroughly every line of the Act, although he may differ with others on the mode and time."[24]

Nevertheless, in March, 1863, McKee and Fishback complained when they were not awarded government printing contracts. They contended that the contracts were being given to secessionists instead of to loyal Republicans.[25] By this time McKee believed that his work for the Union was deserving of every reward. Had he not heard from Lincoln's lips that his paper had been of more service to the Union than ten regiments of soldiers? Did not Union soldiers appreciate the work of the paper? After all, regiments passing through St. Louis frequently stopped in front of the office to give "three times three hurrahs."[26]

In Washington, however, Lincoln with his many problems was sometimes impatient with McKee and the *Democrat*. In his opinion, the paper, and therefore McKee, was "justly chargeable with a full share of the blame" for splitting the Missouri Republican party. In regard to McKee's complaints about the printing contracts, he understood, he said, that by law they were awarded to the lowest bidders; if government agents at St. Louis acted differently, "it would be good grounds" for McKee to prosecute them.[27]

Lincoln was particularly disturbed about the trouble that stemmed from the splitting of the party. He found it necessary to replace General Samuel R. Curtis, the commander of the Department of Missouri, who had become embroiled in the factional fight. Lincoln explained the situation in a letter to General J. M. Schofield, who replaced Curtis:

> Having removed Gen. Curtis and assigned you to the command of the Department of Missouri. I think it may be of some advantage for me to state to you why I did it. I did not relieve Gen. Curtis because of my full conviction that he had done wrong by commission or omission. I did it because of a conviction in my mind that the Union men, con-

stituting, when united, a vast majority of the whole people have entered into a pestilent factional quarrel among themselves. . . . After months of labor to reconcile the difficulty, it seemed to me to grow worse and worse until I felt it my duty to break it up somehow . . . I had to remove Gen. Curtis. . . . Beware of being assailed by one or praised by the other.

It was the publication of this letter on July 10, 1863 that led thirteen days later to McKee's arrest by Schofield.[28]

As has been pointed out, Lincoln believed that the publication of this letter without his or Schofield's consent was not proper, but he also believed that the matter did not deserve the importance being attached to it.[29] A flood of dispatches from prominent St. Louis Union men reaching the President's desk claimed that McKee's arrest was "unkind, unjust, against the spirit" of Lincoln's instructions, and "an insult to the supporters of the Union."[30]

McKee told his *Democrat* readers that he would not have printed the letter if he had thought the President would object. He pointed out that the paper was published for the benefit of more than 45,000 regular subscribers.[31] Strangely enough, though, a small proslavery party, which in St. Louis had "succeeded in securing a considerable degree of favor with the Administration," had no love for the *Democrat*. Editor Hume warned these people that McKee's "foolish and unwarrantable" arrest would in no way spare them from further criticism.[32]

Later, McKee professed surprise at the language used in General Schofield's order releasing him from giving further testimony. He was unaware, he said, of committing a military offense by publishing the letter, and he could not understand how he could be excused from giving further testimony when he had never given any.[33]

Thereafter, the *Democrat* seized every opportunity to criticize Schofield and Lincoln. The President, the paper said, was "engaged in rapidly driving nails into his political coffin" by his policies. He was criticized specifically for not opening trade on the Mississippi River, for his political appointments, and for his failure to take "immediate steps" to relieve the state of anarchy and confusion in Missouri by removing Schofield.[34]

When the Committee of Seventy went to Washington to present the Radical grievances to Lincoln,[35] McKee and Fishback took advantage of the occasion to send a petition to Lincoln. Charles D. Drake, the Committee spokesman, was to hand the paper to the President. Called "A Memorial to His Excellency, the President of the United States," it originated with the *Democrat* proprietors and was signed by representatives of seven other Republican papers in Missouri. They were protesting Schofield's order in which the general had threatened to throttle "the immediate and lawless press" which had criticized him for his Kansas Border policy.

> The undersigned representatives of newspaper journals published in the State of Missouri which have not only at all times given an unconditional support to the Union, but have earnestly sustained the principles of your Freedom Proclamation of January 1, 1863, and the general policy of your administration, would respectfully call your attention to the [order].
>
> [It] has proved the occasion of much exultation to that portion of the press of this state described by the term "Copperhead" and which has at no time given more than a qualified support to the Union, while it has at all times bitterly assailed your political policy which does not hesitate to declare that the order in question is designed expressly to operate against the Radical Union Press of Missouri.
>
> Knowing that the differences of opinion . . . have served to produce a feeling of alienation between him and us and having already unjustly, as we believe, experienced evidences of his personal hostility, we are not persuaded that the order may not hereafter be used for our annoyance and suppression.
>
> We would therefore respectfully . . . ask if we cannot, by some intercession of yours be guaranteed the same security in expressing our views of men and measures which is enjoyed by the loyal press of the nation at large.
>
> . . . . For the abuse of any privilege we ask no immunity. But as evidence of the integrity of our intentions, we point to the past of our journals, which has been one of unsul-

lied loyalty, and to the further fact that the majority of us have risked life and every earthly possession in the cause of the Union.

Very respectfully yours,
McKee and Fishback[36]

Lincoln received the Committee of Seventy on September 30, but it was not until October 5, that he sent his answer to Bates, and not until October 23, that the *Democrat* published it so that its readers might know that the President was taking a middle-of-the-road course. In his reply Lincoln said that he held "whatever commands in Missouri or elsewhere responsible to me and not to either Radicals or Conservatives. It is my duty to hear all, but at least I must, within my sphere, judge what to do or what to forbear."[37]

That Lincoln had no intention of removing General Schofield as he had General Curtis now became clear to the *Democrat*. This attitude was construed promptly as a presidential condemnation of the Radicals and the Radical press. Hume declared that Lincoln's evasion of the problems was merely "plowing around the stumps," and for all practical purposes readers should regard the President as a "Copperhead."[38]

It is little wonder, then, that the *Democrat* began looking around for a new presidential candidate. Lincoln, Hume said, should be willing to "take his chances with other candidates." Hume's statement was the paper's answer to the reported movement to have Lincoln nominated by state legislatures instead of at a convention. "Are there no genuine party members . . . except such as take their hats and swear that Mr. Lincoln must be the next President in preference to any other man?"[39] In addition, the paper censured the formation of Lincoln clubs, saying that it would be better to organize a Union regiment to fight against the rebellion.[40]

As possible presidential timber, Editor Hume suggested at various times Andrew Johnson, General Ulysses S. Grant, Samuel Portland Chase, and General Frémont.[41] The *Democrat* also sponsored a Freedom Convention, held in Louisville, Kentucky, on February 22, 1864, where possible presidential candidates were considered.[42] Hume's article discussing Johnson's qualifications for the office was widely discussed in the Northern press; the editor later attributed Johnson's nomination for vice-president to his editorial.[43]

The *Democrat* still refrained, however, from saying which man it preferred. Hume assured his readers that "we are not yet prepared to say that we shall be either for this one or that one, but this we will say—that whomsoever we may support, he must come up to the standards of our principles."[44]

And Lincoln, according to the *Democrat*, did not measure up to these principles. He was too lenient with his amnesty plan, too soft in his treatment of traitors.[45] Besides, the President's appointments in St. Louis did not please McKee, who wanted his brother named to the coveted position of postmaster. His former editor, Peter L. Foy, was soon due for reappointment, and already McKee had enlisted the aid of Missouri senators and representatives.[46]

Foy was a Blair man, and McKee was jealous of Blair's influence with the President. Through the spring of 1864, the *Democrat* kept up a steady stream of vituperative editorials attacking "that post office clique" and Lincoln's "open, shameless, and unrestricted patronage" in Missouri.[47] The paper protested vehemently when Lincoln restored Blair to the army with a major general's stars. "What infatuation," Hume asked, "has possessed the President to induce him to join with the Blairs?" Surely Lincoln was in bad company.[48] The criticism of Lincoln was continued until he was nominated in June.

Hume headed the Radical delegation at the National Republican Convention and cast Missouri's votes on the first ballot for General Grant. But when he saw that Missouri was the only state not in the Lincoln column, he jumped on the bandwagon, too.[49]

The *Democrat's* influence had not been as great as he and McKee had hoped. Hume was disappointed, he told his readers, in Lincoln's nomination. He promised that the paper would not support the President on a conservative platform. Unless he placed himself fully and squarely and evidently in good faith upon the National Radical platform, the members of the party nominating him would be under no obligation to support him.[50]

This was an idle threat, however; the *Democrat* actively campaigned for Lincoln's election.

Because of its early opposition to the President, the paper was approached about joining a movement to displace Lincoln after his nomination. But McKee declined to become "a party to the proposed insurrection."[51] So the *Democrat* began once more defending Lincoln's policies. His election was termed a Radical victory.[52]

McKee and Fishback were rewarded for their support. In spite of their paper's criticism of Lincoln and in spite of the fact that the *Democrat* sometimes published forged Lincoln letters,[53] the President once more intervened on behalf of a *Democrat* proprietor. In December, 1864, Lincoln ordered the release of Louis A. Walton, a relative of Fishback, who had been tried and found guilty of disloyalty.[54]

The news of Lincoln's assassination reached St. Louis on the eve of a great victory celebration. Already the city was draped with flags. The next day, Saturday, April 15, business houses were to close and a parade and a speaking program were scheduled in the afternoon. But then in the night came the news, and St. Louis was stunned.

> Starting up from their beds, the people rushed into the streets, and with freezing blood and staring eyes read the horrible details of the most damnable deed that has ever blackened the pages of our history. As the news spread, a deep gloom settled upon the whole city. . . . During the afternoon an extra was issued every hour, giving further details of the awful crime, and mingled with the individual regret were feelings of hatred and revenge toward everyone who was supposed to entertain the slightest sympathy for the assassin.[55]

Thus it was that St. Louis mourned instead of celebrating. Flags were lowered to half-mast, business houses remained closed, people spoke in low tones, and churches held special services. Even the lowliest homes displayed mourning symbols. And if an occasional brute expressed gratification at the tragedy, he was punished promptly and severely. The next week schools closed. On

Thursday funeral guns were fired every half hour from sunrise to sunset, and at noon all the bells in the city were tolled.[56]

For six weeks stories and editorials in the *Democrat* told readers the details of Lincoln's assassination and funeral. A two-column story described his death and his lying-in-state. The paper was so "overwhelmed with letters and reports of meetings" honoring Lincoln that Hume was forced to notify his correspondents that it was impossible to find room for one in ten of the most interesting. But someone on the staff wrote the following epitaph in time for the Monday paper:

> God's Noblest Work—an Honest Man.
> The Brave, the Wise, the Good.
> Ambitious without Vanity,
> Discreet without Fear,
> Confident without rashness
> In disaster calm, in success moderate—in all
> things upright and true!
> The Hero! The Patriot! The Statesman!
> The guiding star of the People!
> The deliverer of the bondsmen.
> A victim to slavery,
> A martyr to the cause of Human Liberty!
> He died that his country might be free.
> A grateful Nation will honor his name,
> Perpetuate his principles,
> and
> Remember his virtues.

The funeral itself was well reported. Six hundred St. Louisans attended.[57] The whole nation, Hume wrote, was bowed in grief. "A great and good man, whom the people loved as a father" had gone. Whatever mistakes he had made in "the minor details of his administration were the errors of his head and not his heart."[58] Lincoln was forgiven.

Strained as the relationship with Lincoln may have been at times, it still had taught McKee the advantage of knowing a President. In the four years of the Civil War his paper had become the medium of information between Congress and the West.[59] He was to cultivate and expand this link with other White House occupants in the years to come.

Chapter VII

A Liberal Republican Leader

WILLIAM McKEE, by 1865, no longer had to walk the streets of St. Louis to borrow money to meet his Saturday payroll. Like many of the Black Republican leaders he had emerged from the war years with money. It was rumored that he had made it by buying mules and selling them to the Army, and he may have. But his speculations in real estate were also paying off, and by this time the *Democrat* was operating in the black.

McKee was not a man to parade his wealth before the public. He did not fancy the fine clothes of the period, nor did his wife and daughter wear the diamonds that other wealthy St. Louis women did. When many business men drove fine rigs or rode the horse cars to work, he walked. And on most nights he liked to read to his family from the works of Washington Irving or Nathaniel Hawthorne.

In his office he was always available for advice to budding politicians, laborers, civic leaders, and business men. His counsel was so valued that it was later said many would not name their babies unless they first consulted McKee. It was from here, too, not from caucus rooms or political rallies, that McKee helped plan and direct the emergence of St. Louis from the economic, social, and political turmoil of the Reconstruction era.

Mushrooming into the nation's fourth largest city, with a population in 1870 of 310,864, St. Louis bore the brunt of much of Missouri's strife following in the wake of the war. Into the city flocked destitute families of returning Union and Confederate soldiers. Unemployment of both white people and Negroes climbed, disease swept through the population, and crime increased alarmingly.

Old hatreds were not alleviated with the changing social pat-

tern. The easy-going Southerners, who had lost their fortunes
and lands during the war, no longer dominated the social and
cultural activities. They waited impatiently for the time when
they could again assume leadership.

The preponderant Northern and German influences had infiltrated the schools, the churches, and other cultural activities as
they had the economic and political life of the city. Particularly
the large German contingent, with its Hegelian philosophy which
came to be known as the St. Louis Movement and which for a
time threatened to supplant New England transcendentalism in
American cultural circles, was now contributing cultural and
political leaders. It was this group that gave birth to the dream of
St. Louis as the "Great Future City of the World."

Missouri's political activities evolving from Reconstruction
problems also were centered in St. Louis. Radical leaders such as
Drake, Editor Hume of the *Democrat*, and Chauncey I. Filley
were St. Louis business and professional men. Known throughout
the state as the "St. Louis Clique," they were enjoying their prestige and the political spoils of the victor. Since the proprietors
and staff of the *Democrat* were leaders in the Radical movement,
the paper continued to be as active in state and national politics
during the Reconstruction period as it had been during the war
years.

Yet there was friction within the party, and once more the
Democrat was to shift political positions. As it had turned from
Free-Soilism and Thomas H. Benton to Black Republicanism, as
it had turned from Frank Blair and Conservative Republicanism
to Radical Republicanism, so now it was to turn from Charles D.
Drake and Radicalism to Liberalism. In fact, the *Democrat*, with
McKee the power behind the participating politicians, was to
originate the so-called Liberal Movement.

From 1865, when the new Missouri state constitution was ratified, until 1868, the paper staunchly and vehemently supported
every issue of the Radical Republican platform. Blair, as the
leader of the Conservative Republicans was supported by the
Missouri Republican; his pleadings for a more lenient amnesty
for Rebels furnished the most outspoken opposition to the Radi-

84   ST. LOUIS GLOBE-DEMOCRAT

cals. The greatest controversy arose over the Test Oath in its ap-
plication to the professional classes—lawyers, preachers, and
teachers. The *Democrat* had no patience with the Conservatives'
contention that the Test Oath for preachers violated the First
Amendment to the Constitution of the United States. If the state
had no power to require preachers to be loyal, Editor Hume contended, it had no power to require them to obey the laws in general. There was no necessity to separate the citizens from the
preachers, who themselves were not above the laws of man.[1] Furthermore, the enactment of the Registry Law was regarded as a
triumph second only to the adoption of the new constitution.[2]

The proprietors and staff of the *Democrat* shared the extreme
views of Drake, and through 1867 the paper advanced Drake's
causes. "From 1862 to 1868," Drake wrote later, "the *Democrat*
was my friend and it was through its columns that I was able to
reach the public."[3]

As has been noted, Drake skyrocketed into political prominence when the Republican party in St. Louis split into the Conservatives and the Radicals. A lawyer from Kentucky, Drake was
very religious and became noted for his bitter tirades against the
Rebels.[4] His rapid rise from a minor figure in Missouri politics
was helped by the *Democrat*, which agreed with him on the
emancipation of the Negroes. The paper printed his writings and
speeches, editorially defended his views, and lashed out at the
Rebels, maligning them in the same manner as Drake did. The
Rebel leaders were guilty, according to the paper, of "every possible atrocity." There was nothing they would not do.

> Wholesale massacres and torturing, wholesale starvation
> of prisoners, firing of great cities, piracies of the cruelest
> kind, persecutions of the most hideous character and of
> vast extent, and finally assassinations in high places—what-
> ever is inhuman, whatever is brutal, whatever is fiendish,
> these men have resorted to. They will leave behind names
> so black and memories of deeds so infamous that the exe-
> cution of the slaveholders' rebellion will be eternal.[5]

In the *Democrat's* defense of Radical views, many of the paper's editorials bitterly assailed Blair. In the election in Novem-

ber, 1865, Blair refused to take the Test Oath devised by Drake, but he swore to one he himself had composed. The judges refused to accept his ballot, and Blair sued for $10,000, eventually taking his case to the Supreme Court. The incident gave Drake and the *Democrat* more fodder for their Radical machine. Blair's action was rightfully construed as a criticism of the new constitution; and according to Hume, any such criticism was meant to destroy Drake's influence. He advised *Democrat* readers to stand by their constitution, which was "the only sure protection against rebellism, Copperheadism, and Blairism—three isms that, once fastened in Missouri, would drag her down into the mire where poor rebel-gripped and Copperhead-bitten Kentucky now lies floundering."[6]

Into the midst of this turmoil in the summer of 1866 stepped a new *Democrat* editor. Hume, who had promised to stay with the paper until Missouri was free, resumed his law practice, but continued his active participation in Radical politics, as a Drake lieutenant. Later he was to become a prominent New York broker.

To replace him, McKee and Fishback employed Colonel William M. Grosvenor, a native of Massachusetts. Educated at Yale, Grosvenor had edited the *New Haven Palladium* and the *New Haven Journal-Courier*. During the war he had enlisted in the 13th Connecticut Volunteers and later, as a colonel, had commanded the Louisiana Native Guards (colored troops).[7]

A man of powerful build, Grosvenor was only five feet, ten inches tall, but he had massive shoulders and such a huge head that he wore a size nine and a half hat. His beetling brow, long black hair, and bushy beard made his head seem even larger. He was an expert billiards player; he could carry on three games of chess simultaneously; and he could play remarkable games of whist and tennis.[8] To St. Louisans, he seemed unusually snobbish.

Grosvenor came well recommended to McKee and Fishback by no less a journalistic personage than the editor of *Harper's Weekly*, George William Curtis.

> I do not know how much special knowledge he may have, but I am sure that few men could learn more rapidly what is necessary than Colonel Grosvenor, or use this

knowledge with greater discretion than he. He is a true
Yankee and it is Yankee ingenuity that must rebuild the
country.[9]

The new *Democrat* editor lived up to McKee's expectations.
His editorials, taking up the Radical cause where Hume's had
stopped, soon were attracting attention. Nor was Grosvenor long
in becoming an active party member. By the end of the year he
was recognized as a forceful speaker and a party organizer of
intelligence. But many Radicals resented this assumption of leadership by a comparative stranger. Wrote the editor of the *Ste.
Genevieve Representative*:

> Colonel Grosvenor, the supercilious, newly-imported
> hired editor of the *Democrat* who is patronizingly insolent
> to county papers. . . . chews tobacco very much after the
> manner of country editors. . . . and has a don't-give-a-
> continental air. Should he travel in the rural districts, he
> will probably get a local item from some country editor that
> he will not soon forget.[10]

When he assumed his duties with the paper in 1866, Grosvenor
agreed with Drake that the time had not yet come when rebel
enfranchisement should be made a part of the Radical program
in Missouri.[11] The *Democrat* was pleased in 1868 when Drake
favored a Radical platform that advocated Negro suffrage. But
disenfranchisement of the Rebels was still considered necessary
and justifiable.[12]

Nevertheless, *Democrat* editorials by that time were growing
much milder than they had been two years earlier. In 1867 Drake
was elected United States Senator; with his absence from St.
Louis, a more liberal element in the Radical party began to
emerge. McKee soon became a potent factor in this movement
which was to develop into a party split with far-reaching consequences. In reality the *Democrat* proprietor may have been considering a split with Drake for some time before it occurred. Had
Blair not been leading the opposition, McKee might have taken
a more liberal attitude earlier. Drake had no real conception of
social and economic forces; McKee could see that if St. Louis
was to return to normalcy, these forces would have to be con-

sidered. If the Radical party failed to keep abreast of the times, the *Democrat* declared editorially in 1868, and forget the vindictive spirit which war and reconstruction had fostered, it would lose its power.[13] How different was this attitude from the paper's political views of 1866 and 1867! But McKee was beginning to understand that only in a normal St. Louis could his paper develop into the journal he envisioned or operate with the profit he was now realizing.

Besides, McKee was becoming more and more unhappy over federal patronage in St. Louis. He could not understand why, with the service his paper had performed for the party, his recommendations of men for political appointments were not heeded. President Johnson had not listened to his desires any more than Lincoln had. To McKee this was ingratitude from a man who would not have been President had it not been for the *Democrat's* promotion of him in 1863. Furthermore, the paper had endorsed Johnson when he succeeded to the presidency in 1865.

But by the following year the *Democrat* had become critical of Johnson. McKee had wanted his brother appointed postmaster, but Johnson had renominated Peter L. Foy for a second term and, to pile insult on insult, had nominated Frank Blair as collector of internal revenue, the second most coveted position in St. Louis. Both men were rejected,[14] but this did not lessen McKee's animosity toward Johnson. The *Democrat* used the occasion as a springboard for open hostility toward the Johnson administration. From a criticism of Johnson's appointments and of the President's veto of the Freedman's Bureau bill, editorials grew more and more bitter until it was easy for the paper to advocate Johnson's impeachment, and subsequently to attack Senator John B. Henderson for voting for the President's acquittal.[15]

So it was that the *Democrat* was fertile soil for the liberal ideas of Carl Schurz, who had recently bought an interest in the *Westliche Post*.[16] A tall, lanky German refugee, Schurz had come to the United States in 1852 and had lived in Philadelphia and Middleton, Wisconsin. From the beginning he had been active in the Republican party. He had campaigned for Lincoln against Doug-

88 ST. LOUIS GLOBE-DEMOCRAT

las, had run unsuccessfully for governor of Wisconsin, and had spoken for Lincoln at Cooper's Union in 1860. Lincoln had rewarded him by appointing him minister to Spain in 1861.

During the war Schurz had served as a Union general and later had made a special report to President Johnson on the Southern states. Johnson, however, had ignored his recommendation that Negroes be enfranchised before the readmission of the Southern states. In 1866 Schurz had become a Washington correspondent for the *New York Tribune*. He resigned this job to become editor-in-chief of the *Detroit Post*, a paper just established by leading Michigan Republicans; after one year as editor, he came to St. Louis.[17]

A man of great personal charm, he was known to St. Louisans as an unusually gay, vivacious, and happy person. Nevertheless, he was lonely, for his wife and children were living at the time in Europe. Needing companionship, he was drawn in 1867 to Grosvenor, whose wife had recently died. The two editors had much in common—uncompromising integrity, similar political views, and love of good music, literature, and art. Both were good linguists, and both were later to become New York journalists.

Soon after Schurz arrived in St. Louis he was approached by the *Democrat* on the possibility of his running for Congress. He declined the honor.[18] Shortly thereafter, however, he began advocating a more liberal treatment of the Rebels,[19] and at about that time McKee was considering the same move. Subsequently, Grosvenor and Schurz formed an alliance between their two papers, the *Democrat* and the *Westliche Post*, whereby the Liberal movement was set in motion.[20]

One day as Schurz sat in his room writing to his wife, he thought how pleasant it would be if a group of St. Louis men whom he liked were to dine together occasionally. They could discuss many subjects of interest—music, books, the theater, and current events. Soon thereafter he organized the first dinner meeting of seven men—"journalists, advocates, and a couple of merchants." Grosvenor was one of the group. As Schurz predicted to his wife, these men who met informally for dinner twice a month were to exercise "a decisive influence on the politics of the state."[21]

The members of the Twentieth Century Club, as the organization was named, were united in their dislike of Drake's dogmatic, narrow-minded, intolerant views on enfranchisement. They considered the Senator too dictatorial in party politics and in the control of federal offices in Missouri. It was after the organization of this club that the *Democrat* began to show a more tolerant view toward the Rebels. It would be wise, Editor Grosvenor told his readers, to adopt a more liberal policy; he offered the solution of the Liberal Republicans to enfranchise the Negroes and the Rebels at the same time.[22]

McKee was not a member of the club, but he was kept informed of the opinions expressed in its meetings. Though a sociable and pleasant companion, McKee preferred an unobtrusive role. From his desk in the *Democrat's* office, he directed the affairs of the Liberal movement. He did not want any office for himself, but he was "a great promoter of aspirations in others," and as frequently he "nipped them like untimely frost."[23] Now he gave his approval to a suggestion of the Twentieth Century Club members, and without his approval, perhaps even his initiative, that suggestion would never have been acted upon. At the second meeting of the club, the members were sitting around a table at the Planters' House when someone brought up the question of possible candidates to oppose Senator Henderson in his race for re-election. Grosvenor did not like Drake's choice, General Benjamin F. Loan. Presently someone asked Schurz whether he would agree to run. At first he refused. But finally he agreed that Grosvenor could place a "feeler in the *Democrat*" to see what people thought of him.[24]

Subsequently, Grosvenor became Schurz's campaign manager and an "uncommonly bright, genial, active and energetic champion."[25] The *Democrat* announced for Schurz on December 8, 1868; three days later it reported that twenty-one papers were supporting the German editor. As early as November 16, Schurz wrote to his wife that the great American paper, the *Democrat*, was coming to his aid and that his election was regarded in St. Louis as a certainty.[26]

Grosvenor directed the Schurz forces at the Radical caucus in Jefferson City, January 1, 1869, a meeting which marked the beginning of the split of the Radical Republicans into Radicals and Liberals. For the *Democrat* the events there became one of the biggest political stories of the Reconstruction years. Drake came from Washington to direct the Loan candidacy. He and Schurz engaged in a widely publicized debate before the meeting.

The Grosvenor-Schurz campaign was decidedly different from the usual political maneuvers of the time. The candidate and his supporters refrained from making any abusive utterances against Loan or Drake; they passed out no cigars, champagne, or whisky; and they allowed no noisy demonstrations. Schurz made no promises of offices or other pledges.[27]

In contrast, Drake delivered his usual bitter tirade. He and the Radicals did not believe that Negro and Rebel suffrage were equally urgent. Negro suffrage should come first. He attacked Schurz on the grounds that the editor had not lived in Missouri long enough to understand her problems. He complained bitterly that Schurz's candidacy was an attempt by St. Louis Germans to control the party. He screamed to his listeners that he was being warred on by Schurz and his adherents—"by newspapers, by the *Missouri Democrat*—all backed by the Rebels of Missouri. Aye! Aye! I hear your rebel hisses!"[28]

The Schurz-Drake debate was fully covered in the *Democrat.* After Schurz's nomination the paper reported that neither "the fervor of Mr. Loan nor the froth of Mr. Drake could turn the tide."[29] The work of Grosvenor and the influence of the *Democrat* had paved the way for Schurz's ultimate election over his Democratic opponent. Subsequently, too, Drake deserted the pages of the *Democrat*, sending his writings instead to the *Daily Evening News.*[30]

However, the question of patronage in Missouri, about which McKee was very determined, was probably as instrumental as any other one factor in bringing about the final split between Drake and the *Democrat*. In the presidential election of 1868 the paper had supported General Grant. Before his inauguration the journal predicted that McKee's brother, Henry McKee, would be appointed deputy collector of internal revenue in St. Louis. In addition, Fishback had gone to Washington to secure Drake's aid in getting Constantine Maguire appointed collector of internal revenue. Drake, however, had refused, saying that Maguire had not joined the party until 1864 and had never done a "hand's turn" for it.[31]

The *Democrat* contended that Drake's statement about his interview with Fishback was garbled and unjust to all concerned. Maguire, Grosvenor told his readers, had not been a politician in any sense. Furthermore, he had been loyal and generous in his support of the Radicals since the beginning of the war. It was not because of any supposed defect in Maguire that Drake had refused to support him. Rather, the Senator already had promised to support Chauncey I. Filley for the position. Such things only showed the uncertain and desperate state of Drake's mind. "We do not care," Grosvenor said, "to increase his perplexities by any further references to them."[32] Not by any accident was this editorial printed beneath a notice headed "Drake's Bitters Have Soured," which reported that the St. Louis firm selling this medicine had closed out its stock.

Five days later McKee's paper openly repudiated Drake. Grosvenor claimed that the Senator had forced the Radical party to choose between dictatorship under him and freedom under Schurz. Throughout the senatorial contest, Drake's violence of passion, his narrow vindictiveness, and his utter lack of sense as a party leader were manifest. "Mr. Drake convinced nobody that his despotism would be either wise or beneficent."[33] Schurz's election meant a victory for freedom of thought, progress, good sense, and genuine Radicalism.

The break within the Radical party was not lessened in any way when Grant made his appointments. His failure to yield to the desires of the Radical Missourians was influential, according to Grosvenor, in raising against him "the powerful opposition of McKee, who was highly indignant at his failure to control the collectorship."[34]

To prepare for the split which seemed inevitable the *Democrat* began advocating the removal of disfranchisement after 1870. It was better, editorials declared, to remove the disabilities voluntarily than to allow them to remain a cause of bitter feeling.[35] Early in 1870 other Radical papers were reported by the *Democrat* to favor the Liberal movement.[36] Agitation for the removal of disabilities, which became even stronger during the year, helped widen the gap between the *Democrat*, the mouthpiece for the Liberal movement, and Drake, the leader of the Radical element.

By the time the Radical Convention met in Jefferson City in September, the *Democrat* had prepared its readers for the bolt, which developed over the proscription machinery of the Radicals. Even earlier the Liberals had picked B. Gratz Brown as their candidate for governor. The *Democrat* had reviewed his career, claiming that Drake had forced its former editor into political retirement.[37] On June 17 the paper had announced whole-heartedly for Brown and during July and August had featured editorials praising him.

Then for the first and only time McKee took an active part in a political convention. He went to Jefferson City in September, 1870, several days before the meeting convened, to talk with delegates and direct negotiations between the Radical and Liberal factions of the party. As he was not a delegate, McKee stood in the lobby outside the room when the convention was in session where he watched proceedings and sent messages to the Liberal leaders.[38]

Schurz headed the Liberals, aided by Editor Grosvenor, who, according to one of the delegates, was "the restless and reckless stoker of the whole bolting movement." With his "black eyes lost in a wilderness of black hair, worn *a la banditte*," Grosvenor carried instructions from McKee to Schurz. When the crisis appeared near, he informed McKee, who telegraphed immediately to Daniel M. Houser, because Houser was more favorably inclined toward the Liberal movement than Fishback. McKee and Houser decided to favor a bolt.[39]

When the convention delegates refused to incorporate a plank

in the platform for immediate removal of Rebel disabilities, Mc-
Kee raised his arm and Schurz's group walked out.[40] The bolting
Liberals immediately formed a new convention and nominated
Brown for its gubernatorial candidate. The *Democrat*, abandon-
ing its earlier journalistic practice of publishing only matter concerning its current political affiliations, printed the full proceedings of both conventions as well as Brown's acceptance speech.[41]
Subsequently, aided by the paper, the Liberals were successful
in electing Brown. The next year the Liberal movement which
originated in St. Louis spread across the nation.

Brown, however, had not been Grosvenor's choice, but "Mc-
Kee and Houser demanded him at any cost."[42] Their reason,
Grosvenor rightfully believed, was their strong desire to show
President Grant that "he could not with impunity refuse an of-
fice demanded for the brother of a proprietor."[43]

Editorials in the *Democrat* during the next few weeks sub-
stantiated Grosvenor's contention. On September 14, for example, the paper denounced the existing high tariff and the cor-
ruptness in the government. A week later Grant was warned
half playfully not to meddle in Missouri politics. Then on September 24 the *Democrat* printed a letter from Grant to C. W.
Ford, who instead of Constantine Maguire had been awarded
the position of collector of internal revenue. In this letter the
President accused the Liberals of trying to carry a portion of the
Republican party into the Democratic party. After that the
McKee journal warred openly against Grant, his high tariff, and
the corrupt practices in his government.[44]

Nevertheless, McKee, Fishback, and Company stayed in the
Republican party in 1872 and favored the renomination of Grant
rather than the Greeley-Brown presidential ticket. Several factors influenced this action. After he became governor, Brown
had supported Blair in his candidacy for United States Senator.
Brown and Blair had gone to Cincinnati, where they had made
a deal to have Brown placed on the ticket with Greeley. McKee's
old hatred for Blair alone was probably enough to account for
keeping the paper in the Grant ranks.

But there were other factors, too. Trouble was brewing among the *Democrat* proprietors, and Grosvenor was discharged early in 1871. A small notice on January 24 notified readers that he was "no longer connected" with the paper. Later, many in St. Louis came to believe that since McKee had not been able to control political patronage in Missouri he had joined forces with Grant's appointees in their schemes for graft. It was this shift toward "Grantism" that had caused the rift between McKee and Grosvenor and probably widened the breach developing within the *Democrat* family.[45]

Later that year, J. B. McCullagh, who had started his journalistic career on the *Democrat*, assumed the editorship. His admiration for Grant, acquired during his days as a war correspondent, made it easy for the paper to favor Grant in 1872. Politically, the shifts in the paper's attitude had helped ease old hurts in St. Louis, but at the same time they made possible McKee's later journalistic ventures.

Chapter VIII

News Frontiers of the Reconstruction Era

IN THE seven years following the death of Lincoln, the newspaper business experienced tremendous journalistic advances. More and more journals broke their political party ties and by widening their news coverage opened a variety of news frontiers.[1] The *Democrat* was no exception, although it continued to act as spokesman for the political party with which it was affiliated. As early as 1866 McKee, Fishback, and Houser recognized that their journal, to survive, must function as a communication medium apart from its editorial opinions and long political letters and discussions. They knew that readers wanted a live newspaper—one that reported accurately and effectively facts about events of public interest. Determined to make the *Democrat* such a paper, they boldly ventured into news areas far afield from their political activities.

Much was in their favor. They had a new building and new equipment. The expansion of the telegraph and the successful operation of the Atlantic cable made possible the transmission overnight of news that previously required from two days to two weeks. The work of war reporters had taught the proprietors the value of having their own writers at places where news events were happening. Wide news coverage, of course, took money, but McKee, Fishback, and Houser were willing to spend large sums to obtain facts for their readers. In an editorial on May 11, 1868, they announced their policy.

> Our subscription list is swelling more rapidly than at any other period since this paper had an existence. Every day our club list grows. News dealers in large places and

on cars find the *Democrat* is outstripping our rivals. If this continues, we will have a circulation of not less than 20,000 daily and 40,000 weekly before the year closes. The fact is that in these days people feel as never before that they must have a live newspaper—one that never shirks any expenditure in obtaining facts of public interest, nor suppresses any item of news for personal or political reasons.

Even before this the pages of the *Democrat* bore evidence that McKee, Fishback and Company were not shirking any expense. Week after week the amount of telegraphed news increased. Reports came from such "news centers" as Nashville, Chicago, St. Joseph, Springfield, Washington, and New York. As early as 1866 it was not unusual for as much as six and a half columns of the front page to be filled with news received by telegraph. Some of these reports were Western Associated Press releases, but the majority were marked "special dispatches" and must have been filed by *Democrat* "attachés" or "specials." By 1868 the paper was receiving foreign news by the Atlantic cable and by 1871 had a "special" in Paris.

Not only did the *Democrat* proprietors increase their use of telegraphed news, but they also enlarged their local and state news-gathering personnel. In their "Prospectus" for 1871, they told their readers:

> Journalism must keep step with the fleetest in the onward race and reflect all that is daily accomplished or hoped for. . . . We should engage, with extended plans and with fresh zeal, in the systematic and thorough gathering and the attractive and accurate presentation of the great world's news.[2]

McKee, Fishback and Company further announced that to obtain full news coverage for the *Democrat* the firm was arranging for more daily dispatches; special dispatches from the more important news centers; special dispatches, correspondence, and local reporting in Missouri and Illinois; and special correspondents at various points in the states and territories.[3]

This prospectus, like that of most journals of the period, tended toward elaborate promises that could not be fulfilled. Nevertheless, it was during this period that the *Democrat* first became noted for its volume and quality of foreign news. The close alliance of the paper with the large German and Irish populations in its readership area must have influenced its three proprietors to enlarge their foreign news coverage.[4] Sometimes as much as four columns of an issue were filled with European news. St. Louisans during this period read in the *Democrat* adequate accounts of the Fenian invasion in 1866 and fuller reports, received by Atlantic cable, of the Franco-Prussian War in 1869-1870. A *Democrat* special correspondent described Paris in 1871 and by mail as well as by telegraph reported on European personalities, particularly royalty.

In the United States the big news stories of this period which the *Democrat* covered extensively included the impeachment of President Johnson, the Indian Wars, and the Chicago fire. The political interests of the paper lent significance to the reporting of the impeachment trial. But that alone did not account for the extensive coverage of the event. A *Democrat* reporter was called to testify. When Johnson had spoken in St. Louis on September 10, 1866, the paper had sent one of its best local reporters, Cyrus Walbridge, to cover the event. At the trial he testified that his account in the *Democrat* of the President's speech was accurate. His testimony was reprinted from the *Congressional Globe*.[5] Thus it was that to cover the impeachment of Johnson, McKee, Fishback and Company had in Washington a special correspondent in addition to their regular reporter in the capital. Walbridge's daily telegraphic reports kept *Democrat* readers informed of the progress of the trial during April and May, 1868.

The willingness of the proprietors to spend money to gather news and to employ able correspondents was not an idle boast. The firm picked a journalistic plum when Henry Morton Stanley was employed in January, 1867, to cover "Northwestern Missouri and Kansas and Nebraska."[6] The young English adventurer had distinguished himself as a correspondent with his letters on naval fighting in the Civil War. Then as an "attaché" for the *Democrat* he had traveled in 1865 through St. Joseph, Missouri, across the Great Plains to Salt Lake City, and back to Omaha.

Stanley was praised by the *Democrat* for his letters because he "described events of great public interest."[7]

The next year the young adventurer traveled to Asia Minor. Upon his return to the United States early in 1867, McKee, Fishback, and Houser employed him as a special correspondent to report on the Indian wars, paying him fifteen dollars a week and traveling expenses. In return he supplied the *Democrat* by letter and by telegraph with accounts of "various expeditions against warlike Indians of the Plains."[8]

In March, 1867, the *Democrat* proprietors gave Stanley the special assignments of covering General Hancock's expedition against the Kiowas and the Comanches and in July of accompanying General Sherman and the Indian Peace Commission. His stories, usually signed "Stanley," but sometimes initialed "S," appeared in the *Democrat* almost daily during this period. He told of an Indian attack on a transportation train, described in detail the march from Fort Larned to Medicine Creek and the arrival at Fort Harker, and reported General Sherman's speech and the red men's statements of their grievances. His letters, showing sympathy for the Indians, were filled with personal descriptions, dialogue, and local color. In one letter, for example, he described an Arapaho village and told of the Grand War dance —the beating of the tom-toms, the howling of the Indian dogs, and the shouting of the double row of Indians. Some of his letters ran two columns in length.[9] His last letter, datelined North Platte, Nebraska, November 21, 1867, and published in the *Democrat* a week later ended with the sentence: "Exit." From the *Democrat*, Stanley went to the *New York Herald,* for which he covered the British expedition to Abyssinia. Later, James Gordon Bennett, Jr., sent him to Africa on the famous expedition to find Dr. David Livingston.[10]

Other *Democrat* "specials" and "attachés" sent letters and dispatches covering the Ku Klux Klan developments, the murder trial of Colonel Crane, and the Osage land frauds, which were called unjust to the Indians.[11] "Specials" were in Fort Kearney; Western Kansas; Washington; Omaha; Centralia; Springfield, Illinois; Fort Leavenworth; and Little Rock, Arkansas. The editors even claimed that the reports of the panic news from New York from their own "special" were more accurate than were those of the Associated Press. "N. C. B." reported from Jefferson City. "Xelia" described the Indians at Fort Cobb, and "F. W." sent news from California.[12]

An important local story, the Whisky Ring trials, received thorough coverage in 1869.[13] Reports of these trials were written in a more lively news style than the records of court proceedings as they were usually recorded. Three men—Cutter, Fulton, and Babcock—were accused of tapping lead water pipes in the street in order to pass high wines from a distillery to a rectifying house, thus depriving neighboring houses of water.[14]

Editorials and stories concerning social and economic problems following in the wake of the war were also common during this period. Much space was devoted to the cholera epidemic of 1866. The *Democrat* reported meetings to aid people made helpless by the disease. As many as three or four articles on the prevention of cholera were sometimes printed in one issue. Dr. McDowell announced through a "paid local" that he had left his prescription for cholera with Jones and Sibley, druggists, who could prepare the medicine properly. Instructions were on each package.[15]

Stories and editorials revealed that Missourians were moving to Illinois, that free black labor had created unemployment problems, that returning soldiers were unemployed and destitute, and that Southern office hunters were causing dissension.[16] Long local stories, usually placed on the back page, told of the building and growth of St. Louis. One issue contained reports on river and harbor improvements, the dike at Chain of Rocks, the new City Water Works, and the cleaning of the old reservoir. A picture two columns wide and over half a page in depth of the Chain of Rocks and Cabaret Island was captioned "The Northern Harbor of St. Louis."[17] The introduction of stereotyping had made the use of pictures easier, and the *Democrat* proprietors began to use them more often after 1868.

Also in this period the paper began running church news and local items from neighboring towns. East St. Louis and Collinsville were represented daily with items containing news of people in these places. Church advertisements were printed on Saturdays, and accounts of sermons appeared in Monday papers. The sermon at the Congregational Church filled one-half column on October 24, 1870.

To further the paper's policy of giving its readers a greater variety of news, the firm frequently used supplements and "extras" when the event was considered important enough. For example, a two-column, one-page "extra" used to publish President Grant's inaugural address, without comment, was printed on only one side, and was without a date.[18] Supplements enabled the *Democrat* to bring to its readers such features as "A Journey to New Mexico," "Southern Missouri and Her Railroad Prospects," "Famine in Prussia," and "Are Paper Collars Poisonous?" Mark Twain, Petroleum V. Nasby, and Artemus Ward were familiar to *Democrat* readers.[19]

River news; railroad news, consisting mostly of arrival and departure time for trains; and commercial news and markets, under the direction of Fishback—all received fuller coverage than at any time before. "City Items," once only a column long, was in 1870 changed to "City News," and sometimes filled three columns.

St. Louisans were sports-minded people, and by 1870 few issues of the *Democrat* did not carry a report of some sports activity—races, baseball games, or prize fights. Baseball was increasingly popular, and the *Democrat* reported such games under the head, "The Great American Sport" or "Sporting." A one-column story on October 27, 1870, recorded the defeat of the St. Louis Empires by the White Stockings, 40-10. This was one of the few times that the game was written up by innings. An account of the Abe Hickey-Pete Maguire prizefight was reprinted from the *New York Herald* and ran under the head, "Pugilistic."[20] On July 22, 1870, the editors of the *Democrat* joyously reported that the paper had "scooped the *Republican* on the Steamboat Races."

Phil G. Ferguson, who signed his stories "Jenks," was a city reporter during this period. He became well-known for his humorous sketches, in which "Fritz Bummel," who spoke in German dialect, was a central figure.[21] "Jenks" and "Bummel" investigated a spiritualist, spent a night in the calaboose, and visited the police court and the slough ponds around Frenchtown.[22] Ferguson also traveled with B. Gratz Brown on his speaking tour through the state in 1870 and sent back daily dispatches on Brown's activities.

With the passing of the custom of dueling, newspapers increasingly were forced to defend themselves in libel suits. In 1867 McKee, Fishback and Company were plagued with these suits, which the proprietors claimed interfered with the freedom of the press. The long-time attacks on Blair led to a widely publicized libel suit. On July 22, 1866, the *Democrat* had printed what was called a "mendacious and defamatory attack" on its former proprietor.[23] About the same time James Lindsey had "libeled" Blair in a letter to the *Democrat* editors, which was published July 17, 1866. When the *Republican*, on July 27, announced that Blair had started action for damages, the *Democrat* derided Blair's action.[24] By May, 1867, however, the *Democrat* had publicly acknowledged that its accusations against Blair were unfounded,[25] and Blair dropped his suit against the firm.

In his letter Lindsey had accused Blair of stealing cotton while in command of the 15th and 17th Army Corps, of using Government teams and soldiers to do the hauling, and of using the proceeds to purchase a large stock farm in Mississippi and stock it with three hundred mules. The other *Democrat* story which was said to libel Blair had come from the paper's Washington correspondent. He had reported that facts would soon be published to show that Blair had appropriated silverware and china for his own use while he was on military duty in South Carolina. Blair sued the *Democrat* for $100,000 on each of these counts.[26]

In another libel case, Madame Cora James, a fortune teller, was awarded $1,000 damages from McKee, Fishback and Company for remarks printed about her powers of prediction.[27]

Judge Moody, a lawyer in St. Louis, sued the *Democrat* for $10,000 on a libel charge. The paper had published a statement made by a witness in a suit in which Moody was the defending lawyer. The witness had said that Moody was too drunk to make a speech.[28] Another suit also involved Judge Moody. This one was filed against the *Democrat* by Hudgens, Moody, and Hudgens, lawyers for William C. Robinson. The article in question stated that an insane man named William C. Robinson had assaulted his wife and child. This elicited the following editorial:

> There seems to be a sort of mania for suing the *Democrat* for libel. Like the suicide mania, it exists only among the weak and despairing. It is a favorable indication of the success and enterprise of a newspaper when its enemies attempt to silence it by the gag law of libel. . . .
>
> Other papers may commit errors, may assault public and private character with impunity, but the moment the *Democrat* makes the slightest mistake in a hurriedly written paragraph, somebody pounces down upon it and seeks to make a fortune by suing for enormous damages. . . .[29]

The imprisonment of Samuel Bowles, the *Springfield Republican* editor, resulting from a suit brought by James Fisk, Jr., gave the *Democrat* editors further opportunity to comment on libel laws and a free press. Fisk's action, they told their readers, brought up the question once more of whether or not the press was free.

> When Mr. Fisk muzzles the press, he attempts to make these corporations absolute monarchs of the country. Already they control the Legislature and the courts and threaten to master Congress and tie up the President. Nothing can successfully resist them but a press absolutely free to utter an honest statement, which a regard for the public may prompt.[30]

Democrat editors also hoped that in every state "changes of the libel law—that relic of barbarism"—would be demanded and gained so that every paper would be free to expose scoundrelism even if it controlled powerful corporations.[31]

Although the new frontiers in journalism touched advertising very little, there were evidences that the *Democrat* was trying to offer its readers more attractive advertisements. Pushed off the front page during the war, advertising had returned to the *Dem-*

ocrat's front page by 1867, but with a difference. Now the first two columns on the left side were usually topped by a two-column advertisement with more white space than had been usual, and with larger type. Another device used was to print the copy of a one-column advertisement vertically rather than horizontally. Also making their appearance during this period were the "paid locals," one- or two-sentence notices inserted in the "City News."

Still another innovation was the more frequent use of prices, particularly in clothing advertisements printed as "paid locals." One such item read: "Keep cool and buy the great $1.50 linen coats at Polack's."[32] Overcoats in 1867 were selling for $6.00 to $25.00; cassimere suits, $6.00 to $25.00; pants, $4.00 to $7.00; and vests, $2.00 to $4.00.

To meet the rising cost of production McKee, Fishback and Company increased their advertising rates. They sold one insertion for fifteen cents per line of agate type. The second and third insertions were ten cents a line, and insertions after the third were five cents.[33]

Of significance to later development of the paper was the addition of a new advertising clerk, Simeon Ray, nephew of William McKee. By 1872 he had become the *Democrat's* bookkeeper. Later he was a stockholder,[34] and his son, E. Lansing Ray, was to become the publisher and editor of the paper.

Many of the advances made by the paper during this period can be attributed to Houser. Quiet and unobtrusive, he ran the business end of the paper, while McKee set the paper's news and editorial policies. Yet when Houser made suggestions McKee listened and usually took his advice. One such instance was the suggestion that telegraph operators at various places be used as *Democrat* "specials" or "attachés."[35] In this way the paper was able to expand its news coverage at low cost. Moreover, Houser was a good business man, and able to keep the paper making money. By 1870 McKee was reported clearing $25,000 annually from his half interest,[36] not a small sum for a man who twenty years before had nothing.

Although many of the new journalistic practices had been

started by 1871, it remained for Joseph B. McCullagh to stabilize and develop them. The chunky young newspaper man had gained a national reputation for fairness and reliability with his war reporting. During the battle at Fort Donelson he was one of the first to volunteer to go on the gunboat, "St. Louis," the first boat to pass the fort. His paper, the *Cincinnati Gazette*, refused to print his report of the battle because it discredited the Union soldiers. McCullagh promptly resigned and was immediately employed by the *Cincinnati Commercial* at twice the salary he had been receiving.

He ceased reporting as a war correspondent in 1863 to become the Washington correspondent of the *Commercial*. He also served as the Senate reporter for the New York Associated Press. His stature as a journalist was considerably increased while he was in Washington; he became famous for his use of the interview. Popular with both public officials and the reading public, he was something of a liaison between President Johnson and the public; Johnson often called in McCullagh to "give out" news. An interview which McCullagh had with Alexander H. Stephens was widely reprinted, adding to his reputation.

Before returning to St. Louis McCullagh had for a short time edited the *Cincinnati Enquirer* and with a brother, John W. McCullagh, had taken charge of the *Chicago Republican*. But this journal had been destroyed by the Chicago fire, which had also swept away McCullagh's large library and his other posses- sions. After this disaster, McKee, Fishback, and Houser were fortunate enough to employ as editor of the *Democrat* the man they had trained as a "cub reporter" ten years earlier.[37] The proprietors offered him a small share in the paper to persuade him to stay with them. They knew that with McCullagh in charge the *Democrat* would have every chance of surpassing the *Republican*.

With McCullagh as managing editor, with the paper now advancing in journalistic practices, and with the profits increas- ing each year, it is little wonder that the year 1872 brought the changes that it did.

Chapter IX

Two Sales and a Merger

THE Reconstruction years came to a dramatic close for the *Democrat;* the paper was sold in March, 1872. For some time Fishback had been at odds with McKee and Houser because he was dissatisfied with the management of their journal.[1] The precise cause of the rift between the proprietors was rumored to be political. Credence in this theory probably developed from the fact that Fishback had recently bought an interest in the *Dispatch,* which supported the Democratic party.[2] Certainly Fishback's later re-employment of Grosvenor as editor of the *Democrat* tended to substantiate this belief.

In view of the developments in the next three years it is not unlikely that the proprietors also disagreed on spending large sums of money for gathering news. Fishback was not the enthusiastic adherent of this policy that McKee and Houser were. Moreover, he probably wanted a larger share of the profits. In a time when "the element of speculative mania" was rampant,[3] Fishback no doubt could envision unlimited riches. Would not the first steel bridge in the world soon be spanning the Mississippi River at St. Louis? This connecting link with the East surely would bring more and more Eastern wealth to St. Louis for investment. Besides, he had arranged already for financial backing if he could gain control of the paper. In this "Future Great City of the World," why could he not be the newspaper tycoon instead of McKee?

Whatever the cause, Fishback, who owned one-third interest in the *Democrat,* wanted either to buy McKee's one-half interest and Houser's one-sixth or to sell his interest to them. What arguments must have taken place in the paper's counting room, how many offers made and rejected! McKee, pleasant but unyielding to pleas, refused to accept Fishback's offers and would not set a price on his own interest. Houser, taking his cue from McKee, also refused to come to terms. Finally, the insistent Fishback lost his patience and obtained from Judge Madill of the Circuit Court an order for a sale, whereby an equitable transaction could adjust and close the partnership.[4]

No newspaper in St. Louis had ever been sold like this. In fact it had been many years since any large, established journal in the country had been sold at a direct public sale.[5] How much would Fishback pay? Or how much would McKee pay? What was the influential and profitable *Democrat* worth? These were the questions in the minds of the men who gathered on the morning of March 22, 1872, in the law office of Irwin L. Smith, one of the counsellors for McKee and Houser.

First to arrive was McKee, with his other lawyer, Samuel Knox, and his three friends—James Richardson, William H. Benton, and Henry T. Blow. Then came Theophile Papin, who was to act as auctioneer. Next to appear were Houser and his friends—Constantine Maguire, Thomas Walsh, and ex-Collector Harris. By this time Smith's office was becoming crowded, and extra chairs were brought in. Last to crowd into the room were Fishback, his lawyers, S. T. Glover and H. N. Hitchcock, and his friends, William E. Burr, president of the St. Louis National Bank, A. G. Edwards, United States assistant treasurer, and General J. S. Fullerton.

The door was closed, and the men waited tensely for the proceedings to get under way. Finally, Papin, from behind Smith's desk, asked, "Who will start the bidding?"

A heavy silence settled on the room for an instant. Then Fishback spoke, "$100,000."

McKee raised, "$150,000."

And the auction was on. Fishback raised to $175,000 and McKee to $200,000. At this point each bid was increased by only $5,000 until the $330,000 mark was reached. Then the bidding slowed. Raises dropped to $1,000 a bid, to $500, and at last to $100. Seventy-three times the price had been raised by $100, and the voices were beginning to sound monotonous in the stifling room. Someone raised a window to clear the office of smoke.

McKee glanced at Houser, who shrugged his shoulders. "I bid $456,000," he said and looked down at his half-smoked cigar.

Fishback cleared his throat and inched his chair back. "Four hundred fifty-six thousand and one hundred dollars," he said.

Silence settled in the office. Through the window came the sound of horses' hoofs clopping down the brick pavement. Still the silence continued.

"Is there another bid?" Papin finally asked. But there was no answer. Fishback had bought the *Democrat* for $456,100.

This really meant that Fishback was to pay $304,066 for McKee's one-half interest and Houser's one-sixth. The sale included everything—newspaper, job printing, bookbinding equipment and supplies, subscription lists, good will, shares in the cooperative Western Associated Press, office building, and leases. The land upon which the new building had been erected belonged to two different people and was leased separately at a total of $4,300 yearly. At the time of the sale, rent amounting to $1,625 was due on one of the leases,[7] a debt which Fishback assumed.

Nobody had thought that the *Democrat*, barely twenty years old and in grave financial difficulties only ten years earlier, would sell for such a price. But as the *Republican* on the following day grudgingly commented:

> The actual material in the *Democrat* establishment would be valued at a comparatively small proportion of the price which the journal has just sold for, but this material comprises only a small proportion of the real value of the establishment. The attributes of age, established character, political views, advertising patronage, public influence, and subscription lists, all constitute the substantial elements of value in an established journal. The *Democrat* has its share of the value elements, and they represent a large proportion of the handsome price for which the paper sold.[8]

Terms of the sale were one-half cash, one-fourth in three months, and one-fourth in six months. This agreement had been reached before the sale as well as an understanding that whoever bought the paper was to protect McCullagh's interest.[9] To meet these obligations, Fishback on March 25, 1872, mortgaged all equipment "acquired by court sale," to borrow $232,033.32 in seven separate notes of $50,000.00, $30,000.00, $57,012.50, $32,-012.50, $25,000.00, and two each for $19,004.16. Among those lending Fishback money were Gerald B. Allen, William P. Fishback, Hudson E. Bridge, Elihu K. Shepard, Jesse K. Arnot, and George H. Rea. The notes were payable in thirty days to a year at from 6 to 10 per cent interest variously.[10] Fishback must have had $72,022.00 himself to invest in his purchase.

Three days after the sale the new owner formed a corporation, the St. Louis Democrat Company, with a capital of $500,000. Others in the company were Henry C. Yeager, Richard Holmes, who became secretary, and George P. Whitelaw. The capital stock consisted of and was divided into 500 shares, each having a par value of $1,000.[11] McCullagh was given sixteen shares. Thus was the *Democrat*, established twenty years before on a financial shoestring, now a journal of some note, worth half a million dollars. Its prospects were bright for a prosperous future.

Fishback assured his readers on March 25 that the paper's policy on national issues would remain Republican and that it would continue to support Grant. The *Democrat*, he said, would be, even more than in the past, "a full and complete *newspaper—* a faithful record of the world's history from day to day, and a complete chronicle of all that interests the people in their relations to each other as social and moral beings." He also promised increased attention to subjects pertaining to the commercial and manufacturing interests of St. Louis, of Missouri, and of the Great West.

But Fishback hardly had time to fulfill his further promise of strengthening the *Democrat's* claims "to public esteem as an organ of advanced thought in all that concerns the population,"[12] when he had to face competition from his former partners. Already there were eight other St. Louis dailies to compete for the readership of St. Louis and its area; now there would be another. It would be difficult, Fishback realized, to keep his paper alive.

Within a few weeks after the sale, McKee and Houser began plans for establishing another newspaper. They leased the Finn Building at 118 North Third Street. Houser, who was something of a wizard at newspaper management, laid out the floor plans. On the first floor were the counting room, McKee's office, and the mail room. On the second floor was the editorial department.[13] McKee's office was set off from the counting room by a partition eight feet high, six feet below the ceiling. In the partition was a sash that could be raised and lowered.

In the counting room were five desks, one of which McKee sometimes used. The others were used by Houser, a bookkeeper, and two clerks. A lounge was equipped with chairs for visitors.

The first issue of the new paper, called the *St. Louis Globe*, was published on July 18, 1872, barely four months after McKee and Houser had sold their interest in the *Democrat*. It was the first St. Louis daily in "quarto" form, eight pages each with six columns twenty-three inches long.[14] Within four years three other St. Louis dailies were to adopt this new format—the *Republican*, the *Times*, and the *Dispatch*.

The *Globe*, with its smaller pages, contrasted sharply with the *Democrat's* ten columns on pages thirty inches long. McKee and Houser advertised their journal as the largest paper in St. Louis for its price. It sold for five cents a copy, twelve dollars a year for seven papers a week, and twenty-five cents a week by carrier; Fishback was still selling the *Democrat* for fourteen dollars a year and thirty cents a week by carrier.

The proprietors promised their readers that the new paper would carry daily news in all departments from all quarters of the world, as well as a complete record of local events. The *Globe* was to be a journal of "Western enterprise, intelligence, and opinion, progressive in character, Republican in principle, and national in spirit," with "new features, fresh energies, and a disposition to cooperate with others in the advancement of an expanding St. Louis." McKee and Houser pledged their paper's support for the successful administration of President Grant and his re-election. "In the prevalence or overthrow of the Republican principles," they declared, was "wrapped up the thrift and glory or the ruin and disgrace of the American people." But they pledged that the *Globe* would print "no vindictiveness or ungenerous upbraidings against the South."[15]

Readers were further assured that the proprietors had "abundant means" to carry out these "designs." Neither exertion nor expense would be spared to obtain the most experienced and thorough journalists available to direct the "several departments."[16] Simeon Ray became the paper's bookkeeper. Subsequent to the sale of the *Democrat*, Ray had been appointed district gauger for the distilleries in the St. Louis district of the Internal Revenue Service. With the founding of the *Globe* he returned to bookkeeping for his uncle, McKee.[17]

Edited by Charles R. Davis, who for sixteen years had been a writer for the *Democrat*, the first issue showed how carefully McKee and Houser had planned their paper. The first page had only one column on the right side devoted to advertising, although after this issue advertising disappeared from the front page for more than a year. The other five columns were filled with news stories from "specials" in Washington, New York, Joliet, Chicago, Springfield, and other news centers. The first and third columns on the left side of the page had headlines. One page was devoted to financial news and to market reports. Column headings on the other pages included "Agriculture," "Weather," "River News," "City News," "Railroad News," "Court News," and "Real Estate Transactions." In the second issue a column called "Globules" appeared on page two; probably written by Editor Davis, it consisted of one-sentence paragraphs, which appeared to be satiric references to and humorous remarks about local events and people.[18]

Evidence of sharpened news writing appeared in the reports of the city council, the school board, and various committees. Events were summarized in short paragraphs. Sentences tended to be much shorter than those used in the *Democrat* of previous years. With its new presses and its new, easily handled form, the

Globe was a much more attractive and readable paper than was the *Democrat*.

McKee and Houser were not content to compete with Fishback with the daily alone. On July 26 they began publication on Fridays of the *Weekly Globe*, also in "quarto" form. On Tuesdays and Fridays they issued the *Semi-Weekly*, and they increased to twelve pages their Sunday *Daily Globe*. Sometimes they had so much news that it was necessary to insert a one-sheet supplement. Furthermore, they lowered their advertising rates in an effort to win accounts from Fishback. Where Fishback charged fifteen cents per agate line for one insertion and ten cents for the second and third insertions, McKee and Houser charged twelve and eight cents respectively.

As was to be expected the competition between the two papers broke into the editorial columns. McCullagh, as editor of the *Democrat*, attacked the *Globe* in terse, pungent paragraphs which were to become an outstanding mark of his journalistic career. He called the *Globe* office the "Robbers' Roost."[19] He was referring to two activities of McKee and Houser. In some paragraphs in March, 1873, he hinted that McKee was involved in graft; in others he openly referred to the practice of the *Globe* of reprinting from other papers Western Associated Press news stories when they were a day old. The *Republican* was later to reprint these paragraphs in an attempt to involve McCullagh in graft schemes.[20]

Then in the fall of 1873 Fishback imported Newton Crane, a "young man from the East, of good education, fine address, and considerable ability," with the intention of making him managing editor and McCullagh city editor. But McCullagh had little sympathy with college-trained journalists. "A general doesn't take orders from a corporal," he said.[21] As a result of the disagreement with Fishback that followed, McCullagh was fired in October, 1873.[22]

Almost immediately McKee and Houser sent for him. Editor Davis having died of cholera the previous summer, the *Globe* proprietors offered McCullagh the managing editor's position on their paper. So McCullagh started to work for them under an agreement that he was to remain in this position as long as the circulation of the *Globe* continued to climb.[23] He was still with the paper when he died in 1896.

From the time McCullagh assumed the editorship of the *Globe*, competition between it and the *Democrat* sharpened. Fishback editorially attacked his former editor, claiming that McCullagh had slandered Dr. Stuart Robinson in the *Democrat* and then left the paper for the *Globe*.[24]

McCullagh answered this with one of his infrequent long editorials.

> Does it occur to the editor of the *Democrat* that none but dirty birds ever befoul their own nests? And doesn't that individual know that in publishing the *Old School Presbyterian's* attack upon a person once in the *Democrat* employ, and at present an involuntary stockholder in it, he commits the very offense? The subject matter of the assault is an article in relation to Dr. Stuart Robinson, and the individual assailed is one who was supposed to be managing editor of the *Democrat* at the time of publication. If Geo. W. Fishback was not holding that position at the time referred to, he must have sworn falsely in the partnership then pending. For the first time in the history of American journalism, a newspaper opens its columns to the venom of an exasperated ass directed against itself, and then pats the author on the back. This is impersonal journalism with a vengeance. . . .[25]

McCullagh could cut with a blade of ridicule that went smoothly to the bone.[26] But then, the editor had a personal grudge against Fishback. He wanted the money for his sixteen shares of *Democrat* stock. Eventually he employed a lawyer to try to collect this money.[27]

In the first months of the competition the *Democrat* printed frequent four-page supplements, but as competition grew sharper, supplements became less and less frequent. By December, 1873, the paper was back to a four-page, nine-column journal, although it remained "blanket" size. Fishback tended to fill his space with large pictures. The issue of January 1, 1873, a special ten-column paper, featured an enormous map of the United

States and England. Printed on the inside pages, it was twenty columns wide and ten inches deep and showed the water routes from St. Louis to the Liverpool market. On April 9, 1873, the *Democrat's* front page contained a six-column circus advertisement. The top half of the page had five two-column pictures, and the headline extended across the column rules which were broken every two columns. The news was taken for the most part from the Western Associated Press or was reprinted from exchange papers. The number of stories from *Democrat* "specials" became fewer and fewer. But Fishback never reduced the amount of commercial news in his paper; one page was always reserved for this information.

In the meantime the *Globe*, in spite of its lack of a news press service, continued to be more conservative in its makeup. Its front page was filled with news from "specials," its inner pages with news of St. Louis and surrounding areas. Nearly every issue had theater and book reviews, letters to the editor, and a column or more of miscellany of interest to housewives. Its financial news and market reports, though not as extensive as those of the *Democrat,* still were adequate. Editor of this page was McKee's brother, Henry.[28]

But the *Globe* suffered from not being a subscriber to a news press service. McKee and Houser tried repeatedly to subscribe to the service of the Western Associated Press. But as a unanimous vote by members of the Association in St. Louis was required for admittance, McKee and Houser could never buy a membership; Fishback always voted against them.[29]

In January, 1874, McKee and Houser found a way out for their paper. On January 6 Joseph Pulitzer bought at an auction from William Einstein, A. C. Erfort, and a Mr. Jaegerbuber the entire stock of the German language newspaper, the *Staats-Zeitung*—"type, presses, franchises, assets, lock, stock, and barrel."[30] This paper owned a franchise in the Western Associated Press, and, to secure the right to use its news releases in the *Globe,* McKee and Houser on the same day paid Pulitzer "a little in advance of $40,000" for his new possessions.[31] They proposed to run their paper under the charter of the German-language

paper, and from that day McKee and Houser called their company the Missouri Staats-Zeitung Company, publishers of the
St. Louis Globe.[32]

As soon as the rumors of the McKee-Houser purchase were
made public, Fishback called a meeting of the local board of the
Western Associated Press. "The right, propriety, and fairness of
turning a German newspaper into an English journal was debated
on all sides and from every possible standpoint."[33] McKee and
Houser were, as usual, pleasant, but they insisted on their rights.
Fishback made a "very vigorous but manly" fight against his
rival, but as the *Dispatch* said, "It was finally ended by recog-
nizing the right of the English proprietors of a 'Dutch' newspaper to change its language at their own sweet will, all the
members of the Association but the *Democrat* voting 'aye.' "
Furthermore, Houser was promptly elected secretary of the
organization.[34]

Concerning this, Fishback told his readers:

> The *Globe* concluded, after mature reflection, that it was
> better to buy the dispatches of the Associated Press than to
> steal them and as our local columns show, its proprietors
> have purchased the *Staats-Zeitung* and have changed it to
> an English morning paper under the name of the *St. Louis
> Globe*. This, it is claimed, gives the *Globe* the right to re-
> ceive the dispatches heretofore delivered to its German
> predecessor as will be seen by the proceedings of the local
> Board of the Associated Press. The *Democrat* voted "No"
> on the proposition to admit the *Globe* to the Association.
> We have a prejudice to the effect that a man who steals his
> neighbor's property is a thief; and by our negative vote we
> testified to our opinion that men who confess themselves to
> be thieves are undesirable associates.[35]

Of some journalistic significance is the fact that other St. Louis
newspapers considered the whole affair amusing. Which paper
would outlast the other must have been a common subject of
conjecture among St. Louis newspaper men.

Nevertheless, both the *Democrat* and the *Globe* suffered from
lack of advertising, as did all newspapers of the time. The failure
of Jay Cooke's banking house in New York in September, 1873,

was followed by a widespread demoralization in business circles. Unemployment spread quickly to the St. Louis area, which felt especially the stoppage of construction in the railroad industry. Mechanics, clerks, and lawyers bought only the bare necessities of life. Merchants, already weighed down by bad debts from over-expansion, decreased their invoices and cut their expenses in order to stay in business.[36]

Advertising in all St. Louis newspapers felt the effects of this tight money situation, but the two Republican papers, locked in a death battle, probably suffered the worst. By 1874 advertising in the *Democrat* had been greatly reduced. Instead of about half, now only about one-third of it was filled with advertisements. The *Globe*, by this time, had managed to increase its advertising to only one-fourth of its space.[37]

But the circulation of the *Globe* was increasing steadily. As early as November 2, 1873, McCullagh told his readers that he hoped no newspaper in St. Louis was losing subscribers as fast as the *Globe* was gaining them. Four days later he claimed that the daily and weekly combined circulations of his paper were larger than those of any other St. Louis paper. For the remainder of the month, he kept up a steady stream of paragraphs on the *Globe's* strength. On Sunday, November 9, the *Globe* printed two thousand more papers than did the *Democrat* of the same day. In fact the Sunday *Globe* was adding five hundred readers each week, and every issue of the daily brought eighty new readers.[38] By November 21 McCullagh was claiming a larger circulation than the *Democrat*. The *Weekly Globe* had nearly 40,000 subscribers, he said, and he invited anyone who doubted his figures to visit the *Globe* press room before eleven in the morning and to check the press rooms of other St. Louis papers and compare notes.[39]

Nor did McCullagh allow his St. Louis readers to forget that the *Globe* was as much an enemy of the *Republican* as the *Democrat* had always been. He missed few opportunities to loose his sarcasm on his other rival. He especially liked to jibe at the *Republican's* boast that it was the oldest journal in St. Louis. "The *Republican* flaunts its antiquity as proof of its sagacity," he wrote on November 3, 1873, but age and experience, he thought, were not always guarantees of merit. The *Republican* needed progress, too. He advised the paper to add the letters B. C. to 1808, the year it was founded, because "the Psalms of David were published in it as original matter, and it had the letter list when the Apostles were writing to each other."[40]

Other St. Louis journals entered the fray. The *Dispatch*, McCullagh reported on November 4, 1873, had asked the youngest editor of the *Republican* to tell what good his journal had done in the last few years. This was an ingenious way of trying to get Methuselah to write for the *Dispatch*, McCullagh thought. Two days later the editor reported that the *Evening Journal* was alarmed at the fierceness of the *Republican's* remarks respecting the *Globe*.

But the acquisition of a news service had given McCullagh what he needed to advance the paper. The *Globe* may not have outstripped the *Republican*, but with the money McKee and Houser were investing in their paper, the *Democrat* suffered. Fishback was willing to sell as early as 1874. His paper needed new presses, and he was so far in debt that he saw no use in continuing to fight. One day early in the summer Henry T. Blow, Fishback's lawyer, walked into McKee's office in the *Globe* counting room; McKee had already gone to his summer home in New York, and Blow had to talk with Houser. He had come, he said, as an authorized agent of George W. Fishback to negotiate the sale of the *Democrat*.[41] Houser listened politely. Fishback, Blow explained, was tired of the controversy between the two papers, a controversy that seemed inevitable so long as the two papers existed and McCullagh edited one of them. He would like to sell the *Democrat* to McKee and Houser for about $325,000. Houser promised to take the matter up with McKee when he returned to the city.

When McKee returned toward the end of the summer, he mulled over Fishback's offer for a time. Then he called his editor down to discuss the matter, but McCullagh advised against buying the *Democrat*. Extinction was cheaper than purchase, he told McKee; the *Democrat* could be "sunk" for half Fishback's price. Edited and managed as it was at the time, it was no rival for the *Globe*. The only danger lay in Fishback's selling it to someone with newspaper ability and experience. Many years later McCullagh explained that only in that contingency could the *Democrat* have given "us a lively competition for the supremacy we then held." At that time the *Democrat* was shouting itself hoarse for Gentry, backed by the entire Republican party of the state, while at the same time the *Globe* was indulging in a guerilla war against both tickets and all candidates. As the books will show, however, the circulation and business of the *Democrat* went steadily down, while that of the *Globe* went steadily up.[42]

McKee took McCullagh's advice, and the competition continued. Fishback re-employed Grosvenor as *Democrat* editor, but, as McCullagh pointed out, "with no other perceptible effect than to develop that remarkable person's powers to reduce circulation."[43]

In March, 1875, Fishback tried to borrow five thousand dollars for ninety days from General John McDonald, then supervisor for the Internal Revenue Service in St. Louis. In return, Fishback offered McDonald the support of his paper. He even showed McDonald an editorial commending him and proposed to print it in the *Democrat* the next day if McDonald would lend him some of the government money.[44] According to McDonald's own story, he refused to lend Fishback the money because he did not regard the influence of the *Democrat* as consequential.[45] However, he may have refused because he suspected Fishback of trying to get evidence to prove his dishonesty. On the other hand, Fishback may actually have believed that he could get a part of the graft money himself.

In the meantime McCullagh had started 1875 off with a new quarrel; he later said that he was in a fair way "to make things lively in the bowels of the *Democrat*." Then his attorney, who had been trying to collect McCullagh's equity in the Fishback company, suddenly began trying once more to negotiate the sale of the *Democrat* to McKee and Houser.[46] "Bummer Bill" Grosvenor, as McCullagh contemptuously called the *Democrat* editor, had allowed the journal to drop so low that it now seemed likely

that Fishback would be forced to sell it to some capable journalist. This greatly enhanced the value of the *Democrat* to
McKee and Houser.⁴⁷ Perhaps for this reason, but more likely for
the reason that Fishback had discovered McKee's connection
with the Whisky Ring (as will be explained later), McKee and
Houser decided to buy the *Democrat*.

Accordingly, on May 11, 1875, McKee and Houser went to
the *Democrat* office and offered to buy the controlling interest
of the *Democrat* from Fishback and Otto A. Hasselman, the other
large stock owner, for $325,000, which was $131,100 less than
the *Democrat* had sold for in 1872. The sale, completed May 18,
included a proviso to protect McCullagh's $16,000 worth of
stock. Fishback agreed not to enter the newspaper business in
St. Louis again for a "term of years."⁴⁸ The *Globe* proprietors
apparently held no ill will toward Fishback, however, and years
later advocated his appointment to a federal position in St.
Louis.⁴⁹

The sale was announced in both the *Globe* and the *Democrat*
on May 12. The *Globe* called the sale a "merging of the two
papers." The *Democrat* said that arrangements had been made
whereby the "two papers would be published by McKee and
Houser."

Subsequently, McKee and Houser moved their equipment into
the *Democrat* building, and the two papers were published under
the title of the *St. Louis Globe-Democrat*. The first issue of the
paper bearing the hyphenated title was printed May 20, 1875, in
the *Democrat's* blanket-sheet form. It was not until June 5 that
the *Globe* machinery was set up so that the paper could be
printed in the *Globe's* format. At this time the paper was widened
to seven columns. The Sunday paper was increased to sixteen
pages. By 1876 the paper had two presses.

In the first issue of the *Globe-Democrat*, readers were reminded
that neither the paper nor the owners were new. The paper was
"more a marriage than a birth," McCullagh wrote. He promised
that it would continue Republican in politics and remain "true
to the party, always supposing that the party will be true to the
principles that gave it birth." He aimed to make the *Globe-*

Democrat "as nearly perfect as liberal means, large outlay, and large experience"[50] could make it.

The consolidated circulations, even after making deductions for those who took both papers, "reached a very encouraging figure," McCullagh reported on May 21. A year later he noted that the circulation of the daily lacked only a few hundred of 25,000 and that the advertising was proportionately large. By February, 1878, he could report that the circulation had reached 26,792.[51]

McKee and Houser, immediately after the merger, formed the Globe-Democrat Printing Company, with a paid-up capital of $500,000. McCullagh's holdings in the *Democrat* were increased in the new company to $20,000. Houser owned $166,000 worth of stock; Henry McKee, $10,000; and Simeon Ray, $10,000. William McKee held the remainder of the stock, or nearly $300,000 worth.[52] So successful was the enterprise that in 1878 the net revenue of the paper was said to be a little in excess of $100,000.[53]

The merger of the *Globe* and the *Democrat* ended three years of intensive competition, but it was the beginning of a metropolitan newspaper that was to survive all but one of its contemporaries. Not even the connection of McKee with the Whisky Ring frauds could deter its development or its contributions to journalism.

Chapter X

The Whisky Ring Frauds

A HOT sun was beating down on St. Louis when William
Mckee walked to his *Globe* office on July 4, 1874. He
was earlier than usual, but already the streets teemed with people,
for this was the day all St. Louis had anticipated for five years.
The Eads Bridge, the first such all-steel structure in the world,
was to be opened officially.

This bridge would bring St. Louisans a step closer to the reali-
zation of their dream—St. Louis as the largest, richest, most influential city in the world. This direct rail link with the East would
surely make possible the city's industrial and economic growth.
Chicago, that upstart city to the north, would no longer be a
challenge to the supremacy of St. Louis. But few if any people
that day realized that Eads Bridge, in actuality, would seal the
doom of river traffic, and that St. Louis was destined soon to lag
far behind Chicago as an industrial and transportation center.

For days, both the *Globe* and the *Democrat*, as well as the
other journals of the city, had filled columns with stories about
the gala celebration. Thousands of visitors had flocked into the
city by wagon, by boat, by rail. Business houses were draped
with flags, bands played, and peddlers, dodging the ruffled para-
sols of the women, hawked their wares.

McKee was filled with pride that day. As a member of the
committee for planning the festivities[1] he rode in the parade that
was fifteen miles long and took five and one-half hours to pass a
given point. He sat on the platform in front of the Courthouse
with other notables and listened to speeches by the mayor, the
governor of Missouri, and notables from Illinois. He was one of
more than a thousand passengers who crowded into the first train

to chug through the tunnel which provided the western approach to the bridge.

The next day, both the *Democrat* and the *Globe* devoted almost all of their space to the celebration. The *Democrat* used headlines with twenty-three decks; the *Globe*, having shorter columns, used fewer. Both papers estimated the crowd at more than one hundred and fifty thousand.

In the years of competition between the *Globe* and the *Democrat*, the story of the Eads Bridge celebration was one of two stories receiving prominent display and sustained attention in St. Louis newspapers. The other, the Whisky Ring frauds, rocked the nation with its political impact. But McKee was far from proud of the publicity given the Whisky Ring frauds, publicity beside which that of the Eads Bridge celebration paled into insignificance. Stories of the whisky scandals filled the columns in St. Louis newspapers for more than a year. Oddly enough, it was the *Democrat* personnel who obtained the evidence necessary to reveal the Ring's existence, and it was the *Globe's* chief proprietor who was criminally involved. The combination of these two factors precipitated the merging of the two papers, although this event had seemed probable for more than a year.

Actually the story had been in the making for several years. This particular ring scandal reverted to the older whisky revenue exposures of 1869 and to the political maneuvering of McKee when he engineered the formation of the Liberal Republican party in 1870. McKee had fallen out, as has been explained, with President Grant over the latter's persistence in appointing persons to federal offices in St. Louis whom the publisher believed to be against the best interests of the party. McKee was particularly bitter about the appointment of C. W. Ford instead of Constantine Maguire as director of the Internal Revenue Service.[2] This, as much as any other one factor, may have influenced McKee to bolt the party.

Ford controlled the re-opening of the distilleries, closed in the previous whisky scandals. Many were still shut when General John McDonald, a wartime friend of the President, was appointed district supervisor of the Internal Revenue Service.

McKee, Fishback and Company had been one of more than a dozen St. Louis firms and Missouri dignitaries to recommend McDonald for this position.[3] The firm wrote to President Grant that McDonald was a "brave soldier, a true Republican in the days of our trouble." He had energy, ability, and integrity, and his appointment would "give general satisfaction and particularly oblige your friends here and none more than ourselves."[4] Grant, by this time becoming worried about the virulent opposition of the *Democrat* to his candidacy for a second term, appointed McDonald to the position on February 14, 1870.[5]

This did not end McKee's opposition to the administration, however, and shortly after moving to St. Louis, McDonald talked with McKee about patching up the differences between him and the President. But McKee remained adamant, and on August 28, 1870, published in the *Democrat* an open letter to the President— a stinging criticism of Grant for his political appointments and his attempts to control politics in Missouri. McDonald was to contend later that in his talks with McKee about a political reconciliation with Grant, the publisher had brought up the possibility of organizing a ring among revenue officials in St. Louis, the profits from illicit distilling to be used for a political slush fund.[6] Whether this suggestion really came from McKee or from McDonald is a debatable question.

But in the meantime McDonald had discovered that Ford and John H. Concannon, Ford's deputy, were already busily deriving profits from illicit distilling. When McKee learned this late in 1870, he agreed to the formation of the Ring; and according to McDonald, there was an understanding between him, the President, McKee, Ford, and John A. Joyce, McDonald's private secretary, that the proceeds would be used for a campaign fund to advance the President's interests.[7] McDonald and Joyce had been particularly interested in drawing McKee into the Ring to secure the *Democrat's* support. "It is no use disguising the fact," Joyce wrote to McDonald, "that the *Missouri Democrat* is a great power in this State, and we must secure it for Grant and for 1872."[8] In the Ring also, according to McDonald, were General

E. O. Babcock, Grant's private secretary, and several people in the Treasury Department in Washington.

McKee, apparently having committed himself, then approached Grosvenor about softening the *Democrat's* attitude toward Grant. The editor was later to write that McKee, with significant winks and nods, hinted that such action could prove highly profitable to both of them.[9] The paper did become more favorable to Grant; but Grosvenor's subsequent curiosity, according to McDonald, became so insistent that Joyce gave him five hundred dollars, and in January, 1871, McKee dismissed him.[10]

Even after this, however, McKee still hesitated to believe that McDonald had as much power in Washington as he claimed, and so, in April, McDonald took McKee to the nation's capital, where he dined with the Grants at the White House.[11] It was not until after the visit to Washington that the Ring really started its operation, although Grosvenor claimed that the first illicit money was collected that month for a campaign fund for the municipal elections. Apparently, however, McDonald's contention that the first collection was made in September was correct.[12]

As the months rolled by and the money poured in, two significant events influenced the activities of the Ring. First, on October 25, 1873, Ford died; there were hints later that he had committed suicide. Replacing him was Constantine Maguire, the man McKee had favored originally for the position.[13] Second, McKee and Houser, as has been already related, established the *Globe*. Grosvenor later claimed, as did Chauncey I. Filley, who was to assume leadership of the Republican party in Missouri, that the *Globe* was founded with illicit whisky money because the Ring needed an organ.[14] But granted that the Ring was already in operation, it seems plausible that if it needed an organ that badly McKee would have outbid Fishback for the *Democrat* in 1872. It would have cost him much less to have bought the *Democrat* than to establish a new paper and compete against one already established. Besides, McKee was by this time independently wealthy.[15] But the competition between the *Globe* and the

Democrat was to play an important role in the exposure of the Ring in 1875.

In the meantime the Ring operated by collecting the federal tax of seventy cents a gallon on illicitly made whisky. The revenue officers and the distillers divided the money. The distillers shared their cut with rectifiers and storekeepers. The half that went to the revenue officers was divided into five packages each Saturday in McDonald's office. Two of these packages were given to John Leavenworth, who died before the trials. Reportedly, he was to deliver his packages to McKee, who was to send one package to someone else, never named. In fourteen months each of the five members of the Ring proper was said to have collected between $45,000 and $60,000.[16] McKee's share was said to have been $1,000 a week.[17]

Except for a few interruptions the Ring ran smoothly until Fishback, pressed financially and having had no success in selling the *Democrat* to McKee, decided in 1875 to use his paper to force the issue by exposing the frauds. It is difficult to understand how Fishback could have been unaware of the Ring's existence so long. If he had known about it when he forced the sale of the *Democrat* in 1872, why did he not speak then? In 1874, however, he had employed Grosvenor to edit his paper, and it is possible that he was Fishback's source of information.

On February 8, 1875, Fishback took the initial step in unveiling the St. Louis frauds by writing to his Washington correspondent:

> There has been much talk of late of the fraudulent whisky traffic in the west. If the Secretary [Secretary B. H. Bristow] wants to break up the powerful ring which exists here, I can give him the name of a man, who, if he receives the necessary authority and is assured of absolute secrecy about the matter will undertake to do it and I will guarantee success.[18]

Bristow was interested, but before Fishback took further steps, he tried, as has been noted, to borrow five thousand dollars of government money from McDonald. In view of this action, it seems plausible that he, like almost everyone else of that era, was willing to share in the illicit gains. The confusion and unsettlement following in the wake of the war and the hurried over-expansion of the economy led to alarming public and private corruption. Everywhere speculators and jobbers waxed fat on government money.[19]

After McDonald refused to lend him money, Fishback went to Washington in March ostensibly to further legislation for improving rivers, but in reality to see Secretary Bristow and perfect plans for the exposure of the Ring.[20] On his return to St. Louis, he set in motion the machinery necessary for acquiring the needed evidence. He called in his financial editor, Myron Colony, who was also secretary of the Merchant's Exchange and a director of the St. Louis Cotton Exchange, and gave instructions. Under the pretense of obtaining data for a story on the growth of shipments of merchandise from St. Louis, Colony then listed for several weeks every item shipped from the city. The whisky shipments were secretly separated from the list and forwarded to Washington, where they were compared with the tax receipts in the Treasury.[21]

It took only four weeks for Colony to collect the information that justified the seizure of the distilleries and eventually led to the overthrow of the Ring.[22] His figures indicated that far more whisky was shipped from St. Louis than was indicated in official tax returns. Oddly enough, biographers of Grosvenor later credited him with the compilation of these figures.[23]

The first printed report of the existence of the Ring appeared in the *Democrat* on May 6, 1875. Fishback's paper carried a story datelined Washington—actually it was written in the *Democrat* office—that there were rumors of a graft ring in St. Louis and that an investigation was under way. On May 10 the distilleries were seized, and the next day both the *Globe* and the *Democrat* published stories of this action. On May 12 a story in the *Democrat* gave Colony credit for obtaining the evidence necessary for making the seizures.[24] But the day before, May 11, McKee and Houser had started negotiations with Fishback for buying the *Democrat*. These were rapidly consummated and the merger completed.

One morning a few days afterward, Jacob S. Merrell, a druggist in St. Louis for twenty-five years, picked up McKee, his neighbor, and drove him to town in his buggy. On the way Merrell asked the publisher about the whisky seizures. McKee thought the trouble would blow over. It was too big a thing, he said, bigger even than the government. Then Merrell suggested that Joyce be made the goat and driven into the wilderness as the Jews had done in their early history.

"Oh, hell," McKee said, "he's been in the wilderness for the last three days."[25]

But if McKee thought that by buying the *Democrat* he could end the publicity over the whisky frauds or that the whole thing would blow over, he was mistaken. As usual, McKee spent the summer at his New York farm.[26] While he was gone, indictments were returned against distillers, gaugers, Joyce, and W. O. Avery, a Washington employee of the Treasury Department. Subsequently Joseph M. Fitzroy, an indicted distiller, turned state's evidence and implicated McKee. Very concerned, McKee went to Fitzroy's home soon afterward. In their talk he told Fitzroy, "I hope I am not indicted because then I can be of more service to you."[27] But Fitzroy thought that many bitter stories about him published in the *Times* the preceding summer had been written in the *Globe-Democrat* office.[28] So when he was called to testify before the November session of the Grand Jury, he implicated McKee, who was then indicted for conspiracy to defraud the government.

"My God, what will become of my paper?" McKee exclaimed when he was arrested.[29] He was not tried until January 20, 1876, but in the meantime the press had a holiday. The *Boonville Weekly Advertiser* on November 12 declared that McKee was ruined. Hume, then editing the *St. Louis Evening Journal*, had been the first to strike at McKee and demand his indictment. Now he had visions of the *Globe-Democrat* being forced out of business.[30] Grosvenor, who was dismissed when McKee bought the *Democrat*, went to New York where he wrote stories of the St. Louis frauds for papers in that city. He and the Radical Republicans, led by Filley, the St. Louis postmaster, resented McKee's party leadership and became the publisher's severest critics. Filley was to continue his acrimonious attacks on McKee and the *Globe-Democrat* for another twenty years.

During McKee's trial, which lasted eleven days, excitement ran high. The courtroom could seat only a small portion of the crowd, and Judge Dillon ruled against a standing audience. The corridor outside the courtroom was thronged long before court opened at ten in the mornings. By eight-thirty every seat was filled, and the overflow crowd pushed and shoved their way to windows and doors. On January 30 police were called in to control the mob, but when the doors were opened, a mass of pushing men elbowed inside, leaping over benches and railings for choice seats. Policemen had difficulty in closing the doors against the shoving men. One prominent citizen was heard to say that he would gladly pay fifty dollars to insure a seat in the courtroom.[31]

The excitement was not lessened by the press. The four main St. Louis journals kept readers well informed of proceedings. Under the adroit steering of McCullagh, the story of McKee's trial was handled with admirable fullness and objectivity in the *Globe-Democrat*. Complete trial proceedings were printed each day, while the *Republican*, the *Times*, and the *Dispatch* omitted some of the testimony or summarized it.

The *Times* whipped up interest by running one-column pictures of McKee and his lawyers. In a sketch of McKee's life, its readers were told that the defendant was worth not less than a half million dollars at the time that he merged the two papers. One paragraph of this story was widely copied in the Missouri press.

> Mr. McKee has always been an industrious worker, giving personal attention to all the details of his business. He has never aspired to office, although he has been a great promoter of aspirations in others. He is an active politician in the managing sense, knows all the prominent public men, and is sociable, unobstrusive, a pleasant companion and a man of quiet decision and unbending purpose.[32]

On January 29 the *Dispatch* said editorially that the press had refrained so far from comment and thus far had favored "Uncle

Billy." His previous good character, local popularity, and clever-
ness had earned for him the "sobriquet of Uncle Billy"; aside
from his reported complicity in the crooked whisky business, he
enjoyed a high reputation. The *Dispatch* editor continued with
an interesting analysis of McKee's character. He was then sixty-
one years old. He had simple habits, but his great ambition was
money. He was worth $750,000, but his family did not own two
hundred dollars worth of jewelry. He never rode a street car,
preferring to walk the twelve blocks from his home on Washington Street to his office. He was always generous, however, to his
friends and relatives.

> He has never been a writer and for several years has tak-
> en no active part in the management of his newspaper en-
> terprises. He does the heavy standing around and looks
> after his periodic profits with marked punctuality. He
> stands a good deal in his counting room and watches the
> passing crowd. . . . He is now quite fleshy, decidedly nerv-
> ous, and smokes incessantly. His manner is quick and his ex-
> pression sagacious—two circumstances which make amends
> for the grossness of his physique.[33]

But the *Dispatch* forgot or disregarded the *Republican* when
it declared that the press had refrained from comment or had
favored the defendant in this great case. From the beginning
that old rival had published derogatory remarks about McKee
and during the trial was busily engaged in trying to implicate
McCullagh in the frauds. The *Republican* claimed that McKee
had bought McCullagh's silence by printing many of his
"Robber's Roost" paragraphs written while he was still working
for Fishback. Heading its editorial columns on January 25 was
this cryptic sentence: "Mc-ee to Mc---gh, 'Et tu, Brute!' "

Not only did this journal slant its trial reports against McKee,
but it also quoted other metropolitan papers which did not favor
him. From the *Cincinnati Commercial* came: "Things look black
or at least blue for Uncle Billy in St. Louis," and from the *Chicago Tribune*: "The case of the government against Mr. McKee.
. . . is strong enough to fully justify the defendant's ejaculation,
'It will ruin me here in this community.' "[34]

Nevertheless much sympathy was elicited in St. Louis for McKee and his family. The prevailing sentiment was that if "Uncle Billy" McKee were given a fair hearing it would take more direct testimony to convict him than that given in any of the previous whisky trials.[35] On opening day McKee pled not guilty to the charge of conspiring to defraud the government, and the next day his lawyers filed a demurrer to dismiss the case for lack of evidence. This was denied, however, and the trial proceeded. Among the parade of character witnesses for the publisher were two former governors of Missouri, B. Gratz Brown and Trusten Polk; the present governor, Thomas C. Reynolds; and the mayor of St. Louis, James H. Britton. McKee himself did not testify.[36]

Every day at least two columns on the first page and all the third page of the *Globe-Democrat* were filled with a transcript of the trial proceedings. The lead paragraph noted the time, the weather, and the size of the crowd. Headlines told the significant developments, as:

McKee's Case.

The Most Interesting Day of the
Great Trial.

Judge Dillon Overrules the Demurrer
to the Evidence.

Sanford M. Barton the First Witness
on the Stand.

John H. Concannon, Former Deputy
Collector, Testifies

And is Subjected to a Long and
Telling Cross Examination.

Alfred Bevis and John Bucher
also Examined.[37]

McCullagh, although commenting on the Whisky Ring in general in short editorial paragraphs, refrained from any attempt to vindicate his employer. Toward the end of the trial, however, he did attack sharply the *Republican* for circulating a rumor that McKee's health had been impaired by the trial and for prejudicing the minds of the jury. McCullagh told his readers that McKee was not one of the "breaking down" kind and that his health had never been better for twenty-two years.[38]

The *Republican* on January 31 addressed a long editorial to the jurors, who on that day were allowed to read the newspapers. In this editorial the jurors were told that the *Globe-Democrat* and the *Times* were attempting to better McKee's cause. The *Globe-Democrat* was trying to convey the idea that McKee was an "injured being." The jurors would see in the *Times* a "journalistic wind tempered to the as yet unshorn lamb." But the *Republican*, "mindful of the obligations of a public journal," would not seek to influence the jury, and the efforts of other journals in that direction would be fruitless. The jurors in McKee's case were intelligent and would not be influenced by newspapers.

McCullagh reprinted this *Republican* editorial the next day and editorially announced that its purpose and aims were transparent. It was hard to think, he said, that men "so brave of heart and nature" would print an article of this kind "while the individual at whom it is aimed is on trial, according to law, with what is dearer to him than life or liberty." It was hard to believe that men could be so base and blackhearted as the Knapps, proprietors of the *Republican*. "Their manifestation of hatred is a toothless rage of imbecility. How brave, how honorable, how Knapp-like that article is!"

Referring to the *Republican*, the *Times* declared that the Knapps might not have any personal hostility toward McKee as an individual, but "their gall arises because McKee as head of a paper that by ability and enterprise in a fair field and in an open fight had sent them and their journal from a high rank to a low rank."[39]

Of some significance in legal history is the fact that the jurors actually were allowed to read the newspapers during McKee's trial. Moreover, the jurors already empaneled for the Babcock

The first issues of the DAILY MISSOURI DEMOCRAT, forerunner of the GLOBE-DEMOCRAT, were printed in this building located near Third and Locust streets.

INSET—Frank P. Blair, one of the founders and the first editor of the DAILY MISSOURI DEMOCRAT.

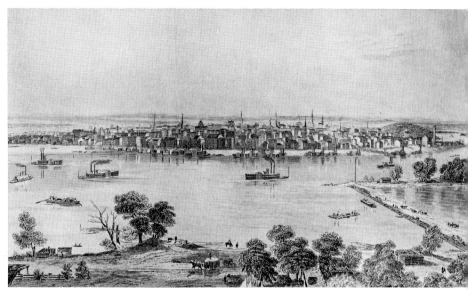

St. Louis in 1854, *two years after the* Missouri Democrat *was founded.*

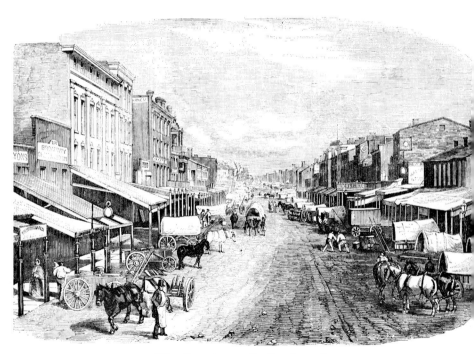

The Broadway, St. Louis, 1858.

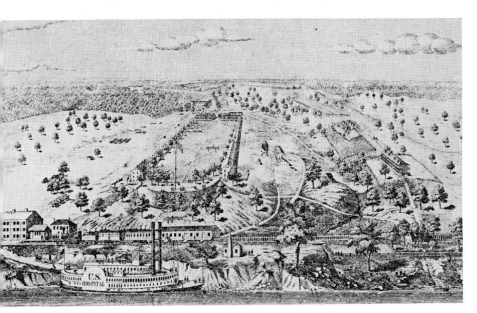

U. S. General Hospital, Jefferson Barracks, Missouri, 1864.

United States Volunteers being attacked by a St. Louis mob. From HARPER'S WEEKLY, *June 1, 1861.*

St. Louis citizens were concerned about the violence in their city. From HARPER'S WEEKLY, *June 1, 1861.*

The tornado which struck St. Louis May 27, 1896, was a big story in the McCullagh era.

The Floral Parade of All Nations during the Louisiana Purchase Centennial
Exposition, 1904, which received extensive coverage in the GLOBE-DEMOCRAT.

Photograph (1873) of the construction of Eads Bridge over the
Mississippi River, one of the big stories of the Reconstruction period,

William McKee

Daniel M. Houser

Joseph B. McCullagh

E. Lansing Ray

trial, which followed, were allowed to go home with a mild admonition from Judge Dillon not to read the newspapers. No objection was raised in either case, yet the trials were called fair.[40]

In instructing the jury the judge pointed out that McKee could be convicted only on the testimony of convicted conspirators. On the first ballot seven jurors voted for acquittal, but when the jury filed back into the courtroom after ten hours of deliberation, the verdict was guilty.[41] As the *Dispatch* said, "McKee had a fair trial and good lawyers, but the jury convicted him."[42] The *Republican* seconded the verdict.[43]

When on April 26 McKee was sentenced to two years in jail and fined ten thousand dollars, McCullagh told *Globe-Democrat* readers:

> We have at no time attempted to make the *Globe-Democrat* the special champion of Mr. McKee. . . . We were unwilling to have it said that he was making use of a newspaper in which he happened to be a large owner, to obtain a vindication before the people, after his vindication or condemnation had been submitted to judicial determination. Now, however, that final action has been taken and final judgment rendered in the courts, we think we but echo the popular sentiment in pronouncing the sentence extremely, if not unwarrantably, harsh and severe, and out of all proportion to the degree of criminality legally established and proved. After pointing out certain well defined circumstances of mitigation, the judge proceeds to assess the maximum penalty both as to fine and imprisonment; after stating the distinction which the law draws between official and non-official offenders . . . he gives a non-official offender four times the punishment he recently gave to an official offender. This seems to us a little remarkable. . . we do not think it will stand the test of reason or fairness.[44]

Few had expected such a heavy sentence, McCullagh said. Most people had believed that six months in the county jail and a fine of five thousand dollars would be the heaviest penalty imposed.[45]

The *Times* believed that Judge Dillon had imposed this heavy penalty in order to save Babcock.[46] If Babcock had been found guilty, the President would surely have been implicated. Many thought that in order to save Grant, McKee was sacrificed.

But McKee served only six months of his sentence. The President then pardoned him and remitted his fine. It was common knowledge in St. Louis during those six months that he spent about as many nights in his home as he did in jail.[47]

The prediction in the *Dispatch* on January 13 that if McKee were convicted the *Globe-Democrat* would no longer continue to be an influential journal proved false. The continued success of the paper could be attributed no doubt to McCullagh's skillful handling of the trial and his ability to give readers a good newspaper. But Houser, too, deserved much credit for keeping the paper prominent. Even the often bitter *Republican* acknowledged his honesty:

> The remarkable prosperity of our Republican contemporary is largely due to a gentleman who, indifferent to public notice and disavowing all credit does not receive his share of the honors that are justly his due. We, of course, refer to Mr. Daniel M. Houser. The old proverb could be literally applied to his case—he got rich by minding his own business. Modest and unassuming to an extreme, Mr. Houser's tireless industry, his great business sagacity and his devotion to his paper for many years contributed conspicuously to its great success.[48]

The increase in circulation of the *Globe-Democrat* seems evidence enough that the public did not boycott the paper because of McKee's involvement in the Whisky Ring. The daily circulation by February, 1878, had reached 26,792.[49] There were also other evidences. A. E. Poteet, for example, wrote to the *Globe-Democrat* that he was a Democrat, but that he could not find any Democratic paper that had half the news that the *Globe-Democrat* printed.[50] Other newspapers from Minnesota and Kentucky to Kansas praised it. It was called the best, largest, and most reliable paper in the West. "Sharp as a singed cat," it was probably unsurpassed by any paper in the country for general news.[51] Furthermore, by 1879, the paper could boast of printing more advertising on December 21 than did the *"New York Herald* of the same date and 20 to 30 per cent more than any other daily paper in the United States of the same date."[52]

But McKee did not live to see his paper outstrip the *Republican*. He died December 20, 1879, at the age of sixty-four. Although few people knew it, McKee had suffered from heart disease and "derangement of the nervous system" for more than a year. But his death was unexpected.

McCullagh was the last person to see McKee downtown. Shortly after noon Mrs. McKee and Ellen had driven to the office. McCullagh had brought out to the carriage a new edition of a book by Washington Irving, one of McKee's favorite authors. Then he helped McKee into the carriage and watched them drive away.[53]

That evening McKee had read aloud from the book to his wife and daughter. Later he complained of not feeling well; when he grew worse, Dr. Love was called. The doctor, in turn, summoned McCullagh and City Editor Irwin, but they arrived too late. McKee died in his sleep shortly after midnight.[54] The funeral procession was said to have been one of the largest the city had ever seen. "Not alone relatives to whom he had been attached by tender ties through a long lifetime—ties to which he had been sensitive and responsive to a degree unusual among men—but friends who had enjoyed his confidence in the busy walks of life which he trod; and best of all, as a tribute to his worth, was the long line made up of those to whom he had been for many years an employer never less than just and often more than kind."[55] Thus did McCullagh eulogize his employer.

McKee's obituary in the *Globe-Democrat* included a history of the paper with this comment:

> In speaking of this great newspaper and its founder, it should be borne in mind that more than one-half the people in Missouri, and one-half the people in Illinois, differ from its political expressions; and there is, therefore, an added significance in its journalistic success.[56]

The *Republican* devoted a half column to an account of McKee's life, and with somewhat restrained praise told how he had often aided his friends in need. Just the summer before, he paid off the debts of a neighbor farmer in New York who was having a hard struggle. Editorially this paper said that the *Repub-*

lican would not be expected to eulogize McKee. Nevertheless "we can truthfully say that in many respects he was excellently calculated to conduct a daily journal, having had, from the printer's case up to the supervision of the whole business of a newspaper, a long and active experience." Yet in his newspaper office he was autocratic. "Probably no paper in the West, especially of the politics of the *Globe-Democrat*, ever reflected a single man's views more completely than the *Globe-Democrat* represented McKee's."[57]

But it was that recent merger and lusty young paper, the *St. Louis Post-Dispatch*, just getting its start under Joseph Pulitzer, that gave St. Louis readers the information they wanted. Besides the usual biography of McKee and the historical sketch of the *Globe-Democrat*, Pulitzer interviewed McCullagh, from whom he learned that there would be no change in the management of the paper. Pulitzer's paper told about McKee's property. The year before, McKee's share of the *Globe-Democrat* profits had been over sixty thousand dollars. Independent of his newspaper holdings, his property was estimated at nearly a million dollars, of which more than $150,000 was in St. Louis real estate. All of his property went to his wife and his daughter, who was an only child.

The facts of McKee's complicity in the Whisky Ring frauds, Pulitzer said, were too fresh to need repetition. But he pointed out that both McKee's friends and enemies were ready and willing to testify to his virtues and to bury old antagonisms. "No man has occupied for so long a time so prominent a position as William McKee; few threw themselves with more vigor into the troubled waters of the last twenty years, but the most bitter opponents of the dead publisher will forget their opposition and find nothing that is not pleasant to remember of the dead."[58]

McKee's death marked the end of an era for the *Globe-Democrat*. In its first twenty years, as the *Missouri Democrat*, it had exerted a powerful influence on city, state, and national politics. Consistently it had advocated political viewpoints of minority groups until they became viewpoints of the majority. At the same time it had evolved into a valuable public service because of its superior coverage of events about which its subscribers wanted to read.

William McKee was the outstanding personality of the paper until his death. Though he was described by his associates as a diffident, retiring person, events indicate that his weakness was a desire for power and wealth. Men who helped promote his paper with their brilliant writing—Thomas H. Benton, Frank Blair, B. Gratz Brown, John Hume, and William Grosvenor—were tossed aside and often bitterly denounced when they no longer agreed with his political views. Even his connection with the Whisky Ring is attributable to his passion for power and wealth. It is the more regrettable that the paper became identified with the corruption of the Grant administration because for twenty years prior to the scandals, it had been an important instrument in the fight for human rights.

Nevertheless, McKee deserves a prominent and permanent place in the history of journalism. His professional career was identified with the struggle against slavery. In establishing a free-soil paper in a slave territory and in using it successfully to further the unpopular cause of abolition, he achieved nation-wide recognition. His newspaper perspicacity in always employing strong editors, his far-sightedness in spending money for news-gathering and in daring to use the new "quarto" form for his *Globe* indicate his significance to journalism. At his death he left a paper that would prosper and live for many years.

Chapter XI

The *Globe-Democrat*
Under McCullagh

"An institution," Emerson said, "is the lengthened shadow of one man." Joseph B. McCullagh is the *Globe-Democrat*. —William Marion Reedy[1]

THE fabulous success of the *Globe-Democrat* in its first twenty years under his management was Joseph Burbridge McCullagh's contribution to the history of American journalism. An acknowledged leader in new journalistic practices, the editor extended the influence of his paper throughout Missouri, Iowa, Kansas, Illinois, Mississippi, Arkansas, and Texas. With his own pithy paragraphs and with a great newsgathering corps at his command, he soon overcame any setback that the paper may have suffered because of McKee's connection with the Whisky Ring. At the time of the merger of the *Globe* and the *Democrat* he had divorced the upstairs, the news and editorial room, from the downstairs, the counting room; and it was not long before *Globe-Democrat* readers realized the absence of censorship over the editorial policies of the paper.[2]

Uppermost in McCullagh's mind in the early days of his editorship was increasing the circulation of his paper. The editor was well aware that the sweep of population into the Southwest and the developing literacy of the masses was opening a vast readership area.[3] To tap this source of subscribers and to extend the influence of the *Globe-Democrat*, he hunted news. When there was none, he created it. For example, soon after McKee's trial, he developed a notable religious controversy.

Bishop Patrick J. Ryan, a St. Louis Catholic priest, delivered

136

on December 16, 1877, a lecture in the Mercantile Library Hall
on "What Catholics Believe." His speech, published in the *Globe-
Democrat* the next day, filled five columns. At a time when newspapers generally were printing less and less religious news,[4]
McCullagh suddenly made it a major project. He called the attention of his readers to the Bishop's speech and arranged for the
Reverend S. H. Sonneschein, a Jewish rabbi, to reply to Ryan
in the same hall. He told his readers that he hoped "the Protestant
divines" would contribute their viewpoints on the "important
controversy inaugurated by the Catholic bishop." He assured
them that the *Globe-Democrat*, "as the organ of all creeds and
denominations," was "anxious for the fullest and freest discussion." It would do "its duty as a religious daily newspaper by publishing both sides."

Thus McCullagh started the "Great Religious Controversy,"
which was to run more than three months. He sent his reporters
out into the city, and by Christmas the *Globe-Democrat* had
published interviews with thirty-two clergymen. Reports of
sermons and letters to the editors answering Bishop Ryan's lecture
filled columns of the paper almost daily. Among clergymen who
entered the controversy were two Presbyterian ministers, the
Reverend W. C. Falconer and the Reverend J. G. Reaser; two
Episcopalian ministers, the Reverend George C. Betts and the
Reverend R. A. Holland; and Bishop Thomas Bowman and the
Reverend John Snyder of the Methodist Church.

McCullagh constantly fanned the flame of interest with his
short editorial paragraphs. "Dr. Snyder must come to the front
now," he wrote on December 28. "A Jesuit father says that he
[Snyder] believes in nothing and also accuses him of insincerity
in the controversy provoked by Bishop Ryan's letters." On January 2 the editor commented that the controversy was "waxing
warm." If these interviews and letters did not cause "a thorough
awakening of St. Louis on the subject of religion" it was not
"the fault of the *Globe-Democrat*."[5] A few days later he invited
the ladies to take part in the "Great Controversy." A master at
creating catch-words, he termed the *Globe-Democrat* during
these days the "Great Religious Daily,"[6] a name St. Louisans

used for the paper for twenty years. The immediate effect of the "Great Controversy" was an increase in circulation. By the end of February McCullagh could claim a circulation of 26,792.[7]

In July of 1879 McCullagh started another circulation-building stunt, which resulted in what was called the "Texas Boycott," an attempt by Texas newspapers to keep the *Globe-Democrat* from being sold in that state. McCullagh and Houser, now president of the firm, employed correspondents in all the cities and larger towns in Texas. These writers were instructed to send in all news of interest, but their reports almost invariably were stories of crime. When Texas editors complained, McCullagh began agitating in his short pungent paragraphs. "If the energy that is wasted in Texas in denunciation of the *Globe-Democrat* for telling the truth about events in that state," he wrote, "were directed to the punishment of crime and the administration of impartial justice there, the reign of lawlessness would soon be over."[8]

Texas editors called for a boycott of the *Globe-Democrat*, and Texas Governor Oran M. Roberts came to their aid. At the time yellow fever had been reported in the Memphis area, and the Governor quarantined trains from that area—the trains that carried the *Globe-Democrat*. McCullagh kept his readers well informed on the situation, calling the quarantine foolish. Since the only case of yellow fever in the United States was that of a man in Memphis who was convalescing, he hoped that "Texas would safely give her fears to the wind."[9] In Marshall, Texas, an old city ordinance prohibited the sale of newspapers on Sundays. This law was invoked against the *Globe-Democrat*, and a newsboy selling the papers was tried and fined twenty-five dollars and costs.[10] McCullagh, however, insisted that the *Globe-Democrat* was "doing good instead of evil for Texas" by printing facts as they were gathered by its correspondents. He told the "chaw-bacon editors of Texas" who were trying to kill the *Globe-Democrat* that in no case had the people of Texas been called responsible for the condition of affairs there.[11] The Marshall incident brought about a natural reaction; the proposed boycott failed, and the *Globe-Democrat's* circulation reached another high point.[12]

Other stunts used primarily to increase circulation included sending Walter B. Stevens to Mexico to write a series of articles about the people, the customs, and the government of that country.[13] Stevens, the Washington correspondent for the *Globe-Democrat* from 1884 to 1903, also directed the "great catechism" that attracted so much attention in December, 1891. He organized, at McCullagh's direction, a corps of more than twenty reporters who interviewed, on Pennsylvania Avenue in Washington, members of Congress on their knowledge of political history.[14] Each reporter wore a badge of silk to identify him. The questions, devised by McCullagh to show how little Washington politicians really knew about the subject, were kept secret even from Stevens until the morning that the reporters suddenly appeared on the street. These interviews filled fifteen columns of the *Globe-Democrat*,[15] and McCullagh considered the stunt a "great success." He hoped that it "worked up the people at Washington."[16]

McCullagh was not the typical newspaper crusader, in that he did not deliberately seek to unearth graft and other malpractices in the government. Rather, he ridiculed in his short editorial paragraphs such practices as gambling and excessive drinking. He campaigned against the "open-house," a custom of St. Louis banks. These institutions kept a dining room open for their biggest customers. Here wines, liquor, and food were served. The editor advised ministers to speak on temperance, and every year just before New Year's day he admonished housewives not to celebrate by serving intoxicants. In 1881 he agitated against a law allowing the sale of beer on Sundays.[17]

Among McCullagh's most famous campaigns was his "gambler's round-up" in 1878 and 1879. Gambling had become big business, being protected by bribes of the police. McCullagh believed that this condition was a blight on St. Louis. Suicides, embezzlements, and thefts, he said, were the results of gambling debts. He cited the example of a St. Louis official who embezzled $143,000 from the city school funds. The editor pounded away until a grand jury was empaneled, with himself as foreman. Subsequently, the gambling ring was smashed, and the Missouri Legislature passed a bill outlawing gambling.[18] This campaign against gambling increased the enmity between the *Republican* and the *Globe-Democrat* because the Knapps, publishers of the *Republican*, were known as big gamblers.

McCullagh constantly agitated for a better St. Louis. The census of 1880 revealed what he had feared for some time—that Chicago had passed St. Louis in population. Chicago was now the fourth city in size and St. Louis, with a population of 350,-518, was sixth.[19] The editor chided "poor old St. Louis," and he "boomed," to use his own word, the city's industries. He called the paper's influence the "towline." The "towline," he wrote, pulled George Bain through as president of the Exchange, but the "towline" could not help "poor old St. Louis."[20]

McCullagh was particularly interested in the railroad industry. The river trade at St. Louis had come almost to a standstill when Eads Bridge provided railway connections with the East. Furthermore, Chicago had become a larger railroad center than St. Louis. The *Globe-Democrat* began a campaign to step up railroad development and service in the St. Louis area. When the Burlington Line started fast mail service, the paper paid two-thirds of the cost of running the business until it became self-supporting.[21] McCullagh sent reporters into the Southwest to observe and write about the effects of railroad service there, and he started a railroad department in the *Globe-Democrat*. Every day McCullagh would give his railroad editor clippings of relevant events in other cities. Six times a week the railroad column kept readers informed about conventions, meetings, and new developments, and entertained them with interviews with railroad personalities. Later the *Chicago Tribune* borrowed this idea for a column, and subsequently many metropolitan newspapers added a similar column.[22]

McCullagh was opposed to mob violence and riots, which were rather frequent in St. Louis in this era. Railroad workers went on strike in 1877 and again in 1885. Broom makers and collar manufacturers were also on strike in 1885.[23] But the *Globe-Democrat's* "towline" defended the right of labor organizations to parade. And in the summer of 1894 McCullagh took a prominent part in the settlement of the railroad strikes. "Move the trains," he wrote. "Surrender first—arbitration afterwards" headed his editorial columns. He acted as a mediator in the labor dispute between the Missouri Pacific Railroad Company and the Knights of Labor. Jay Gould was grateful and wanted to compensate McCullagh. Declining all personal gifts, the editor asked only that St. Louis be given fast train service to the Southwest. In a few days this service was started.[24]

Houser's "pay-any-price-for-news" policy enabled McCullagh to produce the paper that he did. The editor could use large amounts of telegraphed news and keep special correspondents in all parts of the country. By 1884 he could tell *Globe-Democrat* readers that his firm was paying "more money for the collection and transmission of telegraphic news from all parts of the world" than was paid "by any newspaper in any other city of the world, New York and London not excepted."[25] By 1892 the paper was using $400,000 worth of telegraphed news annually.[26]

News gathering became a fiercely competitive business in St. Louis. McCullagh, who loved a vulnerable target, particularly delighted in outwitting the *Republican*. In November, 1890, he devised a scheme to replace that paper in the *New York Sun* syndicate. He hoped to knock out its leased wire arrangement whereby it was able "to get a great deal of news for a small amount of money." If the Knapps were put out of the syndicate they would have to get their news from all points instead of from one agency. If he succeeded in his plan then he and Houser would lease a direct wire "for Washington and New York."[27] Apparently he succeeded, because two months later he wrote to Stevens in Washington that he had completed plans for employing a New York operator for the leased wire to that city, and he instructed his Washington correspondent to employ someone there to operate that wire.[28]

The *Globe-Democrat* probably paid its regular reporters and correspondents better salaries than did other St. Louis newspapers of that time. For example, McCullagh started Theodore Dreiser as a local reporter at twenty dollars a week and raised his salary five dollars when he "scooped" the other papers on the story of a train wreck. The *Republic*, on the other hand, paid beginning reporters only eighteen dollars a week.[29] Stevens was paid seventy dollars a week and expenses when he was in Washington. Later his salary was raised to seventy-five dollars, and he was sometimes told to take his wife with him on his trips, her expenses to be paid by the paper. Washington reporters who worked under Stevens received thirty dollars a week.[30]

Nor did McCullagh and Houser object to the large expenses necessary to "scoop" other papers. On December 8, 1881, for example, Stevens, then the city editor of the *Globe-Democrat*, and four of his reporters outwitted rival journals on a disaster story. In the first place, the "scoop" was made possible because the *Globe-Democrat* kept a correspondent, George S. Johns, in St. Charles, and the other papers did not. Late one afternoon Johns wired the *Globe-Democrat* that the Missouri Bridge at St. Charles had crashed under the weight of a trainload of livestock. When this news reached the office, Stevens and four of his reporters hired a hack and dashed to the river ahead of reporters from other St. Louis papers. There they hired the only two boatmen on the St. Louis side to ferry them across. They even purchased one boat to prevent its owner from returning for their competitors. They also bribed the telegraph operator in St. Charles to pretend weariness and put a *Globe-Democrat* operator in charge.[31] Later McCullagh sent Johns a five dollar bonus.[32]

That the *Globe-Democrat* was paying large sums for telegraphed news was clearly evident in the pages of the paper. News stories were received from special correspondents in London, Vienna, Berlin, and other European cities. Sometimes as many as five columns in a weekday issue were filled with foreign news. Besides news received over the Atlantic cable, correspondents telegraphed reports from such places as Washington, New York, San Francisco, Chicago, and many widely separated news centers.[33] McCullagh often gave more attention to events a hundred miles distant than he did to similar events in St. Louis. Once, William T. Harris, superintendent of St. Louis public schools and a leader in the St. Louis Movement which made the city a center of educational and philosophical ideas,[34] spoke at the Mercantile Library on speculative philosophy. The *Globe-Democrat* gave little space to his speech; but when he gave the same lecture in Boston, it printed long telegraphed reports of the event.[35]

The sensational type of news which the *Democrat* had used in the late sixties, and which McCullagh had so effectively employed before the merger to outstrip the *Democrat*, now became characteristic of the *Globe-Democrat*. McCullagh looked for the colorful, the entertaining, the dramatic. He wanted news that interested but did not detain his readers, accounts that would give them relief from their daily grinds. He found it in disasters, crime, sex, violence, the odd, the religious, the mystical, the different. Day by day, news in the *Globe-Democrat* became increasingly sensational.

The big local news stories during the McCullagh era included the opening and dedication of the St. Louis Union Station in 1894, mob violence in the strikes, and the tornado which struck St. Louis in May, 1896. The day after this great storm the *Globe-Democrat* reported that more than one hundred people were killed. Several hundred were injured, several million dollars worth of property was destroyed, and the city was left in darkness. The front page had four two-column drawings showing the destruction. Silas Bent, then a St. Louis journalist, was to write later that the *Globe-Democrat* had blared the news of the storm in huge banner lines,[36] but in reality only two-column headlines were used, one set on the right side of the paper and the other on the left side. Each headline, however, had seven decks. Much space on the inside pages was devoted to stories about the storm and to relief measures for the victims. McCullagh used the disaster to further his advocacy of placing wires underground.[37]

The destruction by fire of the old Southern Hotel on April 11, 1877, was another disaster story which the paper covered fully. Cliff Sanders, a *Globe-Democrat* reporter, helped save from the burning attic several girls employed by the hotel. Eleven people died in the inferno. Train wrecks and floods, such as the

Mississippi flood on April 30, 1892, made good copy from time to time. When the temperature dropped to five below zero on December 7, 1882, business houses had to close the next day because of frozen water pipes, and many homes were without water.

Sensational crime and sex stories, which McCullagh himself clipped from the exchanges, filled several columns of the paper daily. Such "reprints" were important to the editor, but he never clipped merely to fill space. He sought the sensational item for his readers, and the night foreman learned early never to omit a clipped item with a credit line in McCullagh's handwriting.[38] The big crime stories of the period included a detailed account of a wife-murder and suicide in Chicago and the criminal assault of a white woman by a Negro in Texas.[39] The lynching of four Negroes in Yazoo, Mississippi, December 27, 1883, filled columns for weeks. McCullagh sent a correspondent to Yazoo to cover this story before other metropolitan newspapers awoke to the sensational possibilities of the event. Editorially, he commented: "The correspondent whom we sent to Yazoo City a few days ago seems to have struck an item. The great art of running a newspaper is the art of guessing where hell is likely to break loose next."[40]

St. Louis itself was one of the great sources of crime stories of the time.[41] Local sensational crimes included the disappearance of two small St. Louis children from the home of a miner, and a trunk murder in the Southern Hotel. The latter was sensationally written up and illustrated with sketches of the trunks and a plan of the room where the trunks were found.[42] McCullagh had a knack of turning the serious and the gory incident into humor. For example, he reported on December 8, 1882, that Police Officers Todd and Lunden got into a fist fight at Channing and Olive streets after Lunden charged Todd with invading his "beat" to sell tickets for the Police Charity Ball. They fought it out for fifteen minutes unmolested by a crowd which enjoyed the fight between the two "peace officers."

Spiritualism was one of the oddities that always interested McCullagh. Many Missourians were ardent believers in this philosophy, and the editor printed stories of mediums and spiritualists two or three times a week. One such story concerned a woman in Portland, Maine, who was said to have talked to a dead friend.[43] McCullagh sent Stevens to Boston to cover spiritualists' camps and to New York to report the forty-fifth anniversary celebration of the advent of modern spiritualism held in Carnegie Hall, April 2, 1893.[44] So many stories did he run on spiritualism that at his death it was rumored that the great editor himself was a spiritualist.[45]

Feature stories were important to McCullagh. On Saturdays he ran illustrated articles on animals and snakes. He used so many odd snake stories that the *Republican* printed a cartoon depicting the *Globe-Democrat* editorial room, with a sign on the wall: "50 cts. a Dozen paid for Snake stories."[46] He constantly sought new material. In 1885 he started a column called "The Spoils," a series of biographies about Federal appointments under the Cleveland administration. He directed Stevens to prepare features on such subjects as the census, the cotton state members of Congress, the financial distress in the South brought on by low cotton prices, interesting displays at the Smithsonian Institution, and oddities at the Patent Office.[47]

Interviews with prominent people and with people connected with news events were often printed. McCullagh himself had long been noted for his interviews, particularly when he was a Washington correspondent; historians credit him with driving the first wedge that eventually opened the way to press conferences with public officials.[48] Now as editor of the *Globe-Democrat* he employed the mass interview technique. He first used this device for newsgathering on June 21, 1879, when a group of Ohio editors came to St. Louis on an excursion. McCullagh organized a corps of thirty reporters, who were under the direction of the city editor and the railroad editor. Each reporter wore a badge declaring: "A Soft Answer Turneth Away Wrath, *Globe-Democrat* Interviewing Corps, With Malice for None and With Questions for All." The reporters met the incoming trains; and after each arriving editor was questioned, a yellow card was stuck in his hat band. On it was printed: "Pumped.

Keep this check in your hat to avoid further disturbance."[49]
The resulting interviews of two to four hundred words each
filled eight columns in the *Globe-Democrat* the next day. Mc-
Cullagh called this the "unspoken speech" interview. Later he
used the device so successfully at political conventions that other
big metropolitan dailies adopted the practice.[50]

Expansion of news coverage reached into every department.
In a column called "Third Street Gossip," readers learned about
crop reports and river shipments. McCullagh instructed his correspondents in the rural areas to keep him informed about crop
conditions; once when Congress failed to appropriate funds for
sending out weather bureau reports, he had Stevens wire the
bureau nightly so that the paper could keep its readers informed.[51]

Sports news, which had been lengthened to a full column in
the late sixties, now was expanded still more. By 1892 sports
stories sometimes filled two or three pages, especially on Saturdays and Sundays. Although still run under the head, "Sporting,"
they covered a variety of activities. More space was devoted to
baseball than to any other one game. On May 1, 1877, the St.
Louis Browns of the National League and the Syracuse Stars
battled to a 0-0 tie in a fifteen inning game at Sportsman's Park.
In 1884 the Maroons won the pennant in the Union League, and
the next year the Browns won the pennant in the American Association. In 1886 the Browns won the World Series in six games
with the Chicago Whites. The last three games were played in
St. Louis. The *Globe-Democrat's* Chicago correspondent covered the games played in Chicago, but the local sports reporter,
Frank Shuck, reported the home games. Of the last one, he
wrote: "It was the hardest fought battle of all six games, and
it was not decided until a wild pitch allowed Welch to cross the
plate with the winning run in the tenth inning."[52]

Horse racing and prize fighting were still popular sports.
There were stories on roller skating, rifle shooting, and bowling,
and on walking contests for reporters. Toward the end of the
era, bicycling news was used. A column of interest to hunters
and fishermen was printed on Saturdays. Football stories began

to appear in 1889, and a chess problem was run two or three times a week.

The expansion of society news was probably as effective in increasing circulation as were some of McCullagh's crusades. Social items, which often filled two or more pages, came from Illinois, Mississippi, Kansas, Arkansas, and Iowa. Consisting of one- and two-sentence paragraphs, the items were grouped under the names of the places from which they were sent. Usually from fifty to seventy cities and towns were represented in the Saturday issues.

Since the fifties, the paper had printed news of interest to women, but now this department, too, was enlarged. Sketches were used to illustrate the latest styles in a column called "Women's World." Here ladies read about dresses of mahogany-colored Bengaline silk and figured plush of the same hue; short evening wraps of terra-cotta plush, trimmed with terra-cotta feather bands; and a fur-lined Russian cloak, made of brown striped camel's hair cloth.[53] Also of interest to women were the songs, with words and music, printed in the Saturday and Sunday issues. Popular tunes of the period were "My Darling's Face," "Last Rose of Summer," and "Eva Ray."[54]

Contemporary newsmen agreed that McCullagh won journalistic fame with his system of interviewing public men on timely subjects and with his success as a news gatherer.[55] They admired most, however, his incisive editorial comments. His use of the short editorial paragraph revolutionized the pages of St. Louis journals. On many days the second page of the *Globe-Democrat* had no long editorials, and for a quarter of a century McCullagh's "quotable quotes" in his often biting language entertained his readers. "People read short paragraphs," the editor said, "and don't give a d——d for the long ones." He called profanity with d's and dashes "heat-lightning profanity."[56]

The timely editorial, McCullagh believed, was invaluable; he used current incidents and topics for the basis of his comments. It was in his short paragraphs that the editor chided St. Louisans for their lack of civic pride in not obtaining the Toner Library in 1877, for waiting for someone else to build a new opera house, and for wanting to reduce the park area in the city. It was here that he "boomed" the movement for providing ice for the city's poor in the summer. And it was here that he jibed at the *Republican* which, he often said, had no enterprise, no understanding of what the public wanted. A first-class paper once, now it ranked only as a fifth-class one—a "journalistic anachronism as far behind the times as the press it was first printed on."[57] Occasionally he jibed at the *Post-Dispatch*, but he did not fear it as he did the *Republican*. Even when Pulitzer started his Sunday edition, he did not think it a very good paper.[58]

Although the *Globe-Democrat* remained a Republican newspaper, McCullagh seemed more interested in creating controversies within the party or in ridiculing the Democratic party than in using the paper to promote party policies. As a result, the political policies of the paper tended to become somewhat spineless and conservative. Even McCullagh's campaign of 1880 for a third term for Grant was chiefly a device for promoting the *Globe-Democrat*.

Chauncey I. Filley, leader of the regular Republican party in Missouri, claimed that the paper tried to instigate a revolt in the party every year from 1887 to 1892.[59] In reality, Filley split the party himself at times, and he never allowed anyone to forget McKee's connection with the Whisky Ring. For this McCullagh attacked Filley relentlessly, calling him "Cheeky I. Filley," and "Cranky I. Filley."[60] In the campaign of 1878 he said that the "Republicans of St. Louis might as well spare" the trouble of a campaign under the auspices of the "bummers and the barnacles" who constituted the Central Committee, and that Filley, the chairman, tried to "dictate policy and candidates of the party." The three Missouri Republicans in Congress did not amount to much, he said, but "since God made them, we will call them such."[61] In later years McCullagh and Filley became friends.[62]

From 1877 to 1880 McCullagh satirized the Hayes administration. He went to Washington in 1879 and wrote a series of editorial letters in which he spoke of the dissatisfaction of the Republicans with President Hayes, then suggested Grant for a third term. He kept Grant's name in the paper so much that politicians began seriously to consider the former President for a third term. The *Globe-Democrat* printed what other papers were saying for, as well as against, Grant.[63] Its editor was creating political news.

Although McCullagh had used the word "booming" as early as 1878, his use of it in the Grant campaign made it a common term in the sense that he used it. "The Grant movement is booming," he wrote. "The Grant movement booms more boomingly than ever. . . ." Or "The Grant boom has been taking a rest but it's coming again. The Sherman boom has been weighed and found windy."[64]

A few years later the editors of *Century Dictionary* wrote to the *Globe-Democrat* to find out how the paper happened to use the word "booming." McCullagh said that he once heard it used by a Mississippi riverboat pilot as he watched the river overflowing and sweeping everything before it. "By Jove," said the pilot, "but she's booming." McCullagh liked the word and started using it.[65]

It was at the 1880 convention, too, that the great editor first used his mass interviewing scheme at a national meeting. He sent a corps of "bright, energetic, wide-awake reporters" to Chicago a week before the convention opened. They were given instructions to see every prominent delegate as soon as he arrived, to become acquainted with every delegation, and to learn beforehand just how each was likely to vote. This practice was later followed by Eastern newspapers.[66]

When Garfield was nominated over Grant by a 395-304 vote, McCullagh did not bother with explanations or regret. He headed his editorial column with one word: "Ratification." He followed this with short paragraphs about Garfield, whose biography, he said, read well. The Garfield movement then boomed in the *Globe-Democrat*. Later, James Guiteau's assassination of Garfield became one of the paper's big front-page stories of the era; McCullagh headed his editorial column with Garfield's famous words when Lincoln was killed: "God reigns and the government at Washington still lives."[67]

The same journalistic procedure used in the 1880 campaign was followed in 1884. The columns of the *Globe-Democrat's* front page were filled with the convention proceedings. Inside pages carried stories describing scenes and incidents at the convention, a biography of James G. Blaine, the nominee, and four or five columns of what other papers were saying about the candidates. The paper operated a big bulletin board in front of its building, where large crowds watched the tabulation of the balloting. The big board was later used for posting the election returns.[68]

McCullagh delighted in waving the "bloody shirt" to foment political discord; 1884 was a typical year for this. He said it was an insult to elect as governor John S. Marmaduke, a Confederate major general, and advised the nomination of a non-partisan ticket to catch Greenbackers, prohibitionists, and dissatisfied Democrats.[69]

McCullagh's lack of enthusiasm for Blaine as a presidential candidate was indicated by the meager space given to him during the campaign and by his failure to mention the candidate very often in his paragraphs. But he did not fail to register his dislike for Grover Cleveland. When news of Cleveland's being the father of an illegitimate child leaked out, McCullagh struck with vengeance. It would take only thirteen alibis, he said, to prove Cleveland's good moral character. In another month the candidate would no longer be the "Darling of the Dudes." He was either a libertine of the most pronounced and conscienceless type, or he had been lied about by citizens of good standing as a man never was before.[70]

Nor did McCullagh care for Cleveland's inaugural address, which, he said, contained little about the practical questions of government. The President had urged "in a general sense the virtue of simplicity and those 'prudential economies'" which were always safe to talk about. Regarding Cleveland's plea for a return to the "plain way of life," McCullagh commented: "The American people can be honest and prosperous and altogether worthy of their mission without going back to the style of living which characterized their ancestors."[71]

Several state issues also drew fire from McCullagh's editorial pen in the eighties. One concerned railroad legislation. He criticized Governor Crittenden's plea for a liberal policy toward railroads and attacked the railroad lobby in Jefferson City for preventing passage of a bill to regulate freight rates and for helping to block a bill which would force railroad companies owning switches in cities to lease them to other railroad companies at reasonable rates. Failure of the legislature to pass these two bills, he believed, caused the bloody strikes of 1886. But he approved the passage of a law that allowed the designation of a standard method to calculate wages of railroad mechanics.[72]

Several third-party movements which were becoming prominent in Missouri at this time complicated political issues. The farm bloc, desiring free coinage, was back of most of these movements; both the Republican and the Democratic parties tried to devise platforms that would draw the votes of these minority groups. McCullagh, always ready to foment trouble in the Democratic ranks, delighted in the break between the "Young Democrats," led by David R. Francis, who later became governor, and the "Ed Butler machine" Democrats, led by Charles H. Jones, then editor of the *Republican*. McCullagh declared that the Democratic platform in 1888 was interesting for what it did not contain—no silver plank. He gloriously waved the "bloody shirt," with such terms as "hard cider," "log cabin," and "Tippecanoe." The candidates for both parties were good men, he said, but the campaign would be waged on economic and business issues. In an attempt to alienate the farm bloc vote, he called Francis a grain gambler, but he advised the people of St. Louis to vote against the Democrats so that they could keep "this man Jones" from tightening his grip on the city.[73] He gleefully told of the communication system of Wheeler's Alliance, an agrarian movement, whereby orders from the state office reached every member in two days. Mossback Democrats and Ultra Republicans, he said, sat side by side in a Texas county convention.[74] Later he charged the Democrats with having a hundred-thousand-dollar fund to bribe editors of Populist party organs.[75]

In the panic of 1892 McCullagh declined to join the "partisan pirates" who were trying to make political capital of the tight-money situation because it was occurring under a Democratic president. "We can all recover in time from a Democratic president, but a financial crash would leave such distress" that there would be no recovery.[76]

The editor believed that a newspaperman should not be a politician. He advised Senator G. G. Vest to retire from politics if he wanted to start a newspaper.[77] Once when it was rumored that McCullagh was being groomed to run for the United States Senate, he was interviewed by James C. Espy, a reporter for the *St. Louis Republic*, as the old *Missouri Republican* was then called. McCullagh, however, denied the rumor. He told Espy that he considered being an editor as high an honor as being a senator.[78]

In newspaper circles it was considered a privilege and an education to work under McCullagh. When John T. McEnnis was city editor of the *Chicago Globe*, he told Theodore Dreiser that working under "Mac" was one of the best opportunities that could come to him. McEnnis, who had worked on the *Globe-Democrat*, said that it was "one of the greatest papers and McCullagh was one of the greatest editors that ever lived."[79]

Dreiser said that when he started working on the *Globe-Democrat* in November, 1892, there were about fourteen or fifteen reporters on the paper. Among these was one Negro. Tobias Mitchell was the city editor. Casper S. Yost, an assistant editor, had charge of the Sunday edition. Captain Henry King was an associate editor and chief political writer. McCullagh had brought King, already a noted Kansas newspaperman, to the *Globe-Democrat* in 1883.[80]

Other McCullagh men not already mentioned included: W. A. Kelsoe, William Spink, Harry James, John N. Edwards, Tom Gallagher, H. B. Wandell, George S. Ochs, O. H. Lake, O. K. Bovard, W. A. Hobbs, and W. C. Brann. Richard Wood was the best of three artists who drew illustrations for stories and political cartoons for the editorial pages. Otis Hall, a clerk in the paper's business office, wrote society news in the early part of the era. Later, Mrs. Maria L. Johnston wrote the society news, and Mrs. D. N. Burgoyne assisted her. Miss Julia Crawford had charge of the religious news.[81] Many McCullagh-trained men such as Dreiser, Yost, King, Bovard, and Brann later became noted journalists.

McCullagh called the *Globe-Democrat* the best journalism school in the country. He believed that a good news story should have clearness, simplicity, force, and fullness. It should be so clearly written that it not only could be understood, but could not be misunderstood. His staff believed that he delighted in catching their errors in figures or in quotations. "Always verify; always verify," he told them.[82] Frequently he edited proof-sheets for wordiness and called the attention of the city editor to errors in figures, names, and statistics. He insisted that names and initials be correct. His correspondents were instructed to send in only what he ordered. They had to query him about stories; then McCullagh would wire how many words to send.[83] He passed on the importance of all news matters, and his authority was absolute.[84]

Even his best reporters were always reminded to keep their stories short. To Stevens, he once wrote:

> Your service has been in general so efficient that I do not like to complain of special matters. But you sometimes expand a little too much, as in the matter of the Hyde papers, which I have just received, and the matter of the Dumont Corporation which I had to kill on account of its length. Please state facts and avoid elaboration as much as possible.[85]

Again, when McCullagh sent Stevens to Mexico, he told his Washington correspondent to employ a good man "to attend to affairs in Washington," but to instruct him that the *Globe-Democrat* expected "all the news and no essays."[86]

The editor insisted that his men carry out his orders implicitly. Once he sent John T. McEnnis to New York by a specific train. But McEnnis, to save six dollars, took an earlier train, and thus missed the Johnstown flood. For this McCullagh was said to have dismissed him.[87] McCullagh's manner to his subordinates was gruff, but no more so than to others. He did not encourage familiarity. He answered questions without taking his cigar from his mouth or his eyes from what he was reading. He did not encourage familiarity. No member of his staff, however, hesitated to ask "the chief" a second time what he had said because it was well known that he preferred that sort of annoyance to having his directions misunderstood.[88]

As an editor McCullagh was a "journalist recluse in his sanctum, where he worked harder than when he was a reporter."[89] He was so punctual in his duties that his staff declared that they could set their watches by his movements. In the early days of his editorship he lived at the Southern Hotel and walked every day to his office, arriving exactly at twelve-thirty in the afternoon. At three he left for an hour and at seven-thirty he clamped his derby hat over his eyes, took his cane and went to dinner at the Southern. Spotless white socks always gleamed above his black shoes. At five minutes past nine, the faint squeak of his shoes set flat upon the floor told the editorial staff that the chief had returned. From then until after midnight he worked at his desk, but exactly on the stroke of twelve-thirty, he could be heard squeaking down the hall. His twelve-hour day was finished. In later years he had rooms on West Pine Boulevard, and for many years he walked the same route to the office. At night he took a carriage home, accompanied by a friend, Louis C. Bohle. It was said facetiously of him that after the paper moved to its new building on Sixth and Pine streets he got lost on his way back from dinner the first day and had to retrace his steps to the old building to get his bearings.[90]

His office was not very large; besides his desk and the shelves of books that he always kept around him, there was only one chair. Over this was a sign, "Have a seat," but to discourage this, he kept the chair piled high with exchange newspapers. His personal contacts were slight, and except for his telegraph and city editors, he seldom saw his other employees. When he did it was only for brief periods. Hour after hour he sat in his office smoking, reading, and writing. He never learned to use the new typewriters.[91]

Among newspaper people of St. Louis, McCullagh acquired the reputation of being liberal with his own funds, but parsimonious with his paper's money. He never gave more nor less than the market value, and he had a thrifty idea about the market value, they believed. Some thought erroneously that he would take a reporter's resignation before he would give him a raise. He praised his men for good stories, and raised salaries for good work, as he did for Stevens and Dreiser. He once gave Dreiser a twenty-dollar bill as a bonus for his work on a train wreck story.[92]

Eugene Field summed up the opinion of journalists about McCullagh and the *Globe-Democrat* in his poem "Little Mack."

> This talk about the journalists that run the East is bosh.
> We've got a Western editor that's little, but O gosh!
> He lives here in Mizzoora, where the people are so set
> In ante-bellum notions they vote for Jackson yet;
> But the paper he is running makes the rusty fossils swear,—
> And best of all, the paragraphs are pointed as a tack.
>   And that's because they emanate
>   From Little Mack.
>
> In architecture he is what you'd call a chunky man,
> As if he'd been constructed on the summer-cottage plan:
> He has a nose like Bonaparte; and round his mobile mouth
> Lies all the sensuous languor of the children of the South;
> His dealings with reporters who affect a weekly bust
> Have given to his violet eyes a shadow of distrust;
> In glorious abandon his brown hair wanders back
>   From the grand Websterian forehead
>   Of Little Mack.
>
> No matter what the item is, if there's an item in it,
> You bet your life he's on to it and nips it in a minute!
> From multifarious nations, countries, monarchies, and lands,
> From Afric's sunny fountains and India's coral strands,
> From Greenland's icy mountains and Siloam's shady rills,
> He gathers in his telegrams, and Houser pays the bills;
> What though there be a dearth of news, he has a happy knack
>   Of scraping up a lot of scoops,
>   Does Little Mack.
>
> And learning? Well he knows the folks of every tribe and age
> That ever played a part upon this fleeting human stage;
> His intellectual system's so extensive and so greedy
> That, when it comes to record, he's a walkin' cyclopedy:
> For having studied (and digested) all the books a-goin',
> It stands to reason he must know about all's worth a-knowin'!

So when a politician with a record's on the track,
   We're apt to hear some history
   From Little Mack.

And when a fellow-journalist is broke and needs a twenty,
Who's allus ready to whack up a portion of his plenty?
Who's allus got a wallet that's as full of sordid gain
As his heart is full of kindness and his head is full of brain?
Whose bowels of compassion will in-va-ri-a-bly move
Their owner to those courtesies which plainly, surely prove
That he's the kind of person that never does go back
   On a fellow that's in trouble?
   Why, Little Mack!

I've heard 'em tell of Dana, and of Bonner, and of Reid,
Of Johnnie Cockerill, who, I'll own, is very smart indeed;
Yet I don't care what their renown or influence may be,
One metropolitan exchange is quite enough for me!
So keep your Danas, Bonners, Reids, your Cockerills, and
   the rest,
The woods is full of better men all through this wooly West;
For all that sleek, pretentious, Eastern editorial pack
   We wouldn't swap the shadow of
   Our Little Mack![93]

As the years passed McCullagh, never very tall, grew fatter
and fatter. He was afflicted with both asthma and a kidney ail-
ment, and after a serious illness in 1893 he did less and less work
at the office. It was as if he had achieved his purpose in life. The
Globe-Democrat had become recognized nationally as a great
newspaper. Financially it was a success. The new journalistic
trends which he had started in the seventies had mushroomed,
by 1896, into "yellow journalism." Even Joseph Pulitzer had
known that if he were to compete with the *Globe-Democrat* he
had to employ editors who could meet McCullagh's methods of
sensationalism. Now there seemed little more that McCullagh
could do for his paper. He did not approve of some of the "yellow" journalistic trends. He refused once to print an expensive
six-thousand word cable from England because it reported scandals that were not fit for *Globe-Democrat* readers. He would not
use colored comics on Sundays until he heard his six-year-old
niece crying for them, and he once promised Jim Butler's mother

not to ridicule her son when he was running for office on a Democratic ticket.[94] McCullagh was too old, too tired, too ill to compete as vigorously as he once had.

Other events also depressed the editor. Simeon Ray, McKee's nephew, and Henry McKee were both dead. Mrs. McKee, the widow of the former owner, died in 1893. Then McCullagh's closest friend, Judge Normile, committed suicide. At that time McCullagh wrote a long essay on "The Philosophy of Suicide."[95] After his illness he moved to the home of his sister-in-law, Mrs. Kate McCullagh, where on December 30, 1896, he committed suicide by jumping from his bedroom window.

He had been confined to his room since November 10 with acute asthma, complicated by a nervous depression that had resulted from his arduous labors in the recent elections. His physician, Dr. C. N. Hughes, saw the editor a few minutes the night before his death. McCullagh had said at that time that he was sleepy and wanted to be left alone. Dr. Hughes made the odd statement that "his brain was affected from his illness" but that "his intellect was all right."[96]

Earlier in the night, McCullagh had tried to take his life by turning on the gas, but Mrs. McCullagh had discovered him in time to thwart this. Later he leaped from his third-floor bedroom window onto the concrete court beneath. His twisted body was found the next morning by Mrs. McCullagh's stable boy.

Houser told a reporter from the *Post-Dispatch* that he believed McCullagh jumped from his window, but a little later, in an interview with a *Republic* reporter, he denied this, saying that he thought McCullagh fell from the window in a fit of asthmatic coughing. Neither Louis C. Bohle nor Walter Stevens admitted that it was suicide.

In the last year the editor's only exercise had been walking to his carriage. "I used to urge Mac to take exercise," Houser told reporters, "but he absolutely refused. Of late years, he had the idea that his legs would give way if he attempted to walk much. But the truth was, I believe, he was somewhat indolent on account of his increased weight."

The news of his death stunned the journalistic world. The

Post-Dispatch, because it was an afternoon journal, flashed the news to St. Louis first and boasted of its "scoop." Big black headlines and pictures with "X marks the spot" bared every gruesome detail. The next morning the *Republic*, though using smaller headlines, printed more interviews and ran more details about McCullagh. Even the *New York Times* used the news as one of its three main stories on the front page. Condolences to the family poured in from people such as General H. V. Boynton, veteran Washington correspondent; Melville E. Stone, general manager of the Associated Press; John Russell Young of the Union League; Victor Rosewater of the *Omaha Bee*; and W. C. Harrison, an old Cincinnati friend.

McCullagh wore out his life at his profession, the *Post-Dispatch* commented. The *Globe-Democrat's* glory was his glory. The *Republic*, which McCullagh had fought so hard for so long, called him one of the most prominent figures in newspaper circles in the United States. His career was more memorable because "in the complex organization of the modern newspaper, the factor of individual influence becomes more and more obscure." It would be long before there was "another company of Greeleys, Raymonds, and Weeds." It would be just as long before there was "a counterpart of Joseph B. McCullagh." His fame rested on his achievement in developing the "now established system of interviewing public men on timely questions," the "incisive style of his editorial comment," and on his success as a "gatherer of news" for the great paper the *Globe-Democrat* had become. The *New York Times* called him a "keen, shrewd, thorough journalist of the type that, at will, plods or soars." Undoubtedly contemporary journalists considered McCullagh one of the greatest editors in the United States. In the minds of many of them he surpassed Joseph Pulitzer, perhaps because they considered that Pulitzer was only following in the steps of McCullagh.

McCullagh never married, though it was rumored that he was engaged twice. Once, about 1874, he was said to be an ardent admirer of Miss Jennie Brown, the adopted daughter of Joseph Brown, then mayor of St. Louis. She lived in a beautiful home on Chouteau Avenue and was a member of the "ultra-fashionable set." But the Mayor objected to the hours that McCullagh worked, and Miss Brown married someone else. McCullagh was said to have been engaged sometime later to a young woman in Terre Haute. He wrote to her regularly and visited her, but this match, too, was broken off. When he died his whole estate, including thirty shares of *Globe-Democrat* stock, was left to his eight-year-old niece, Gladys McCullagh.[97]

Perhaps McCullagh's chief weakness lay in the fact that his greatest stunts and crusades, while adding to the prestige of the *Globe-Democrat*, lacked any particular social value. Yet his influence in bringing better railroad service and other improvements to St. Louis cannot be overlooked. Nor can it be denied that he created a newspaper of great reader interest, and in so doing was instrumental in making the *Globe-Democrat* one of the outstanding papers of the time. Something of McCullagh's nature can be seen in his refusal to accept from a group of business men a $25,000 gift to buy him a home. The offer was apparently made without ulterior motives and in gratitude for the great services he had rendered the St. Louis area. If these men wanted to give him something, he said, they could give it to the poor and needy. As a result $18,000 was collected, and McCullagh distributed this among the poor and among the charitable institutions of the area.[98] Later commenting on his refusal to accept the personal gift, he said that members of the group might some day want him to do something which was against his judgment as a newspaper editor.

McCullagh's ability to recognize and appraise news; to make news by creating controversies and by developing and exploiting insignificant items; to develop fully the mass interview of politically important men, thereby giving access to information never before available; to foresee and have reporters on the spot where "hell is likely to break loose next"; to recognize at an early period in pictorial journalism the value of illustrations and to exploit them extensively; and above all to write short, terse, timely paragraphs—these abilities earned for him the right to be called the *Globe-Democrat's* greatest editor and one of the really great editors of American journalism. Certainly he can be credited with being a chief originator of what the *New York Times* later called "the great tradition in St. Louis journalism."[99] Since his death, the *Globe-Democrat* has found it difficult at times to maintain the national stature that "little Mack" gave to it.

Chapter XII

Daniel M. Houser and Management

D ANIEL M. HOUSER, who at William McKee's trial right-
ly called himself a "newspaper publisher," had come a long
way from the time when, as a thin, shiny-faced teen-ager, he had
walked the dusty blocks between the *Union* office and Thomas
H. Benton's home with proofs for the Senator to read. In 1890
he was fifty-five years old. His drooping mustache, like his thin-
ning hair, was beginning to gray, and he was paunchy; but he was
still robust and healthy. His round red face and red nose was a
familiar sight in St. Louis where he took vigorous walks daily.

At the *Globe-Democrat* office he no longer sat on his high
stool in the counting room adding up figures. The business office was well staffed with bookkeepers and clerks. He liked, however, to wander about the *Globe-Democrat* building and watch,
without saying much, what was going on.

McCullagh's dynamic personality had seemed to those who
worked for the paper to overshadow Houser. But his reputation
as an honest, successful newspaper executive was already extend-
ing far beyond St. Louis. Shortly after McKee's death he became
president of the Globe Printing Company, and Henry McKee,
William's brother, was named vice-president. But when Henry
died in 1887 McCullagh became spokesman for the McKee interests in the paper and was made vice-president. As such, he
was allowed to increase the number of his shares to thirty and to
pay for them out of their dividends.[1] Thus McCullagh had quite
as much to say about the paper's policies as did Houser.

Nevertheless, at the *Globe-Democrat* there was as near a separation of the editorial and counting rooms as could be found in newspaper offices in the eighties. McCullagh expended his energies in hiring and firing reporters, in the collecting and collating of the news, and in its distribution and arrangement in the final product—"the popularization of the commodity," as Henry Watterson once called it.[2] Houser, on the other hand, as president and publisher, put the finished commodity on the market: framed and executed contracts for advertisements, for printing-paper and ink, for typesetting and press work; handled the money and the credits; organized telegraphic and postal service; and supervised the machinery and provided new equipment and adequate quarters.[3]

From the first Houser had shown an unusual aptitude for the commercial side of the newspaper business. His rise from a mere messenger boy in the old *Union* office to the presidency of the firm, his laying out of the plans for the efficient *Globe* office, and his scheme for hiring telegraph operators to act as reporters for the paper testify to his great executive ability. Without Houser's "pay-any-price-for-news" policy, McCullagh could not have developed his "Texas Boycott," could not have published the columns and columns of personal items from small towns, could not have built the sensational paper that he did. Nor could the *Globe-Democrat* have made the meteoric rise in circulation that it did.

Furthermore, Houser led the way in St. Louis journalism toward more modern advertising. He used his big circulations as leverage to raise advertising rates, so that by the time of the death of McCullagh, advertising probably accounted for a giant portion of the paper's income. The tremendous growth of department stores and the use of national advertising during the eighties and nineties proved a boon to Houser, as it did to all newspapers of the time.[4] As early as 1885 he had employed a special agent, Thomas W. Woods, to seek advertising in the St. Louis area. Woods made estimates and drew up contracts with advertisers. In New York the publisher employed F. T. MacFadden and the Consolidated Eastern Bureau as advertising agents and distributors.

In 1887 the daily issues of the *Globe-Democrat* still devoted from two to five columns of the front page to advertising, and the front page of the Sunday issues was entirely filled with advertisements. Frequently one firm bought the entire front page for a display advertisement printed in large type that cut across the seven columns in headline effect. Such displays were rather modern in layout and in copy; articles for sale were grouped in classes and marked with prices. Column rules were often broken, and many illustrations were used. Classified advertisements by this time often filled as many as five pages.[5]

Two firms often using full-page advertisements were D. Crawford and Company and William Barr Dry Goods Company. Other big advertisers in the *Globe-Democrat* included Scruggs, Vandervoort and Barney, A. H. Fuch's, May Stern and Company, and E. C. Meacham Arms Company. By the early nineties bicycles sold from $13.50 to $35.00. Point-lace bridal veils were listed at $1,000, but ladies' fashionable hats sold for only $1.95 to $3.45. Parasols for the races were advertised at $1.50 to $6.00, and James Means' shoes at $3.00. English serge sold for seven and a half cents a yard, forty-four-inch cotton plaids for seventy-five cents, and French tricot for fifty cents. Bedroom suites were priced at $7.90 and extension tables at $5.00. A dining room could be completely furnished for $36.00. Monogram cigars, Whitaker's sugar-cured hams, and Royal Baking Powder were advertised almost daily.[6]

After the turn of the century, Houser continued to develop the paper's advertising, and by 1915 the *Globe-Democrat* could claim that it was printing daily 334,925 lines of display advertising and 136,025 lines of classified.[7] Houser was not averse to the extensive advertising of patent medicines and of medical doctors whose practices bordered on quackery. Carter's Little Liver Pills positively cured sick headaches and regulated the bowels. The "very worst cases of nervous debility" were absolutely cured by Perfecto tablets, and Professor Jules Laborde had a wonderful French preparation that restored lost manhood. Dr. Spinney promised women to cure all their ills with vegetable remedies and electricity. For a small fee Dr. Meyers and Company promised cures for almost every disease. This physician could cure rheumatism for $5.00 to $45.00 and falling hair for $6.00 to $10.00. Dr. Miller and Dr. Fayne cured catarrh for fifty cents a treatment and furnished the medicine free. Dr. Schreiner treated out-of-town patients by mail for one dollar a week.[8]

By 1910 automobile companies had become large advertisers in the *Globe-Democrat*. The Willys-Overland firm announced its 1911 line of cars in a five-column display advertisement with pictures of its five models. The Winton Motor Company's Winton Six, which sold for $3,000, cost only seventy-seven cents per thousand miles to drive. The White Limousines and the White Landaulets were called the "aristocrats of fine cars" and were equipped with dome electric lights, toilet articles, and silk curtains for plate glass windows. For $750 a business man in St. Louis could buy a Ford coupelet, a practical all-the-year-round two-passenger car. Other automobiles advertised were the Chalmers Victorian Cabriolet, the Reo, and the Landau Studebaker.[9]

The terrific competition in news gathering of the eighties and the expansion of news coverage and of advertising necessitated the enlarging of the *Globe-Democrat*. Whereas immediately following the merger, Houser and McCullagh had been content to use an inserted supplement to take care of the increased news, by 1885 they had enlarged the week-day paper and the *Weekly;* the *Semi-Weekly* was enlarged to twelve pages. In 1890 the *Semi-Weekly* was dropped because its circulation was only 1,500, but the *Weekly*, with a circulation of 96,500, was published in two parts, on Tuesdays and Fridays. This paper and the Saturday edition of the daily were increased to sixteen pages. The Sunday edition had thirty to forty-four pages.[10]

Prices of newsprint dropped during the McCullagh era.[11] This, plus the desire to gain on his competitors, influenced Houser to lower the price of the *Globe-Democrat*. As early as 1884 he reduced the price from five cents a copy to one cent for issues of twelve pages, two cents for twenty pages, and three cents for twenty-two to twenty-four pages. The Sunday paper remained at five cents. By 1892 issues of even forty pages had been cut to three cents.[12] It was not until the paper shortage of World War I that the prices of the daily issues were standardized.

In spite of the huge sums paid for gathering news the *Globe-Democrat* made money. By the end of 1879 Houser had paid off all debts incurred by the competition between the *Globe* and the *Democrat*, and the firm had a bank balance of $90,000.[13] Houser was not content, however. As new inventions were developed and new equipment needed, he plowed much of the profits back into the paper. In 1883 he added two Hoe presses costing $80,000. With a capacity of fourteen thousand copies an hour, the new presses brought the total capacity to forty-eight thousand.[14] Telephones and typewriters were also installed. In 1884 one telephone was listed for the business department and one for the editorial offices. By 1885 the business department had two telephones, and by 1893 it had three.[15] In 1890, the *Globe-Democrat* installed a photo-engraving plant, the first St. Louis newspaper to do so.[16]

By this time the paper had grown and prospered to such an extent that Houser realized his paper was outgrowing the composing and press rooms. Consequently, he began looking around for a suitable site for a new building. In 1891 he bought the Dozier Bakery property on the southwest corner of Sixth and Pine streets and started construction of a new building which was to house the latest equipment.[17] The new structure, which McCullagh liked to call "The Temple of Truth,"[18] was completed in May, 1892, and the paper moved into its new quarters. Houser believed that the ten-story building would be large enough to fill the paper's needs "until the end of time." Two floors were under ground; the business, editorial, and mechanical departments occupied five of the floors above the ground.[19]

Houser's almost unprecedentedly lavish spending for news, his proper placing of competent agents, his provisions for new equipment and ample quarters, and his careful attention to details in the counting rooms,[20] together with McCullagh's editorial management, enabled the *Globe-Democrat* to contend successfully with its rivals. Only two St. Louis journals ever became serious competitors of the Houser newspaper—the *Repub-*

lican and the *Post-Dispatch*. Both of these papers, however, suffered serious reversals by the turn of the century, while the
Globe-Democrat continued its remarkable progress.

The *Missouri Republican*, traditionally a bitter foe as well as
a contender for newspaper readers, was far in the lead of the
Globe-Democrat in circulation at the time of the merger, though
exact circulation figures were never released, and press foremen
were sworn to secrecy on the number of copies printed.[21] But
instead of concentrating on news gathering as had Houser and
McKee, the Knapps had invested their money in expensive machinery, even purchasing a Walters press in London.[22] Then, in
the eighties, a series of difficulties with editors had developed.
Colonel George Knapp died, and William Byars, the *Republican's* long-time editor, resigned. Byars was replaced by Frank
O'Neill, who lasted only a short time because he disagreed with
the publishers. In 1888 Charles H. Jones of Florida purchased an
interest in the paper and persuaded the Knapps to turn over
complete control to him. One of his first steps was to change the
name of the paper to the *St. Louis Republic*.[23] Of course, it had
long been Democratic in politics, and its old title was perhaps a
misnomer. Jones made of the paper "a personal journal," and the
circulation, which had suffered during the earlier trouble with
the editors, dropped still more. Subsequently, after the new editor
attacked Governor David R. Francis in an article and the two
men came to blows on the street, Francis purchased an interest
in the *Republic* in order to remove Jones as editor. Charles W.
Knapp then resumed editorship of the paper.[24]

By this time, however, the *Globe-Democrat* had surpassed the
Knapp journal in circulation. In 1885 the circulation of the
Republican was reported at 27,000, while that of the *Globe-
Democrat* had reached 37,000.[25] But Knapp set out to make the
Republic a rival in circulation as well as in politics. As a result,
by 1895 the two papers were about equal in both daily and Sun-
day circulations. *The Republic* reached its peak in 1902 when
its Sunday and daily circulations surpassed those of the *Globe-
Democrat* by more than 10,000, both Sunday papers having circulations of more than 100,000 and the daily *Republic* also ex-

ceeding 100,000.[26] After this, however, except for another good year in 1912, the circulation of the *Republic* fell consistently, while that of the *Globe-Democrat* climbed steadily. By 1915 the *Globe-Democrat* could claim a daily circulation of 26,277 more than the *Republic* and a Sunday circulation of 79,083 more than its rival. In addition, the Houser newspaper was printing annually 151,280 more lines of display and classified advertising.[27]

The fact that the *Globe-Democrat* gave its readers more news than did the Knapp paper partially accounted for the decreasing popularity of the *Republic*. But other factors also contributed to its decline. The Knapps had failed to take into consideration that the business district of St. Louis would move west when they constructed their new building on Chestnut and Third streets. They spent huge sums of money in rebuilding the Southern Hotel and the Merchants' Exchange to try to halt the westward movement of the city, but finally they were compelled to open an "uptown office" for the *Republic* on Olive Street.[28] Furthermore, they were going deeper and deeper into debt. In 1901 Francis talked to Joseph Pulitzer about combining the *Republic* and the *Post-Dispatch*. Pulitzer valued his paper at two million dollars. Francis thought that this was too high, but he is said to have lent two and a half million dollars to the Knapps.[29] It was about this time that the circulation of the *Republic* soared. Still the paper could not maintain its financial standing, and in 1912 it suspended payment of dividends to stockholders.[30] Nor were the Knapps able to maintain the *Republic's* standing with the Democratic party. In the presidential campaign of 1895, it favored the views of St. Louisans in advocating "hard money" and thus alienated its rural readers.[31]

In the meantime the *Post-Dispatch* had emerged as a formidable foe of the *Globe-Democrat*. In 1878, after Joseph Pulitzer had turned from Republicanism to Democracy, he bought the *St. Louis Dispatch* for $2,500. The next day he consolidated it with the *Post* and announced that he would "oppose all frauds and shams." His paper was not to be an organ of Republicanism, but an organ of truth.[32]

Because the Pulitzer paper was an afternoon journal, McCullagh had not been so concerned with the *Post-Dispatch* as a rival as he had with the morning *Republic*. On occasions he somewhat jokingly approved of the Pulitzer newspaper. Once when the *Post-Dispatch* threatened to print the names of the delegates who were drunk at a political convention, he commented editorially that the Pulitzer paper could save money by printing the names of those who did not get drunk. Again, when Editor Hyde of the old *Republican* knocked Pulitzer down on a St. Louis street, McCullagh used the occasion to attack Hyde rather than Pulitzer for what his paper had printed: "If the editor of the *Republican* was as nimble with his pen as with his fists, his columns would be much more interesting than they are now."[33]

In 1879 Pulitzer bought the *Evening Star* and imported John A. Cockerill, a man of wide newspaper experience, as the most likely man to compete with McCullagh. Thereafter, it was a race between the two editors,[34] but the *Post-Dispatch* had a long way to go before it could compete with the *Globe-Democrat* on even terms. In 1880 the Pulitzer paper had a circulation of only 8,740 in comparison with the *Globe-Democrat's* 24,000. Moreover, the *Post-Dispatch* suffered a temporary setback when Cockerill killed a prominent St. Louis attorney in a quarrel over an article printed in the paper in which the attorney's personal and professional honor had been attacked.[35] Pulitzer later took Cockerill to New York to edit the *World*.

It was not until 1892 that the *Post-Dispatch* began to be a serious competitor of the *Globe-Democrat*. At that time it had a daily circulation of 33,804 while the *Globe-Democrat* had 53,352. Pulitzer, hoping to compete more effectively with McCullagh, sold a part interest in his paper to Charles H. Jones, the man who had profited so much while editing the *Republic*. In 1893 Jones lowered the price of the *Post-Dispatch* to two cents and in 1894 to one cent.[36] This was ten years after the price of the *Globe-Democrat* had been cut to one cent. Immediately the circulation of the *Post-Dispatch* soared, and by 1897 it exceeded that of the *Globe-Democrat* by eight thousand. But the *Post-Dispatch* did not maintain this margin for long. Pulitzer and

Jones disagreed over editorial policies. When Jones refused to obey Pulitzer's order to stop agitating the silver question, Pulitzer had to go to court to regain control of his paper. During this controversy the circulation of the *Post-Dispatch* slipped until, in 1899, it surpassed that of the *Globe-Democrat* by only 2,653.[37] After that the *Post-Dispatch's* circulation had soared again; by 1914 it had reached 176,659, while that of the *Globe-Democrat* was only 134,671.[38]

The Houser paper also faced strong competition from the Sunday *Post-Dispatch,* which Pulitzer started on October 2, 1887.[39] As has been stated, McCullagh termed this paper a "great failure." But he was mistaken, and rivalry between the two Sunday papers soon became intense. By 1900 circulations of both papers had passed the 100,000 mark,[40] but by 1915 the *Post-Dispatch* was far in the lead.[41] Unlike McCullagh, Houser had recognized the *Post-Dispatch* for the potent rival that it was. He tried unsuccessfully to get the Knapp brothers to help prevent the Pulitzer journal from getting a Sunday Associated Press franchise.[42]

Other competition from St. Louis newspapers was negligible. In the eighties, the *St. Louis Times* merged with the *Journal.* McCullagh liked to refer to the "semi-annual sale" of the *Times-Journal.* Later the *Republic* absorbed this paper, reducing the number of English morning dailies in St. Louis to two, the *Republic* and the *Globe-Democrat.*[43] The *St. Louis Star* and the *St. Louis Times* were evening papers published after the turn of the century, but they presented no appreciable competition before 1915.

Despite competition, Houser, by 1905, had made the *Globe-Democrat* a million-dollar business. Exactly how prosperous the Globe Printing Company had become was apparent after the death in 1905 of Miss Ellen McKee, only daughter of William McKee, the founder. Miss McKee, noted in St. Louis for her donations to charity and to educational institutions, left an estate with an estimated value of two million dollars. She owned the controlling stock, two hundred and ninety shares, of the Globe

Printing Company. This accounted for at least half of her estate.[44]

Her stock was left in trust for twenty years. The dividends during this time were to be divided among her thirty-three heirs, some of whom lived in Scotland. At the expiration of twenty years the executor of Miss McKee's estate was to sell the stock for the best price obtainable in blocks of not less than ten shares, and the proceeds were then to be distributed equally among the heirs. The executor of her will was her cousin, Charles H. McKee, vice-president of the firm since McCullagh's death. One of the heirs was E. Lansing Ray, son of Simeon Ray, a former secretary-treasurer of the company who had died in 1891.[45] Among some St. Louis people at the time there was a feeling that Miss McKee placed her stock in a trust fund to prevent the Housers from gaining control of the paper.[46] However, Daniel M. Houser was one of the witnesses of the will, which was made March 29, 1905, shortly before Miss McKee's death.

Other deaths also struck the Globe Printing Company. Houser's two sons by his first wife, both of whom worked for the paper, died. Daniel M. Houser, Jr., died of typhoid fever in November, 1899. Three months later, William McKee Houser, who had been secretary-treasurer of the company since the death of Simeon Ray, died of tuberculosis.[47] Then in 1915 Daniel M. Houser, "Uncle Dan" as he was affectionately called, died of cancer. He had been ill for two years, but as had McKee and McCullagh, he kept coming to the office as long as possible. He had been accustomed to return to his office at night, working often until midnight, but for more than a year before his death he came only for brief periods during which he was accompanied by his nurse.[48]

For days after Houser's death the *Globe-Democrat* columns were filled with messages of condolence. They came from such people as former President William H. Taft, former Supreme Court Judge Henry Lamm, and Oswald Garrison Villard, editor of the *New York Evening Post*. One of the greatest tributes came in an editorial printed in the rival *Post-Dispatch*: "Since 1851—sixty-four years—the late Daniel M. Houser has been identified with practically the same newspaper interests. The record is perhaps without parallel in American newspaperdom. . . . He was an honest newspaper man and he ran an honest paper. From the age of 18, he was a good man for St. Louis."[49]

For many years Houser had been a director of the Western Associated Press, serving on the same board with such famous newspapermen as Murat Halstead, Richard Smith, W. N. Haldeman, and Joseph Medill. In St. Louis he was recognized for his public spirit, having given much time to civic projects. He was one of the originators and incorporators of the St. Louis Exposition and of the Music Hall Association. He served as director of the latter for fifteen years until November, 1897, when he was publicly eulogized for his service.[50] Though not an active politician, he was long a potent influence in national and state politics, not only through the *Globe-Democrat*, but through his own efforts. Always a staunch Republican, Houser was honored by his party in 1900, when he was made one of the four delegates at large from Missouri to the Republican National Convention.[51]

Though always in the background, Houser is a part of the tradition of the *Globe-Democrat* and of St. Louis journalism. Only once was he known to have interfered with McCullagh's editing. On this occasion he ordered an editorial on the railroad strikes to be killed.[52] Cheerfully he expended huge sums of money in gathering news, provided modern equipment, and devised new schemes for acquiring news. His ability and his standing were recognized by his greatest rivals. Indeed, had he not placed his paper on such a sound financial standing, it would not have been possible for the *Globe-Democrat* to have withstood the vicissitudes of later years.

After Houser's death the second generation of McKees and Housers took up the task of keeping the *Globe-Democrat* the successful and influential paper that it had become. On the McKee side, Charles H. McKee, trained as a reporter under McCullagh, was to become president of the firm. E. Lansing Ray, McKee's nephew, who was later to become president, had been working on the paper for twelve years. On the Houser side,

Douglas B., Houser's son by his second wife, had started as a cub reporter in 1914. A grandson, W. C. Houser, was also working in the business office.[53] These were the men who were to direct the paper through the problems of reporting world wars and to cope with the growing complexities of the newspaper business.

Chapter XIII

Captain Henry King and
Yellow Journalism

A FTER McCullagh died there was much speculation in St.
Louis newspaper circles as to who would succeed the
great editor. The *Post-Dispatch* reported that Walter B. Stevens
was a likely candidate. A former city editor of the paper and now
its noted Washington correspondent, Stevens was a favorite of
Miss Ellen McKee.[1] But as Houser pointed out to a reporter for
the *Republic*, there were other good men on the paper—Captain
Henry King, the leading political and editorial writer, and Casper
S. Yost, who had done such notable work as editor of the Sunday
paper.[2] It was King who shortly thereafter received the appointment.

When he had come to the *Globe-Democrat* in 1883, King was
already a well-known newspaper man. As a child in Illinois he
had learned the printer's trade; and his first assignment as a reporter had been to cover the Lincoln-Douglas debates. After
having served four years in the Union Army and attaining the
rank of captain, he had become editor of the *Whig*, a newspaper
at Quincy, Illinois. Later he had moved to Kansas where he had
edited the *Kansas State Record*, the *Weekly Commonwealth*,
and the *Topeka Daily Capital*. He had also contributed historical
and literary articles to such monthly magazines as the *Century*.[3]

When King started writing for the *Globe-Democrat*, he came
to the office only on specified days. Although McCullagh had
employed him as his leading political and editorial writer, he also
gave his new man extra assignments. Once he sent King to cover
a performance of grand opera. King protested that he knew noth-

173

ing of opera. That did not matter, McCullagh said; he wanted reports by someone who did not understand opera, so that the reviews would not be cluttered by technical terms. King's subsequent articles on the performances drew much favorable comment.[4]

When King took over McCullagh's roll-top desk in 1897, St. Louis was a throbbing city of nearly a half-million people. It fanned westward from the river to encompass a new palatial residential area and the fourteen-hundred-acre Forest Park, which was a civic showplace. With the decline of the river traffic after 1880, the importance of the levee district had declined, and the business section of the city was in the process of inching west from Fourth Street. Already a few buildings pushed twelve stories into the smoky, murky air. Others, to be even taller, were under construction. Bordering this area was an old section of mansions now being vacated and converted into small stores and factories. The wholesale district teemed with men in fancy vests and derby hats and women in high-necked dresses with leg-o-mutton sleeves.

Everywhere, business was flourishing. Department stores were expanding. The steady but rapid industrial development, however, had ushered in many municipal problems. Already the city was outgrowing its transportation facilities, even though red, yellow, blue, green, and orange streetcars clanged and wheezed through the streets twenty-four hours a day. Eads Bridge was no longer able to care for the ever-increasing traffic, and a new bridge to the north was slowly inching across the river. The city government was infiltrated by grafters and bribe-takers who were getting rich. Market Street divided the city into a North and South side, with the people of each side distrusting the other when issues concerning badly needed municipal improvements arose. As a result, little was being accomplished to clean up the crime and disease-breeding tenement districts.

With all its hustle and bustle, however, St. Louis still retained signs of a leisurely life. Rocking chairs lined the sidewalks in front of the Lindell, Southern, and LaClede hotels. Verandas circled the homes of middle class people who were living a comfortable, easy life. Sunday afternoon walks and buggy rides through the parks were popular pastimes.

The Germans, who were the largest immigrant group in the city, were still potent politically. They worked in breweries, frequented numerous beer gardens, and clung to many of their old-country customs. An intellectual group as a whole, they were contributing much to the development of music, art, education, recreation, and amusement facilities and activities.

But flocking into the city were thousands of illiterate Europeans from Russia and the Balkan countries, destitute Negroes from the Southern states, and uneducated white people from the hills and mountains of neighboring states. All lived in overcrowded, unsanitary tenement districts, which abounded in illegitimacy, divorce, child neglect, gambling, drunkenness, and disease. Wages were low, rents high, and industrial accidents frequent.

For the most part the European immigrants were poor and unaccustomed to living in a democracy. They learned the English language with difficulty. Few brought their families with them. They lived in cheap, overcrowded lodging houses with inadequate sanitary facilities. Sometimes as many as seven men occupied one room, sleeping in shifts. Two and three families sometimes occupied one apartment and shared one outside water faucet with the occupants of other apartments in the building. But it was said that the slums of St. Louis were not as bad as those in other large cities.

To care for these people there were more than one hundred philanthropic organizations. The city was particularly proud of its doctors and nurses, who were working so hard to lower the infant mortality rate, and to reduce tuberculosis and nutritional diseases.

This was St. Louis in 1897; King had come to know the city well in his years as the chief editorial writer for the *Globe-Democrat*. Now he was to be the paper's editor, and the eighteen years of his editorship were to prove almost as momentous in the history of the paper as had the years of the McCullagh era. Whereas McCullagh had widened the news coverage and changed the editorial page with his short paragraphs, King now developed the paper into a more well-rounded, modern journal. His use of certain "yellow journalism" practices and recent technological improvements contributed largely to Houser's success in building the Globe-Democrat Company into a million-dollar business.

The new editor had a plain newspaper creed. He believed that there was such a thing as a newspaper standard. To him, getting the news was very important, but printing opinions which had no merit in themselves and which were sensational because they assailed something or someone did not meet this standard.[5] Of the crusading and muckraking current in journalism at the turn of the century, he said:

> We happen to be living just now in an era of accusation and exposure. The air is crammed with yellow particles of commercial and social iniquity. . . . The pessimists are striving with all their benumbing power . . . to persuade us that the canker of vice is at the heart of everything. . . . whatever reforms are really needed, they will undoubtedly be made. . . .[6]

King thought that the average newspaper in 1915 was better than it had been formerly because news reports were more accurate, and editors took more pains to give every side a hearing.[7] He based his philosophy of the press on "the greatest good for the greatest number"[8] and defended newspapers against the frequent accusation that they were controlled in policy and purpose by their advertisers. Speaking before the Commercial Club of St. Louis in 1907, he said:

> In so far as this implies a sacrifice of principle in return for patronage, it has no foundation. But newspapers are influenced in a measure by the business interests of the community. . . . What is best for such interests is best for the city and all classes of the population. . . . I feel that it is my duty, as it is always my pleasure, to consult and cooperate with the business men of St. Louis, because I have learned that their success is indispensable in promoting welfare and progress. If they advertise, so much the better for them, I am sure, as well as for the newspaper.[9]

From 1897 to 1915 the *Globe-Democrat* reflected these ideas, and under King the paper became known as the spokesman for the business interests of the area.

Like McCullagh, the new editor kept the *Globe-Democrat* staffed with a corps of brilliant writers—Charles M. Harvey, Fred H. Collier, Donald C. Maurice, and Tubman K. Hedrick, who in 1897 became the paper's first columnist. He was able also to entice the capable editor, Joseph J. McAuliffe, from the staff of the *Post-Dispatch*.[10]

Another interesting figure whom King employed to write for the paper was David R. McAnally, Jr., son of the famous editor of the *Christian Advocate.* McAnally had first worked for the *Globe-Democrat* in 1875; McCullagh had employed his young friend as a literary and editorial writer. But after two years McAnally had resigned to become head of the English department at the University of Missouri. There he had instituted a course in journalism. Called "History of Journalism," it was really a course in writing and became the forerunner of the University's present School of Journalism. After he left this teaching position in 1885, he began contributing literary and historical articles to the *Globe-Democrat*, probably on a free-lance basis. Then during King's editorship, he wrote regularly for the Sunday magazine section, though he never had a desk at the *Globe-Democrat* office.[11]

Not a little of the success of the *Globe-Democrat* under King came from his own writing. His editorials, as a rule much longer than McCullagh's had been, became a marked and distinguishing feature of the paper. Of his writing, Nobel L. Printiss once said:

> If he didn't lisp in numbers, he editorialized in petti-coats. . . . To write . . . with him is an art like music or painting or acting. His thoughtful devotion to form does not run to pedantry or finical word picking but is a result of the man's constitutional nicety and daintiness of mind, which portrays itself even in the clear, legible, and rather peculiar handwriting in manuscripts that know no "outs," "doublets," or any blots of interlineations.[12]

178   ST. LOUIS GLOBE-DEMOCRAT

Typical of his style was an editorial in which he referred to
Governor Lon B. Stephens as the "sapient son of a sainted sire."
In another, he wrote that the police were "so deeply occupied
assessing the force and making presents to the police board that
reports of burglaries" annoyed them.[13]

A study of the newspapers of twenty-one metropolitan centers at the turn of the century showed that St. Louis was one of
the notable centers of the "yellow journalism" movement of
that period and that three of the city's newspapers were definitely
"yellow."[14] Unquestionably, the *Globe-Democrat* was one of
these journals. It had many characteristics of "yellowness," but
at the same time the conservative King refrained from using
many "yellow" techniques.

In reality it was but a short step from McCullagh's sensationalism to "yellow journalism." Crime, sex, scandal, and sports news
—all characteristic of "yellow journalism"—were as important
to King as they were to McCullagh. The new editor, however,
discarded McCullagh's use of reprints of such stories from other
papers. Instead, he increased the amount of Associated Press
news reports. Typical of the crime and scandal stories were the
reports of the Frank Baruto trial, the elopement of Rathell Ulrich, the Bates Boys' trial, and the suicide of B. T. Browning.[15]
He printed good accounts and gave spectacular picture coverage
to such local disasters as a fire in the heart of the wholesale district that destroyed more than a million dollars worth of property and a Mississippi River flood that inundated property in
Missouri, Louisiana, Mississippi, and Arkansas and left hundreds
of people starving.[16] He also widened the coverage of sports
news to include accounts of yacht races, golf, tennis, checkers,
whist, hunting, and fishing. Advance stories on racing, football,
and baseball came into use. People of St. Louis were always
sports lovers; for them King filled at least two pages in daily issues and often five in Sunday issues with sports news. Such spectacular events as the Corbett-Fitzsimmons prize fight in 1897
pushed almost all other news from the front page for several
days.[17]

The Spanish-American war news in the *Globe-Democrat* ushered in large black headlines and a more lavish use of illustrations—both characteristic of "yellow journalism." Under McCullagh headline type in the *Globe-Democrat* had remained small, whereas, in the *Post-Dispatch* large, black letters screamed exciting news as early as 1896.[18] But beginning with the report of the blowing up of the "Maine," King began using bigger and blacker headlines. Nevertheless, they never reached the glaring proportions of such banner headlines as those used by the *New York Journal*.[19] It took only eight days for King to change from the one-column headlines which announced the "Maine" catastrophe to the one-line, three-column headline, printed in inch-high, black capital letters, that cried out: "FLOAT MINE THE AGENCY." After that, two- and three-column headlines became commonplace in the *Globe-Democrat*.

In the lavish use of illustrations the paper appeared particularly "yellow." McCullagh had first started this practice in the eighties, even though he had been much slower to use chalk-plate illustrations than had other St. Louis newspapers. He had no staff of chalk-plate artists, as did the *Republic* and the *Post-Dispatch*. Although he used such engravings extensively, they were made outside the *Globe-Democrat* office, usually by Miss Lillian Brown, daughter of B. Gratz Brown, early editor of the paper.[20] But after the installation of a photo-engraving plant in 1890, illustrations became more profuse. It was not unusual for King to use more than a dozen drawings three or four columns wide to illustrate a flood, a prize fight, or a similar sensational event. With the availability of better cameras, halftones became predominant over sketches, which then were used largely to illustrate features stories and to make borders for photographs. Pictures of women on the society pages were usually embellished with elaborate scroll work.[21] By 1904 there was scarcely a page of any issue of the *Globe-Democrat* that did not have from one to five pictures, and by 1915 a few spot-news photographs were being used.

King also used cartoons extensively. During the war he stirred emotions by printing three-column cartoons on the front page.

These were patriotic in theme, such as the one on February 21, 1898, which showed Uncle Sam talking to a Spaniard and had the caption: "Thank you, senor, but I'll conduct this investigation myself."

Illustrations were so important to King that he would send at least four artists to national political conventions. Edward Exsergian (Eddie Eks) drew cartoons for the sport pages. Richard Bieger, another cartoonist, drew a series of sketches depicting life on the "Great Religious Daily." Other artists who worked for the paper under King included Armond Wickler, Harry Martin, Peter McCurd, Richard Wood, Clare Briggs, and Elmer Donnell, who drew political cartoons.[22]

Other journalistic practices instituted by King showed that he was well aware of the better characteristics of the so-called "yellow journalism." As early as 1898 he was running a table of contents on the front page, and by 1904 he began printing in a "box" on the front page one-sentence summaries of the late news events. On the society pages he emphasized local events and included descriptions of the food served and the clothes worn by the women. He also initiated a real estate section in the Saturday and Sunday papers. Usually a two-column picture of a house illustrated articles on real estate sales. He continued McCullagh's railroad page; enlivened the popular bicycle page, called "Wheels and Wheelers," with art work by Clare Briggs, and introduced a "page for the man who laughs," with sketches by De La Bruyere.

It was the *Globe-Democrat's* Sunday edition, however, with its pseudo-scientific and superficial articles and its colored comics, which even more flagrantly exhibited "yellow" characteristics. McCullagh had appointed Casper S. Yost the Sunday editor in 1890,[23] probably to counteract the growing popularity of the Sunday *Post-Dispatch*. Yost, who was to add great prestige to the paper, had come to the *Globe-Democrat* the year before. Prior to that, he had learned to set type at the age of eight at the *LaClede County Leader* in Lebanon, Missouri, and had been a reporter and telegraph operator on the *St. Louis Daily Chronicle* and the *Missouri Republican*.[24]

Already recognized as a promising young writer, Yost remained editor of the Sunday paper under King. The two men enlarged the Sunday *Globe-Democrat* until by 1900 it was being printed in four sections with a total of sixty pages. Five years later a fifth section was added. No expense was spared in providing readers with news from over the world. On one Sunday in July, 1897, for example, 100,172 words of telegraphic matter were printed, including 65,172 words of "specials" and 35,000 words of Associated Press reports. Twenty thousand words came by cable.[25]

The first three sections of the Sunday paper contained the news, editorials, and classified advertising. The fourth was the magazine supplement, with a colored cover page, usually drawn by Alfred Russell.[26] The fifth section consisted of from four to six pages for the juvenile set and four pages of colored comics. Called "Our Boys and Girls Magazine," it was printed in tabloid form. Comics included "Brownie Clown of Brownie Town," "Bob, He's Always to Blame," "Simon Simple," "Aunt Tina," and "Br'er Rabbit."[27]

Yost, who was to become nationally famous for his own writing, was particularly noted for his Sunday magazine supplement. Fiction, essays, historical articles, popular scientific reports, and articles of interest to women, all well-illustrated, filled from ten to sixteen pages every Sunday. Later the *Globe-Democrat* added a semi-monthly Sunday magazine, with syndicated articles by such people as Henry L. Stimson, former Secretary of War, and Florenz Ziegfeld, Jr.; fiction by Richard LeGalliene, Gilbert Parker, and E. Phillips Oppenheim; poetry by Madeline Bridges; and the writings of Ed Howe and Fred C. Kelley. Such articles and essays kept *Globe-Democrat* readers informed on a wide variety of subjects—why and how alcohol made a man drunk, how farmers would soon be able to inoculate their fields with bacteria and reap immense crops, how to pick a husband, how the Jay Goulds lived, and how Uncle Sam would clean house for Santo Domingo.[28] Yost himself wrote an article for nearly every issue. His column, "In the Smoking Compartment," was widely read. Each described an incident on a train or reported a conversation between people on a train and revealed in dramatic, fictional form an historic event, such as the founding of the Salvation Army, or a current problem, such as the consequences of the financial panic of 1907.[29] Many of his columns and essays were collected and published in book form.[30]

It was in the Sunday supplement, too, that Yost promoted the story of Patience Worth into national prominence. One hot day in July, 1913, a St. Louis woman, Mrs. John Curran, and a friend sat with their hands on a ouija board. Suddenly the pointer darted from letter to letter. It did not take long for news to reach the *Globe-Democrat* that a spirit had spoken to Mrs. Curran. Yost, who like McCullagh was interested in spiritism, investigated, sat in the chair opposite Mrs. Curran, saw Patience Worth's quaint Anglo-Saxon messages spelled out, and was fascinated.

The *Globe-Democrat* flashed the news of Patience Worth to the world. Doctors, scientists, authors, and reporters from New York, Boston, Los Angeles, and Chicago came to St. Louis to investigate, to doubt, to wonder, and to be chastened by Patience Worth. To the many who believed or wanted to believe in spiritism, Patience Worth became almost a reality. They waited impatiently for the next Sunday *Globe-Democrat* to read her latest story or poem. Other papers and magazines jumped on the bandwagon, and ouija boards became one of the fastest selling items across the nation.

In his book, *Patience Worth, A Psychic Mystery*, which was favorably reviewed by even the *Atlantic Monthly*, Yost neither accepted Patience Worth as a spirit nor rejected her as a hoax.[31] Rather he examined her logically as something that could not be explained. Not until the country became embroiled in World War I did people begin to forget Patience Worth, and it was not until 1928 that she faded entirely from the pages of the *Globe-Democrat*.

But the two biggest stories during King's editorship, as far as coverage was concerned, were the Spanish-American War and the Louisiana Purchase Centennial Exposition held in St. Louis in 1904. Even before the death of McCullagh the American press had started its sensational treatment of certain incidents that aggravated the strained diplomatic relations between Spain and the United States.[32] McCullagh had not failed to attack Spain in his editorial paragraphs. When the first news of the "Allianca" affair, in which a Spanish gunboat tried to search an American steamship and shot across her bow, was flashed to the paper on March 13, 1895, the editor declared that Spain was rash in assailing the United States because the Cuban affair was all that she could manage at the present. "Third-rate nations are not in a good position to attack first-rate nations."

By early 1897, however, when King had full control of the news and editorial policies of the paper, the *Globe-Democrat* was clearly foreseeing more trouble with Spain. Nevertheless, the new editor devoted quite as much space to the current British-Greek controversy as he did to the Cuban troubles. He did use stories written by Sylvester Scovel, a reporter for the *New York World*, about atrocities in Cuba which were carried out under Spanish General Valierono Weyler, but he did not take part in the uproar that followed Scovel's arrest in Cuba. Republican that he was, the editor blamed Cleveland's supineness for outrages committed on Americans in Cuba. He predicted that McKinley would act where Cleveland had not. Spain would not find quarreling with the United States a "remedy for its misgovernment in all parts of the world."[33] Though he continued to print reports of atrocities in Cuba, King relegated these to the inside pages in order to emphasize patronage in the McKinley administration, European news, and local disasters.

Nevertheless, by early 1898 King knew that war was inevitable and long since had arranged for his own correspondents to cover the action. On February 1 that year he wrote that the more ships Spain sent to America, the greater would be her embarrassment. The United States, he hinted, would win easily in a war with Spain. Two weeks later, he was more outspoken. The time was near, he told his readers, when the United States must intervene. Spain belonged to the past, rather than to the present, and Cuba, he thought, was "necessarily American in feeling and impulses." But he took a somewhat conservative stand when the sinking of the "Maine" brought war closer. There was no proof that Spain had caused the disaster. Still, the situation needed watching; the Navy needed more liberal expenditures.[34] Every vestige of doubt had disappeared on February 18, however. Americans, he said, must stand up for their rights.

The prominent display which King gave to the war itself has already been mentioned. During this time, 80 to 90 per cent of the front page of the *Globe-Democrat* was filled with war news and illustrations relating to the war. Feature stories about the fighting, about the armed services, and about personalities in Washington concerned with the conduct of the war crowded the usual feature and literary material from even the inside pages. Houser's policy of paying large sums of money for news-gathering was never more apparent than at this time. The paper did not share its war news-gathering facilities with other newspapers as had the *Democrat* during the Civil War, although Houser did buy a few copyrighted stories from the Press Publishing Company. At least two *Globe-Democrat* correspondents were in Cuba: Lon V. Chapin was reporting from San Pedro Harbor as early as March, 1897; and Jewel H. Aubere, who was later to replace Stevens as chief of the paper's Washington Bureau, remained most of the time in Key West, where he directed the transmission of the news to St. Louis.[35]

Cable tolls ran as high as a dollar and a half a word. Only once did Houser groan to King about the high cost. Then he said, "Try not to break us, King, but, of course, we've got to print the news."[36] The *Globe-Democrat's* new building could accommodate twenty or more telegraphers and their instruments;[37] from the amount of war news in the paper, it would seem that all were kept busy.

News about the Louisiana Purchase Centennial Exposition, the other big story of the King era, filled many columns in the St. Louis newspapers. From the time of its organization in June, 1901, until its closing in December, 1904, the *Globe-Democrat* printed the equivalent of 1,006 pages of news about the celebration. Of this, four hundred pages were printed during the period of the exposition itself. The coverage averaged five and one-half columns daily for the entire period.[38] These figures compared favorably with those of the *Republic*, 1,012 and 421 pages respectively, and slightly surpassed those for the *Post-Dispatch*,[39] 988 and 328 respectively. At one time, however, Houser and King complained that the publicity committee was giving the *Republic* more releases than the *Globe-Democrat*.[40]

A schedule of events was printed daily in a box on the front page. Special events were reported, and columns such as "The World's Fair as a Woman Sees It" and "Sights and Echoes of the Exposition" were daily features. Each day a prominent St. Louis woman served as official hostess, and her picture was printed on the society page. Outstanding events which the *Globe-Democrat* reported in detail included balloon races and a trip made by Megargel and Harrison in an eight and one-half horsepower automobile from New York City to St. Louis. They left New York on May 18, 1904, and arrived in St. Louis on July 1. During the exposition horse racing was featured daily at two tracks, the Union and the Fair Grounds. Races at both tracks were fully covered with advance stories as well as with reports on the results.[41]

The Fair attracted 428 conventions, all of which were reported in the paper. Among these were the Democratic National Convention, the meeting of the National Association for Education, and the World's Press Parliament. King, as chairman of the executive committee of the last group, took a leave-of-absence from his office. He lived on the World Fair Grounds in a suite in a Washington University dormitory and devoted his full time to making arrangements for the meeting. He gave the opening address before five thousand newspaper people from the United States and thirty-seven foreign countries.

Other members of the *Globe-Democrat* staff worked for the success of the exposition, too. Houser was director and vice-president of the Louisiana Exposition Company. As one of seven of the original committee to raise funds, he went several times to Washington to help secure Congressional approval for the celebration. Walter B. Stevens resigned as head of the Washington office to become publicity director for the exposition.[42] Stevens did not return to the paper; nor did W. A. Kelsoe, who had joined the *Globe-Democrat* in 1893 but had resigned to become an assistant to Stevens.[43]

At the turn of the century when newspapers were seeking readers, rather than readers seeking newspapers, the unmasking of graft and corruption in government was a common means of bidding for reader interest.[44] The *Post-Dispatch* increased its circulation by its exposé of the Folk scandals, so-called because Joseph Folk investigated and prosecuted the corrupt officials.[45] As long as Folk was engaged in investigating and prosecuting corrupt city and state officials, King praised him. He thought, however, that Folk should prove the sincerity of his campaign against corruption by denouncing the Democratic party. Later, when Folk was trying to get the nomination for governor on the Democratic ticket, King delighted in criticizing him. He reported with relish that Folk and his Democratic opponent nearly came to blows when they met. He also accused Folk of compromising on the ticket and platform and of accepting contributions from Democratic "Boss" Ed Butler, who had come under fire in the Folk investigations. King deplored the persistent search for corruption and insisted that the virtues of the city and state should be emphasized.[46]

But King himself had an eye for corruption on occasions. His insinuations about the members of the Missouri Supreme Court brought accusations of "mud-slinging" to the *Globe-Democrat*. His charges that the State Democratic administration was dishonestly dissipating school funds and squandering other public money caused Governor Dockey to address an open letter to the paper, in which he defended his administration and invited King to make an examination of the auditor's books. King ignored the letter.[47] Once, however, he arranged to visit City Hall after hours where he examined the auditor's books for several hours to see whether there was collusion in the granting of contracts. Later he complained editorially of the daily cost of sixty-six dollars for expenses of the Circuit Attorney's office in ferreting out frauds. For this, Circuit Court Judge Ryan and the Grand Jury publicly criticized the paper.[48]

Indeed certain charges of fraud led to the Sam Cook libel case, the most costly libel suit in the history of the paper. The libelous article was written by Donald C. Fitzmaurice, a *Republic* reporter who wrote political articles for King under the *nom de plume* of "The Old Politician." It was printed on February 12, 1905, at the time when Cook was president of the Central Missouri Trust Company in Jefferson City. Fitzmaurice charged that Cook, who had been Secretary of State for Missouri for four years, had sworn that he had contributed a sum of money to a campaign fund, when, in reality, it had been contributed by another man whose name Cook wanted to conceal. Cook was also charged with "selling out" legislation in advance in exchange for campaign contributions.

The case was first tried in November, 1905, at which time Cook was awarded actual damages of seventy-five thousand dollars and punitive damages for the same amount. The Globe-Democrat Printing Company appealed the case, and on March 31, 1910, the Supreme Court of Missouri reduced the actual damages to twenty-five thousand dollars and punitive damages of a like amount with interest. Cook actually received about fifty-five thousand dollars.[49]

In King, the *Globe-Democrat* once more had an editor who was active in Republican politics. He was not content to sit in the press section, as had McCullagh, to report or to foment political news. As his editorials show, King, like Brown, Hume, and Grosvenor, participated actively in the Republican party and was deeply concerned with promoting its policies. Nevertheless, he did not hesitate to criticize Republicans who, he thought, were not good for the party. He said, for instance, that C. I. Filley, McKee's old rival for political "boss" of the Republican party in Missouri, should realize that the clock had struck twelve "on his scheme to boss a party" and at the same time abuse it.[50] King was commenting on statements made in an interview with Filley printed in the *Post-Dispatch*, in which Filley had pointed out alleged danger signals in trusts. King's editorial caused Filley to refer to King as "Dan Houser's *Globe-Democrat* hired man," who was trying to boss the party.[51]

In presidential campaigns King markedly showed his Republicanism. He sometimes used more space to criticize Democratic nominees than he did to promote Republican candidates. William Jennings Bryan became a special target for his derisive editorials. He told his readers in 1900 that Bryan forgot all about New York "when he made his imperious fight for the silver plank in the Kansas City platform." Bryan could not repair the damages now "with his silver tongue."[52] In the 1904 campaign King pointed out that Bryan was more efficient than ever as a vote-loser. The editor noted that Bryan advocated more greenbacks when he was in Nebraska, but when he came to Missouri, he joined "the Bourbons for strict regularity."[53] Again, in 1912, King ridiculed: "In his Chicago speech, Colonel Bryan pleasantly referred to the time when he first began to run for the presidency. Seriously, will he kindly inform an indulgent public when he proposes to quit running?"[54]

On the other hand, when William Howard Taft visited St. Louis on October 6, King was among those greeting him. "The jubilant honk of the farmer's automobile," he wrote, was an "advance note" for Taft's victory.[55] Woodrow Wilson was always referred to as "Professor" in the Globe-Democrat. King wrote in 1912 that "Professor Wilson's party record and his own queer notions" were trailing the candidate on his tours. "The Democratic effort to find something remarkable in Professor Wilson" was progressively frantic. In contrast, President Taft and his old-fashioned supporters believed in only one kind of Republicanism —"the kind that had made the most of history in the past fifty years."[56]

Before the 1916 campaign King was dead. He had resigned his position on the Globe-Democrat three weeks before his death on March 15, 1915, only seven months before Houser's death. King had not been well for several years, but over protests, he had insisted on appearing regularly for duty. He had rather be sick at the Globe-Democrat office, he said, than well elsewhere.[57] His death brought to an end the last of the one-man editorships of the paper; the Globe-Democrat had become too big and too modern for one man to direct both its news and editorial policies.

King's contemporaries believed that he had made the Globe-

Democrat a great conservative force in American journalism at a time when "yellow journalism" was rampant. Always interested in young journalists, he delivered the first lecture in a series preparatory to the establishment of the School of Journalism at the University of Missouri. He was the first president of the Missouri Republican Editorial Association and was re-elected to this position annually.[58] Twice he might have been a United States senator, once by appointment in Kansas and once as a compromise candidate in the Niedringhaus-Kerens fight in Missouri, but twice he declined. As had McCullagh before him, King preferred the newspaper profession to a political career.[59] A newspaper editor, he believed, should not become an office-holder and thus sacrifice his influence with the public or limit his independence.[60]

Regrettably, King's vituperative editorials seemed to have little effect in improving the Republican party's political machine, nor did they conspicuously champion the causes of the common people. Yet his awareness that "the yellow particles flying around" were merely a passing phase of journalism, his conviction that his newspaper had an economic responsibility to St. Louis and the country, and his belief in the value of college training for journalists were laudable. His impact on the *Globe-Democrat* is indicated by the paper's remarkable prosperity under his editorship. Undoubtedly Captain King kept the *Globe-Democrat* a leading newspaper, while his executive ability and his writing won for him recognition as an outstanding editor.

Chapter XIV

New Faces, New Problems

WITH the deaths of Houser and King, new faces, new policies, and new problems appeared at the *Globe-Democrat*. Taking over as president of the Globe Printing Company was affable Charles H. McKee. Trained under McCullagh, he knew the St. Louis area, understood the newspaper business, and was fully cognizant of the managerial problems confronting a newspaper that had skyrocketed into a million dollar enterprise. He also knew rather well the personnel of the other highly competitive papers in St. Louis. As early as 1906 Joseph Pulitzer, who feared the *Globe-Democrat*, which he called the "Vampire," had suspected that when Charles McKee took over the reins of the paper he would entice O. K. Bovard from the *Post-Dispatch*.[1] Pulitzer was correct in his suspicion that McKee would raid his staff; however, it was a man other than Bovard who was chosen.

Another new face was E. Lansing Ray, who was promoted to the vice-presidency of the company. Ray was perhaps more ambitious and energetic than his cousin, Charles McKee. A somewhat slight, studious-looking person, he had abandoned plans to enter Princeton University, and before he was twenty he was hard at work in the business office at ten dollars a week. In 1904 he had been promoted to cashier and advertising manager.[2]

One of the first tasks of these new officers was to find a replacement for King. They moved Joseph J. McAuliffe from city editor to managing editor and Casper Yost from Sunday editor to director of the editorial page. They could have searched long without finding a better man than McAuliffe. When he had come to the *Globe-Democrat* in 1913, probably to be groomed for managing editor, he was thirty-six years old and had worked for the *Post-Dispatch* for sixteen years. There he had been trained under Charles Chapin, known as a "hard-boiled, cynical, sarcastic, driving editor." The work of the "cub" reporter in covering a murder-suicide story his first day and a train wreck that night had gained Chapin's respect, and in 1901, McAuliffe was sent to Jefferson City as political correspondent for the *Post-Dispatch*.[3]

His service at Jefferson City covered a period when corporation lobbying and political corruption were rampant. McAuliffe exposed the baking powder trust scandals and led the successful fight in 1905 for the repeal of the "race track bill," which resulted in curbing gambling on races.[4]

By the time McAuliffe joined the staff of the *Globe-Democrat* he was already recognized as an excellent political prognosticator. One day in 1908 he stood in the Planter's House Bar discussing the approaching presidential election with Al Kennedy, a cigar manufacturer. McAuliffe insisted that Taft would carry Missouri. Kennedy disagreed. "What'll you bet?" McAuliffe asked.

Kennedy puffed furiously on his cigar, and answered confidently, "A trip to Europe against all the money in your pocket."

McAuliffe pulled out his change—five dollars.

Later he called this his luckiest bet, 500-1.[5]

As managing editor of the *Globe-Democrat* he made elections a study, placing great confidence in the country correspondents of the paper. He said that they were the true prophets 90 per cent of the time. It was through them that he was able to forecast correctly the Wilson-Hughes election and Senator Reed's "comeback" in 1920. In fact, from 1910 to 1940, he forecast only two presidential elections inaccurately, and he guessed wrong on the Missouri governorship only once.[6]

In 1915 it was the lot of McAuliffe and Yost to put into effect the news and editorial policies of the new publishers. They were faced almost immediately with the problem of reporting World War I. Yost had a particularly difficult and touchy situation in commenting on the war. The early alliance of the *Democrat* with the German press in St. Louis had laid a foundation of friendliness toward the *Globe-Democrat* on the part of the large German population in the area. As late as 1916 the paper could boast of having the largest German-American constituency of any paper in the English language.[7] Neither the publishers nor the editors wished to alienate these subscribers. The new personalities at the *Globe-Democrat* were not the isolationists that King and Houser had been, yet like them, the publishers were aware of the social and economic ferment being brewed by the war in Europe. Only New York exceeded St. Louis in the number of women married to foreigners, and daughters of the same family often were married to men fighting in opposite armies. Furthermore, many Missourians, such as the Adolphus A. Busch family, had kept up social and cultural ties with their native lands by maintaining summer homes in Europe. Too, many Missourians of foreign birth had served in European conscript armies and were enrolled in reserve units. Many had returned to defend their homelands. War had become the foremost topic of conversation "in every foreign quarter of St. Louis, in the clubs, on the street corners, and in the homes."[8] In August, 1914, the *Globe-Democrat* had set up a Sunday War Bureau, staffed by fifteen telephone operators who gave the latest war news to St. Louisans. On one Sunday they handled 2,500 calls, which the paper estimated supplied information to 20,000 persons.[9]

King had viewed the war in terms of military strategy, not moral or philosophical issues. He believed it was a commercial war, and that all involved nations were culpable, but he suspected that the Allies would burden Germany with the entire responsibility in order to justify peace terms that would otherwise shock the world.[10]

King had been concerned especially with the economic interests which would suffer from the war. He pointed out that meat packing, cotton trade, shoe manufacturing, and other such industries depended on international markets. He correctly forecast a depression and widespread unemployment in the area.[11]

When Yost assumed management of the editorial page in March, 1915, the paper became more pro-Ally.[12] Yet the *Globe-Democrat*, with strong protests against competition between the government and private enterprise, led opposition to a merchant marine. Yost argued that a merchant marine would destroy traffic on the Mississippi.[13] The paper also continued its isolationism by objecting to the government's lending money to France and England and by condemning the "starvation" blockade of the Central Powers by the British. Yost said the United States would sacrifice its neutrality by lending money to the Entente Powers. He regarded Germany's announcement of unrestricted submarine warfare as "a reprisal in kind" against the British strangulation policy and believed that Germany would never fire on an American ship.[14]

It was not until the torpedoing of the British "Falaba" that the *Globe-Democrat* really began wavering in its attitude toward Germany. Yost called submarines "the assassins of naval warfare."[15] However, he insisted on a wait-and-see policy. "We do not want war," he wrote. "We have before us now, and have had for months, an illustration of the unparalleled horrors of war in this day and time. The United States is happily outside that maelstrom of murder. We will not be drawn into it if we can with honor avoid it."[16] Although within a week he was anticipating this possibility, he still clung to the idea of neutrality until the torpedoing of the "Sussex," an unarmed cross-channel steamer. Then he declared that the loss of American lives in the sinking of peaceful ships was intolerable and that "the government would be false to its trust if it did not take vigorous action when measures of diplomacy have been exhausted, as they seem to have been at this time."[17]

In contrast to the patriotic fervor of most papers, the *Globe-Democrat* deplored the Wilsonian concept that Americans should enter the war to serve humanity and to fight for justice. There was no cause for action, Yost said, beyond that of American interests and rights. "If we are compelled to fight, it will be for America, and America alone. Any other claim is hypocrisy, and weakening to our cause."[18] For this position, the *Republic* called the *Globe-Democrat* "a heathen newspaper."[19]

By this time preparedness had become the key to much activity in St. Louis and the theme of many editorials in the *Globe-Democrat*. The paper was glad to settle the score with Eastern newspapers which had been criticizing the indifference of

Missouri to preparedness. Missourians were neither excitable nor easily alarmed, Yost said, but when an emergency arose, they always had been the first to answer a call to arms. He pointed proudly to their record in the two most recent wars and boasted of the appointment of a Missourian, John J. Pershing, to command the Southern Military Department.[20] As one of the first Missouri papers to champion national preparedness,[21] the *Globe-Democrat* early insisted on building submarines rather than battleships. It approved the expansion of the air force and the addition of battle-cruisers and scout-cruisers to the navy. The paper also advocated universal military training as a necessity.[22]

Meanwhile, the 1916 presidential campaign had become an important issue in the *Globe-Democrat*. The paper gave no encouragement to the "draft Roosevelt" movement and exposed a plot on the part of Missouri Republican leaders to deliver the state to John W. Weeks and Charles W. Fairbanks.[23] It did not desert the Republican ranks, however, and campaigned for Charles Evans Hughes, even while apologizing for the content and style of his speeches.

In opposing Wilson the *Globe-Democrat* maintained that the President did not deserve much credit for keeping peace with Germany because the Reich had given ample evidence of its intention to avoid trouble with the United States, and too, countries much closer to Germany such as Norway and Denmark had managed to stay out of the conflict. Yost called Wilson's course in Mexico "wobbly," and declared that Wilsonian prosperity was based almost exclusively on exports of war munitions. He termed the eight-hour work day, which a "frightened" Wilson had urged, the "most pusillanimous act in the history of American Congress."[24] Although the *Globe-Democrat* from the first had supported Wilson's plan for enforced submission of international disputes to arbitration, Yost doubted the wisdom "of entangling plans for insuring peace with the complicated problems" of the war, as the President had suggested in his League of Nations speech to Congress. It would be better first to secure universal approval of submitting disputes to arbitration and leave war issues to be worked out later.[25]

It was not until Germany announced that it would resume unlimited submarine warfare that the *Globe-Democrat* was convinced that friendly relations with Germany were improbable. But it agreed with the *Post-Dispatch* that only a "limited liability" war would be necessary. The participation of the United States should be confined to sweeping sea lanes of submarines and to convoying merchant ships. This country, Yost said, should dissociate itself from the territorial ambitions of the Entente Powers.[26] The publication of the Zimmerman note which proposed a German alliance with Mexico completely converted the *Globe-Democrat*. Thereafter, the paper abandoned any vestige of desire for neutrality and declared that when Congress convened on April 2 it should declare war.[27] From then on Yost voiced unswerving loyalty to President Wilson. He successfully suspended partisan politics and devoted his editorials largely to the patriotic necessities of winning the war.[28]

To McAuliffe fell the problem of news coverage of the war. From July 25, 1914, when the *Globe-Democrat* printed numerous stories from European capitals which told of Russia's supporting Serbia and Germany's supporting Austria-Hungary, the European war was headlined on the front page. With the torpedoing of the "Lusitania" in May, 1915, McAuliffe began using banner headlines, a make-up practice which became common thereafter.

War news soon dwarfed all other reports. Even the few society items reflected the war. On May 27, 1917, a society writer noted that women did not have the heart for the usual gaieties in the face of the present conditions. Everywhere—in the clubs, on the verandas and lawns—little groups of women were doing their bit by knitting or sewing for the soldiers or sailors.

The *Globe-Democrat* not only used war reports of the Associated Press and other agencies but also had a corps of its own "specials" in the field and a New York office to coordinate the news-gathering.[29] Chief among the *Globe-Democrat* correspondents at the front was George W. Seldes, who sent long stories telling about what American fighters did between battles, how Americans treated German prisoners, and what American aviators were doing. Other correspondents for the paper included Major J. C. Street, Clair Price, Teddy Wick, Alured F. Ozanne, Captain R. F. Rees, Lieutenant J. B. Morton, John Loyd Balderston, Hayden Church, and a woman, Eleanor Heitkamp. Don Martin and Percival Phillips reported the war for both the *Globe-Democrat* and the *New York Herald*. A column signed "Lady Mary" began on October 10, 1918, telling about St. Louis people in England.

In addition, E. Lansing Ray was one of the publishers invited by England to tour the American-British fronts in the fall of 1918. On a troop ship in a convoy menaced by storms, submarines, and influenza, he traveled with eleven other publishers, including C. A. Rook of the *Pittsburgh Dispatch*, E. B. Piper of the *Portland Oregonian*, Robert W. Patterson of the *Chicago Tribune*, and Frank R. Kent of the *Baltimore Sun*. In London, the group sent a telegram to President Wilson protesting the overcrowded conditions of their ship. On the previous crossing the crew had been ill with influenza, and since only part of a new crew was obtained, soldiers had to assist in all classes of work. The ship had not even been fumigated.[30]

The publishers agreed to send, from time to time, telegrams which they were all to write, but which were to be sent in Ray's name. They were to be cabled to the *New York Herald* and then relayed to the various newspapers.[31] The first of these was published in the *Globe-Democrat* on October 13, 1918, under E. Lansing Ray's by-line. In reality, this particular story, which told of the British seeking American good will, was written by E. B. Piper.[32]

While the group was in London the *London Daily Mail* asked each publisher to write a twenty-five word opinion of President Wilson's reply to Germany's request for surrender terms. Ray wrote: "President Wilson has indicated plainly that America insists on full reparation and ample assurance, for the future. Germany must 'come clean.' Temporizing is *verboten*."[33] Ray discovered that Wilson was "strong" in England and France, where most people believed that the President held the "key to the situation." Wilson, the publisher believed, would have a "wonderful opportunity not only for himself but for America."

For more than a year the *Globe-Democrat* published a miniature paper twice a month for the men in service. A four-page paper, six by nine inches, with three columns to the page, it was called "Special Soldiers, Sailors, and Marine Edition." The editors claimed it was the first of its kind "in all the world" and soon other metropolitan journals adopted this practice of printing miniature papers for distribution to service men. Through publicity in the *Globe-Democrat*, parents in the St. Louis area were invited to get all the free copies they wanted. Thousands were enclosed in letters to service men overseas.[34]

The *Globe-Democrat* did not make the mistake of many papers, including the *St. Louis Star* and the *St. Louis Times*, of printing on Thursday, November 7, the false story of the signing of the armistice. Instead, in its "extra final" edition it reported that Berlin "was said" to have accepted the terms of the armistice. The *Post-Dispatch* reported that the armistice was not signed. In a full-page advertisement in the *Globe-Democrat* on November 9, the *Post-Dispatch* pointed out these facts and labeled November 8 as "Sad Friday." Because of the premature celebration as the result of the stories in the *Star* and the *Times*, the advertisement stated, the influenza epidemic had increased and the mayor and health authorities had closed all retail stores and theaters for four days.

Shortly after Ray returned from his trip to Europe, Charles McKee died. At this time Ray became trustee of the fund set up under the provisions of Miss McKee's will. As trustee he had control of the major shares of the Globe-Democrat Printing Company and in December, 1918, was named president of the company. Douglas B. Houser was elected vice-president and William C. Houser, secretary and treasurer.

Douglas Houser, who was educated at Yale University, had started on the *Globe-Democrat* as a "cub" reporter four years earlier. After his father's death he had joined the paper's staff in Washington as an assistant correspondent. But he did not like reporting and returned to St. Louis in the fall of 1916 to work in the bookkeeping department. Here he learned who the paper's advertisers were and later, as supervisor of advertising, brought many new accounts to the *Globe-Democrat*.[35]

William Houser was a graduate of Western Military Academy at Alton, Illinois, and of the University of Missouri. He had started working in the classified advertising department in 1911 and had only recently returned to St. Louis from his service in the Army when he was named to his new position.[36]

Hardly had St. Louis returned to normalcy after the war when the city was shocked at a major development in its newspaper world. That "Black Republican" *Globe-Democrat* had bought and absorbed the Democratic *Republic*. "Old 1808" breathed its last on December 12, 1919.

Its death was inevitable. In its last year the *Republic* had lost half of its circulation. A mere 30,000 mail subscribers remained on its books. Even the *Star* and the *Times* had surpassed it.[37] The Knapp journal had lost further prestige with the Democratic party in the 1916 election, when it had sold space to the Republican National Committee.[38] The paper was at least $700,000 in debt. David R. Francis, who had been Ambassador to Russia, returned to St. Louis in 1916 and claimed that the *Republic* owed him $800,000. It was losing money at such a rate, he said, that if he had kept on advancing money to it, he would soon be "broken." He was willing to give up all of his stock if someone would pay the debts of the paper.[39]

Negotiations for the sale took about three weeks. The purchase price, though not announced, was $733,812.74, and the sale included everything but the building.[40] Thus came the end of one of the longest and most vituperative rivalries in the history of American journalism.

Ray pointed out that the purchase was an absorption, not a merger. To his department heads, he wrote:

> Today marks a distinct turning point in the *Globe-Democrat's* career. It has been built upon fair and constructive lines until it is an immense power for good in the community. The purchase of the *Republic* adds to the *Globe-Democrat's* strength and, consequently, to its value to the community. It will be the sincere purpose of the ex-

ecutives to continue the same course of constructive policy as in the past.[41]

It was rumored that a new morning paper would be started in St. Louis. There was persistent talk of William Randolph Hearst's starting such a paper.[42] As the *Democrat-Tribune* in Jefferson City pointed out, "The *Republic* was not a strong paper, yet it was a metropolitan daily allied to the Democratic Party," and it was not likely that St. Louis would remain long with only one morning paper.[43]

But the *Globe-Democrat* remained the only morning paper in St. Louis. Possibly one of the reasons that another morning paper was not started by the Democratic party leaders was Ray's change of editorial policy. Desirous of retaining Democratic readers as subscribers, Ray had already made the *Globe-Democrat* "less opinionated" as a Republican paper, and he changed it even more now. Ray assured his readers on December 12 that the paper would continue as "an independent Republican newspaper, basing its editorial policy upon what it believed to be right and printing the news accurately and fairly without fear or favor."

Even the word "Republican" soon was dropped from the publisher's announced policy, however. Ray called upon Yost to frame the following declaration:

> The *Globe-Democrat* is an independent newspaper, printing the news impartially, supporting what it believes to be right and opposing what it believes to be wrong, without regard to party politics. On the other hand, we try to be considerate in all things and charitable in many, particularly in regard to the human element.[44]

The first sentence of this statement began appearing on the paper's masthead on May 24, 1922.

After the absorption of the *Republic* the *Globe-Democrat* claimed its daily circulation had increased to well over 200,000, far above that of the *Post-Dispatch*, with its 160,043.[45] Thus with McAuliffe and Yost to direct the news and editorials and with the Housers to handle the advertising and finances, Ray could look forward with anticipation to the "flush twenties."

Chapter XV

The "Flush Twenties"

A N OLD paper with new ideals in an old city with new ideas—that was the *Globe-Democrat* in that fitful decade that followed World War I. If McKee or Houser or McCullagh could have seen St. Louis or read their paper then, what they would have seen!

Liberation from wartime controls on food and fuel and from regulations of private businesses brought on a period of optimistic expansion in St. Louis. The population was rising steadily past the three-quarter-million mark. Skyscrapers were climbing up and up in the business district, which within a few years would stretch from Fourth Street as far west as Fourteenth and extend between Market Street and Delmar Boulevard (once called Morgan Street). Commercial hotels, theaters, clubs, office buildings, restaurants, and drug stores with fountains for dispensing soft drinks, sandwiches, and ice cream seemed to spring up almost overnight. Surrounding this area, wholesale and jobbing houses and factories for the production of shoes, machinery, garments, drugs and medicine kept creeping into the former residential areas. Residences were pushing farther and farther into the hills west of the city. With the average construction cost for dwellings about three thousand dollars, more and more families were becoming home owners. It was not until 1929 that building began to slow because of tight money.[1]

In 1923 the city voted an $87,372,500 bond issue to finance public improvements. Soon a remarkable civic center began to take shape in a square bounded by Market, Olive, Twelfth, and Fifteenth streets. Here work progressed steadily on a six-million-dollar Memorial Plaza and a five-million-dollar municipal auditorium. The city enlarged its waterworks and purchased new garbage-disposal equipment.

St. Louis became one of the "wet spots" on the Mississippi after national prohibition went into effect in January, 1920. Brewing, a major industry of the city, came almost to a standstill; and the Germans, who resented the new law as an intrusion on their personal rights, suffered economically the most. But the people of St. Louis discovered speak-easies and bootleggers and learned how to make "home-brew." The college crowd and the wealthier people carried silver hip flasks.

Natural gas became the new fuel, and electricity was taking over in the homes. Housewives learned about installment buying, and St. Louis homes were being equipped with radios, electric refrigerators, washing machines, and phonographs. Automobiles were crowding horse-drawn vehicles off the streets. Narrow streets were widened, and graveled roads were paved with concrete. Another bridge now crossed the river. Motor busses were competing with street cars for city transportation, and out in the residential districts immense carriage houses were converted into garages.

Pleasure-loving people of St. Louis flocked downtown to ornate, gaudy theaters to see such movies as "The Iron Horse," "The Covered Wagon," "The Sheik," and "When Old New York Was Young." When "talkies" arrived, Al Jolson became a favorite of movie-goers. Grand opera came to the municipal auditorium, and the St. Louis Symphony played to full houses. In the summer thousands of families roamed through the fabulous zoo in Forest Park. The wealthy traveled to Europe.

Women emerged from the confinement of corsets and long skirts. They wore their dresses to their knees, bobbed their hair, wore silk stockings, and learned to use cosmetics. The young ladies, called "flappers," smoked cigarettes in the open, and with the young men talked in a breezy slang, danced the Charleston to the popular jazz, and "petted" in cars. The older people of St. Louis shook their heads at the changing order of life in the city.

Over the city also swept one of the biggest crime waves in its

202   ST. LOUIS GLOBE-DEMOCRAT

history. Each year it had more robberies than all of Great Britain.[2] Jewelry stores, banks, and restaurants became the targets of gangsters who would hit and escape in high-powered cars. The St. Louis police were overworked by hundreds of cases of thefts, frauds, forgeries, swindling, and the activities of racketeers. The disease-ridden slums and tenements of the city only helped foster crime.

Immediately following the war St. Louis suffered from frequent violent strikes in the coal, steel, railroad, and textile industries. Unemployment rose, and there was much talk of high cost of living and the Bolshevistic influence on labor. Business seemed at first to stand still. But business men banded together to seek foreign trade markets and to fight for direct air mail routes to the East Coast. Then came the building era of the mid-twenties, and unemployment dropped, not to become a municipal problem again until 1929.

Almost all business prospered in these flush times, and the *Globe-Democrat* was no exception. In a way, the absorption of the *Republic* marked the beginning of a new era for the *Globe-Democrat*. E. Lansing Ray, the youngest publisher of a metropolitan daily in the United States,[3] had proved already his capabilities as a leader. Now the way was clear for him to introduce changes. First, however, he wanted to be sure that the paper would remain in his family—a heritage that he could hand down to his son. It was then, in 1919, only six years until the termination of the McKee trust fund, when the controlling shares of the company could be sold at the discretion of the president of the company and the publisher of the paper. As Ray was serving in both capacities, he was in good position to negotiate for their purchase. Operating on a shoestring, and with the support of the Housers, the young publisher by 1925 had paid $1,305,000 for the shares belonging to over fifty heirs.[4]

In the meantime the stockholders had changed the name of the organization to the Globe-Democrat Publishing Company and increased the capital stock to $1,000,000. This was accomplished by transferring to the capital account $500,000 from the $1,245,-269 of surplus funds and declaring a hundred per cent stock

dividend. Thus in 1922, Ray, as owner and trustee, controlled
600 of the company's 1,000 common shares. Soon afterward the
stockholders also issued 10,000 shares of preferred stock with a
par value of $100 and increased the number of common shares
to 10,000, dropping their par value from $1,000 to $100. These
actions gave the company a paid-up capital of $2,000,000 and
assisted Ray in his purchase of stock from the heirs of the McKee
estate.[5]

With these financial arrangements out of the way, Ray could
now devote himself to the editorial development of his paper.
As he explained to his staff on several occasions, he did not approve of the paper "dictating or lecturing" on every controversial issue. He wanted the *Globe-Democrat* to present factual
news accounts and interesting, valuable editorial comment that
would allow readers to make up their own minds.[6]

In this Ray was supported by Yost, who was serving as the
first president of the American Society of Newspaper Editors,
an organization he had recently founded which was devoted to
improving the professional ethics of journalism. Ray and Yost,
both somewhat idealistic, believed that newspapers were obli-
gated to serve society; that journalists had responsibilities to the
Constitution of the United States as great as, if not greater than,
those of lawyers; and that it was the solemn duty of journalism
to maintain the freedom of the press.[7]

Yost might easily have been describing the *Globe-Democrat*
when he wrote in 1924:

> [The newspaper] presents a continuous, never-ending
> moving picture of the world and its occurrences, of man-
> kind and its conduct, depicting comedy, tragedy, vice, vir-
> tue, heroism, devotion, enterprise, discovery, calamity, be-
> neficence, sorrow and joy—human life in all its kaleidoscopic
> and inexplicable changes. And accompanying all this, edi-
> torial comment upon the news, interpreting the meaning of
> events, associating views with information, opinions with
> fact, and thereby aiding the reader to a better understand-
> ing and to an opinion of his own which becomes an element
> in the creation of public opinion, that "sovereign mistress of
> effects" which rules the modern world.[8]

In general the political stand of the *Globe-Democrat* in the twenties was Republican. It regularly supported the Republican presidential candidate, but its editorial pages were conspicuous for their lack of comment on presidential candidates, perhaps in deference to readers acquired through the absorption of the Democratic *Republic*. Only occasionally did Yost speak out. In 1920 he campaigned against the League of Nations because he objected to Article Ten, which called for each member of the League to protect all other members from external aggression and to defend their existing political independence. This article, Yost believed, would lead the United States into war.[9] And in 1924 he told railroad workers that they were "foolish" to support Robert La Follette, presidential candidate of the National Progressive party.[10] But his conservative, dignified editorials were neither bitter nor recriminatory.

Although it could hardly be called a crusading paper, the *Globe-Democrat* did conduct lively campaigns. One of the most spirited was against the soot that hung like a pall over the city. Yost labeled the inadequate city ordinance for diluting the fog "Old Smother" and criticized the Smoke Prevention Bureau of the City Council because chemicals used to dilute the fog resulted in "smarting eyes and sore throats."[11] In 1923, the paper fought for the passage of a city bond issue of $87,372,500, and it was the *Globe-Democrat* that raised $51,864 to over-subscribe the St. Louis Community Fund Drive when it was in danger of failing in 1930. Of special note also were Yost's Christmas and Easter editorials. Printed in a box on the front page, they became a tradition of the paper.

Since the days of the old *Democrat* the paper had fought vigorously for better transportation—improved harbors, good bridges, more railways, better streets and roads. Now it took up the fight for better air service. Yost pressed for regular airmail routes to Chicago and New Orleans and commended the St. Louis Chamber of Commerce for employing an air site expert to survey the city for the best location of a modern airport. He rejoiced when a transcontinental air transport office was set up in St. Louis, which he believed was a sign of great things to come.[12]

In fact it was this interest of the *Globe-Democrat* in promoting aviation that in 1927 rocketed the paper and its publisher into international prominence. In St. Louis in the twenties, a tall, thin, red-headed young man was flying mail to Chicago in an old army warplane and dreaming of flying the Atlantic Ocean alone in a single-engine plane to prove that trans-oceanic air transportation was feasible.

But young Charles A. Lindbergh needed financial aid, and Major Bill Robertson, who was the young flyer's employer, suggested that he ask the *Post-Dispatch* to put up enough money to pay for the whole venture. No, said the editor, when Lindbergh went to see him, the *Post-Dispatch* would not think of taking part in such a hazardous flight. "To fly across the Atlantic Ocean with one pilot and a single-engine plane! We have our reputation to consider. We couldn't possibly be associated with such a venture."[13] "Slim" Lindbergh was not discouraged, though, and Harold H. Bixby, a banker who was interested in aviation and who owned the most modern plane in St. Louis, took over the financing for what was to become the Spirit of St. Louis organization. He raised $15,000 for the venture, Ray giving $2,000 of that amount.

When or how the banker solicited Ray's aid is not known. Later, the *Globe-Democrat's* managing editor McAuliffe was said to have suggested the plane's name.[14] Lindbergh, however, did not learn that Ray was one of the eight St. Louis business men who were helping to finance his flight until he flew into St. Louis on May 11 on his record-breaking, non-stop, fourteen-hours-and-twenty-five-minutes flight from San Diego, where the plane had been built. While the flyer sat drinking coffee with Bixby in the little cafe at Lambert Field, the banker told him that E. Lansing Ray, who ran the *Globe-Democrat*, had joined the backers. Only a few friends, a half dozen pilots and mechanics, and several St. Louis reporters had been there to greet the man who in a few days was to make aviation history. The *Globe-Democrat* did not even send a photographer.

It was not until Lindbergh landed in New York and the news-papers there started "big play" handling of the story that the *Globe-Democrat* began using banner headlines to tell St. Louis about Lindbergh. And it was not until May 20, the day before the flyer took off for Paris, that the city learned that Ray and the *Globe-Democrat* were financial backers.

Meanwhile, in New York, reporters and photographers mobbed the young flyer. A tabloid editor wanted to buy the ex-clusive rights to the flight story for several thousand dollars. Lindbergh thought that if there was to be an exclusive story "my partner, E. Lansing Ray, should have first right to it for his *Globe-Democrat*, but we could sell the rights outside of St. Louis to someone else." He told the editor that he would telephone Bixby and ask for his advice on the matter.[15] Whether he did or what the advice was is not known, but in the end the *Globe-Democrat* published Lindbergh's story exclusively in the St. Louis area, and the *New York Times* bought rights to its publi-cation elsewhere.[16] The *Globe-Democrat*, Yost wrote on May 21, was glad to have been a part of the great adventure.

In the twenties people of St. Louis donned their raccoon coats in the fall months and flocked to football games and in the summer rode the street cars or drove their Model T Fords to baseball games. This interest in sports was reflected in the expan-sion of the sports pages in the *Globe-Democrat*. By 1929 educa-tors were deploring the emphasis on football in college. The paper believed in the value of college athletics and defended its position by conducting an investigation which revealed that most schools employed recruitment plans and that American students needed financial aid.[17]

On September 23, 1926, the St. Louis Cardinals won the National League pennant, and St. Louis was a "bedlam of re-joicing." Nothing like it had been seen since the "hysteria of Armistice Day." The first two games of the ensuing World Series were played in New York against the Yankees. When the two teams came to St. Louis, the pages of the *Globe-Democrat* helped whip the excitement of baseball fans to a fever pitch with full pages of action pictures, screaming banner headlines, and so much baseball copy that even the story of the parade of the Veiled Prophet was crowded into four inches.[18] The paper boasted of its "sports extra," which was issued eight minutes after the Cardinals won the Series. In the city-wide celebration that followed, four people were injured and one man was killed.

On the night of September 29, 1927, a tornado ripped through St. Louis. Six square miles were devastated, 74 people were killed, and 671 were injured. Losses were said to have exceeded ten million dollars. The staff of the *Globe-Democrat* went into production, and a "storm extra" hit the streets early the next morning with scores of pictures from two to six columns wide, detailed accounts of the catastrophe, and stories of heroism in the rescue work that followed in the wake of the storm. For two weeks the paper continued to print additional reports of the storm damage and backed a campaign for relief to the victims.

In those days when there were only unsatisfactory crystal radio sets in a few homes, thousands of St. Louis people seemed to think that they could not exist without their morning *Globe-Democrat* from which they could learn the latest news about the rum-running gangsters or Hollywood scandal. The popularity of the paper soared. Ray emphasized accurate and wide news coverage. The *Globe-Democrat* not only used the facilities of the Associated Press, the *New York Times* news service, the *Chicago Tribune* news service, and the North American Alliance features, but it also had correspondents in Jefferson City, Washington, D.C., and New York; special writers in foreign countries; and "contacts" throughout an area which embraced all of Missouri and parts of Illinois, Kentucky, Indiana, Tennessee, and Arkansas.[19]

It was not long before the publisher's news and editorial changes were helping to increase circulation. In 1929 the combined daily and Sunday circulation passed the half-million mark and brought in $1,472,800.[20]

To increase the efficiency of his company Ray made other changes. First, in 1927, he suspended publication of the *Weekly Globe-Democrat*, although in 1925 it had a circulation of 245,157.[21] But transportation facilities had improved so much that the daily could now serve the areas which once had depended mostly on a weekly. Then at the beginning of the period, when prices of newsprint were increased and wages for pressmen were raised, Ray boosted the prices of his papers, the daily to three cents an issue, and the Sunday paper to ten cents. By 1930 the daily was again selling for two cents and the Sunday for five cents.

When Douglas Houser started working in the advertising department in 1916, only four or five salesmen were employed.[22] But with the "flush" times of the twenties the number of salesmen was increased, and advertising alone became a million-dollar business. In 1929 this source of income brought the Globe-Democrat Publishing Company $4,612,196, or 75 per cent of its total income.[23] Department stores, particularly Stix, Baer, and Fuller, remained the big advertisers of the period; running a close second were the large, national manufacturers of automobiles, cigarettes, and toilet soaps, whose products were endorsed by prominent movie and stage personalities.

So taxed were the *Globe-Democrat* facilities by the increased circulation that in 1929 Ray started plans for a new building. For two years, members of the Globe-Democrat Publishing Company visited big newspaper plants in the country, and the best features of these were included ultimately in the blueprints. Regardless of the financial crash that year, the company decided to proceed with its building plans "to demonstrate its faith in the community." Accordingly, ground for the new building at 1133 Franklin Avenue was broken on March 12, 1930.

The structure, a six-story building with two basements, was and is considered ideal for the distribution of papers, and is convenient for receiving and storing newsprint and other supplies because railroad cars can be shunted directly into the basement.[24] Located on the first floor, the pressroom had huge windows which enabled passersby to watch the papers being printed. Here were installed two rows of huge Duplex Super Duty black-and-white presses. One row contained sixteen units and four folders; the other had five units and one folder. There was also a Goss eight-cylinder multicolor press for printing the comics and magazine sections of the paper.

The sub-basement contained, besides electrical equipment, ice machines, and air conditioning units for the pressroom, two tanks capable of storing 5,220 gallons of ink each and space for storing 7,000 tons of newsprint. The need for this large storage was evident because, in 1930, the firm was consuming 24,000 tons of paper and 585,000 pounds of ink annually.[25]

For two weeks after the move into the new building, which took five days in November, 1931, the columns of the *Globe-Democrat* were filled with congratulatory messages. Among the prominent people who sent congratulations were President Herbert Hoover, William Randolph Hearst, Adolph S. Ochs, Joseph Pulitzer, Charles A. Lindbergh, Jim Londos (world's wrestling champion), Charles G. Peterson (world's billiard champion), senators, business men, publishers, mayors, and other well-wishers.[26]

Thus at the beginning of the depression, the *Globe-Democrat*, then eighty years old, was ready to face the problems of the depression and World War II from a new building.

Chapter XVI

The Depression Years

IN COMMON with all newspapers of the nineteen thirties, the *Globe-Democrat* suffered from the economic depression. No sooner had the paper moved into its new building than falling circulations and a decreasing advertising income began lowering the profits of the Globe-Democrat Publishing Company. The circulation of the Sunday paper dropped in 1933 to a low of 185,934, a loss of 72,065 from its circulation in the peak year of 1929. The biggest slump came in 1935, when the circulation of the daily dropped to 211,906, a loss of 66,227 from 1929.[1]

Every effort was made to keep circulations up. In 1932 the *Globe-Democrat* appeared in a new type which was so much easier on the eyes of readers that the paper was flooded with letters of praise from physicians and educators.[2] Other innovations designed to draw readers included the addition of the Associated Press telephoto service and the expansion of the women's pages. On May 1, 1934, the *Globe-Democrat* began printing a page or more of telephoto pictures daily, and on the women's pages appeared a column on marriage problems, fashion and beauty features, and additional information on food and menus. One must assume, too, that such public service projects as the sponsorship of the annual Golden Gloves boxing matches and the annual Soap Box Derby, both initiated in 1936, were mainly designed to promote the paper.

In spite of these projects, however, in 1937, the year of a new high in aggregate newspaper circulations the country over, the daily circulation of the *Globe-Democrat* had climbed to only 213,705 and the Sunday paper to only 215,316.[3] Still, these circulation figures compared favorably with the figures of the paper's two St. Louis competitors, the *Post-Dispatch* and the *Star-Times*.

In daily circulation the *Globe-Democrat* and the *Post-Dispatch* were fairly even. In 1935, for example, the *Post-Dispatch* surpassed the *Globe-Democrat* by only a few thousand; five years later this trend was reversed and the *Globe-Democrat* was leading by a few thousand.⁴ The Sunday *Post-Dispatch* proved a more formidable opponent, however; its circulation during the thirties always surpassed that of the Sunday *Globe-Democrat* by more than 50,000. The *Star-Times*, which did not publish a Sunday issue, was a less serious contender for area readership. Its daily circulation reached a peak in 1940 with only 158,907.⁵

The income from advertising of the *Globe-Democrat* during the depression years, however, did not rebound as did that of other St. Louis newspapers. As early as 1926 the percentage of the total income of the *Globe-Democrat* derived from advertising had begun a steady decline. In that year advertising accounted for 78 per cent of the total income. By 1940 advertising income had plummeted to only 54 per cent, and the total revenue had dropped more than a million dollars.⁶ Although the biggest display advertisers during this ten year period remained department stores, and automobile and cigarette manufacturers, such advertisements were reduced in number and size. There was also much less classified advertising.

Production costs mounted in spite of attempts at retrenchments. The reportorial staff was reduced. More and more the *Globe-Democrat* used national and international news services rather than its own staff members. Publisher Ray even used the *New York Times* news service for Washington events, though stories from the paper's own New York Bureau appeared until late 1940. Yet increased salaries and shorter working hours required by the National Labor Relations Board kept raising production costs.⁷ In 1937 reportorial and editorial wages alone reached $312,625 and by 1940 had climbed to $330,192, while salaries and wages for mechanical workers reached $813,881. Net profits dropped from $320,506 in 1932 to $177,723 in 1940, and were to go even lower.⁸

Thus in the thirties Publisher Ray found it necessary to alter his news policies. The *Globe-Democrat*, with its reportorial staff

cut in the large news centers of the country, began adapting
itself more specifically to its readership area. Not so much emphasis was placed on sensational sex and crime stories. As a conservative publisher and a scrupulously high-minded gentleman,
Ray steered clear of "big play" coverage of such events.[9] Aside
from the events leading to World War II and the reports of the
industrial and economic depression, the big stories in the paper
during this period included the kidnapping and murder of the
Lindbergh baby in 1932, the California earthquake in 1934, the
Ohio and Mississippi river floods in 1935, the disappearance of
Amelia Earhart in a plane over the Pacific Ocean in 1937, and
"Wrong-Way" Corrigan's flight across the Atlantic Ocean in
1938. Perhaps the leading tragic events in St. Louis were the
dramatic death of an eight-year-old boy, Raymond Breden-
poeller, who was killed when the wall of a cave he was digging
crumbled and buried him alive, and the sleeping sickness epidemic
in 1933 which caused the deaths of 194 people and sent 1,042
to hospitals.[10]

    In its national political outlook the *Globe-Democrat* turned
from its mild bipartisanism in the early thirties to staunch Republicanism. Editor Yost criticized many of Roosevelt's New Deal
policies, but he supported the President's foreign policies, particularly the repeal of the embargo law, the passage of the lend-
lease bill, and all-out aid to Britain.[11]

    One of the biggest problems of the depression years was un-
employment. Bread lines lengthened in St. Louis, but to the
Globe-Democrat this was a local, not a federal problem. To im-
plement this position the paper sponsored a wrestling match for
the benefit of the unemployed in the St. Louis area, and its sports
editor suggested a Cardinal-Brown baseball game for the same
benefit. These two events raised $62,529.[12] The paper also sup-
ported a $4,600,000 bond issue in November, 1932, to relieve
the suffering among the "unemployed and otherwise unfortunate
of St. Louis."[13]

    But in the months that followed the *Globe-Democrat* vacil-
lated in its stand toward relief measures. In 1933 it rejected as
unsound and not needed a city proposal for a $5,000,000 bond

issue to widen city streets, a project which would have provided jobs for many.[14] Yet the next year it advocated the passage of a $16,300,000 city bond issue to build hospitals, sewers, streets, and parks, because this construction would provide employment.[15] The paper also wavered in its attitude toward Roosevelt's request for $4,880,000,000 for direct relief and for financing construction enterprises to provide work that would take 3,500,000 people off relief rolls. It recognized that in not paying relief workers what private industry was paying, the administration was trying to eliminate competition between private enterprise and the government. But "We are not at all sure," Yost wrote, "that the work relief plan is better than direct relief."[16]

Nevertheless, the *Globe-Democrat* commended the city fathers of St. Louis for acting promptly to bring a public works program to St. Louis. Never had there been such an opportunity for improvements at such small cost to the city. At the same time, Yost was advocating the taking of a census of the unemployed, one which would omit the names of people who would never work again.[17] These people he called a "new class of mendicants." Later he referred to the projects of the Works Progress Administration as useless and to the people employed on these projects as "reliefers." The paper admitted that the distresses of the depression had been too great for communities to cope with unaided, but it believed that a community knew better than any government agency who was actually in need; the unemployment problem should be returned now to the states and communities because there "must be a cutting-down on relief."[18]

The *Globe-Democrat*, never especially noted as a spokesman for farmers, opposed the New Deal's two-year moratorium on farm loans. The measure, Yost wrote, was fundamentally unsound, detrimental to the permanent interests of borrowers as well as lenders, and was designed, along with other clauses of the farm act, to restore agricultural prices to the 1910-11 level. But as prices were near this point, it was unnecessary to force acreage reductions on farmers.[19]

The paper's Republican leaning, not very apparent in 1932, grew pronounced and progressively bitter by 1940. This change was particularly evident in the presidential campaigns. In 1932 news coverage was nonpartisan, with equal space being given to both parties. Only the campaign speeches in St. Louis were covered by *Globe-Democrat* writers; Roosevelt spoke there October 31 and Hoover, November 4. Crowds at each of these events were estimated at twelve thousand. The paper never came out openly for either candidate, and editorially Yost criticized both of them. He believed the Reconstruction Finance Corporation, created in the Hoover administration to grant loans to agriculture, commerce, and industry, and to stem the tide of destruction in the banking system of the country, had been successful, and he denied that it had been created to benefit big city bankers. Nonetheless, he criticized Hoover for not revealing the exact date when he discovered that, unless a remedy was put into effect immediately, the country would have to go off the gold standard within two weeks. He praised both political parties for their handling of the situation.[20]

Hoover's difficulty, Yost wrote, in his typically long sentences, stemmed from "having to struggle with world-wide economic conditions of unprecedented complexity, with adverse economic forces of unprecedented sweep and power, bewildering in their causes, movement, and effects," and having to battle against them with instruments that were "unfamiliar and largely incomprehensible to the common understanding."[21] The closest the editor came to saying that he favored Hoover was in an editorial about Calvin Coolidge's attack on the Democratic leadership. The former President's speech unfortunately came too late to change public opinion, Yost said.[22]

Criticism of Roosevelt was also mild. The Democratic candidate, Yost told his readers, exaggerated conditions of the country. He was too vague about the bonus problem. He should have said "no" outright instead of merely stating that he did not see how a country in debt twelve million dollars could pay a bonus.[23] But the editor agreed with Roosevelt's ideas on tariff reciprocity. What the country and the world needed was a "gradual lessening and readjustment of trade restriction and the opening up of international commerce to larger opportunities of exchange."[24]

After Roosevelt's election, Yost wrote: "We do not share in the feeling expressed in some quarters, that the triumph of the Democratic party imperils the welfare of the nation or the permanency of its institutions."[25] After all, there was not much difference between the two parties. The *Globe-Democrat* found much that was reassuring in the new President's inaugural address, and urged its readers to support Roosevelt. "We would certainly give support to the President in case of war, and it is not less necessary in the situation which now confronts us. We must trust him, and we must help him."[26]

Moreover, for nearly a year the *Globe-Democrat* did support the New Deal policies of Roosevelt. Roosevelt, Yost said, acted with commendable promptness in dealing so quickly and promptly with the banking crisis. He was not apprehensive over giving the President too much power because the country was in a situation comparable to that of war. To be sure, the paper warned that the provisions of the industrial recovery act that authorized Roosevelt to require business concerns doing interstate commerce to take out licenses was revolutionary and dangerous. It would carry "governmental bureaucratic domination beyond all justification, even as a temporary emergency measure."[27] But even so, the paper was not yet ready to turn away from Roosevelt, and three weeks later told its readers not to deprecate the work of the President. After all, the depression was world-wide, and the United States was "coming back" more quickly than the rest of the world. "Much of that we may be sure is due to his action."[28]

But by 1934 the *Globe-Democrat,* suffering economically itself, was complaining bitterly of Roosevelt's placing "hampering restrictions on honest business."[29] This was the paper's strongest objection to Roosevelt's re-election in the 1936 campaign. If the people had known that the President had meant to change the whole political and economic system, they would not have elected him in 1932.[30] Editorials maintained that Roosevelt had no authority for many of his actions and accused him of being more Socialist than Democratic. In his steps toward public ownership of the means of production, as in the Tennessee Valley

Authority and in the grants made by the WPA for the erection
of municipal power plants, he had gone far toward the control of
economic activity by government. This was socialism. Furthermore, the *Globe-Democrat* labeled the Guffey Coal Act, the
Social Security Act, and the Wagner Labor Act as socialistic and
said that Roosevelt's most influential advisers, particularly his
"braintrusters," were certainly "attached to socialistic principles."[31] In contrast, Governor Alf Landon, the Republican
presidential candidate, was praised for his attacks on the Democratic party leadership and for his proposed solutions to the relief problems.[32]

The paper's attacks on Roosevelt in 1936, however, were mild
in comparison to its bitter fight against him in 1940. Not since the
days of McCullagh and King had the *Globe-Democrat* taken
such a strong stand. Yost, who had resigned as editorial page
editor in 1935 because of ill health, returned in the fall of 1940 to
direct the paper's editorial campaign to help defeat Roosevelt.
"To stress the importance to every American of the election of
Wendell Willkie to the presidency of the United States," Yost
wrote a series of thirty-five front page editorials.[33] The first
appeared on October 2, and the last on November 5, election day.

With his "arsenic-and-old-lace" style,[34] Yost deplored the
organization of a campaign group to high-pressure Missouri
farmers into donating a percentage of their soil conservation
benefits to re-elect Roosevelt, whose New Deal had not benefited
farmers, nor raised prices substantially, nor reduced surpluses.
Many issues in the campaign were vital, he told his readers, but
none transcended in importance that of the "malicious perversion
of the third term tradition."[35] He pleaded for the election of
Willkie, who would emphasize production, would bring labor
and business together with the government in a united, free
people, would be a good manager for total preparedness, and
would restore free enterprise. On November 2 the editor listed
twenty reasons for not voting for Roosevelt. Under his leadership
the country had been carried to the brink of war and was likely
at any moment to be plunged into war, notwithstanding his promises to the contrary. Under him, recovery from the depression

had been deliberately retarded, and free enterprise had been suppressed by vicious requirements. On the following day Yost listed twenty-two reasons for voting for Willkie. His election was essential to defeat Roosevelt's dictatorial policies. Under him, preparations for defense would go forward more rapidly and a "rebirth of freedom" would result.

But the *Globe-Democrat's* campaign proved ineffectual. Roosevelt carried Missouri "in excess of 75,000 to 100,000 votes," and St. Louis gave him a majority of 50,000.[36] His election, however, did not alter the *Globe-Democrat's* convictions, the paper told its readers. Willkie had not triumphed, but neither had he wholly failed. Now the President needed and would get the united support of all.[37]

For eighty years the *Globe-Democrat* had stressed foreign news; the thirties, in spite of retrenchments in the paper's reportorial staff, were no exception. But for the first time in many years, the foreign news was not reported by special correspondents. Almost all such news came to the paper through the Associated Press. As early as 1932, the paper was editorially criticizing Japan for defying the world, and early in 1933 it began attacking Hitler for his treatment of the Jews and the Catholics.[38] Nor was the *Globe-Democrat* the isolationist that it was prior to World War I. This time it spoke out for subsidies to the Merchant Marine, which were needed for the promotion of foreign trade, for maintaining trade in the event of war among other nations, and "in case of war ourselves, absolutely necessary, as we found out in the last war."[39]

From the time of the proclamation of the Rome-Berlin axis in 1936, the *Globe-Democrat* brought its readers full coverage of the European conflict, often printing "extras" for such events as the declaration of war by Italy and Greece. By 1939 editorial comment was frequent and partisan. The promises of "der Fuehrer" were not to be trusted. He was a "Nazi madman riding hard toward far horizons," and eventually he would be challenged.[40] When Great Britain and France formally declared war on Germany, the *Globe-Democrat* told its readers that this was the "darkest hour in human history."[41] The issue was clear:

It is a war between civilization and the instincts and practices of savagery. In such a war the American people cannot
be indifferent. They are not involved in it, and we earnestly
pray they will never be. But they are profoundly concerned
morally in this issue, and their sympathies are almost unani-
mously with the forces now arrayed against all that Hitler
stands for.[42]

This was no isolationist's stand, although Yost had written in
1935 that if war came in Europe Americans should determine not
to be drawn into it.[43] Now the paper called for "cool heads in
Washington" to give all-out aid to the Allies without, if possible,
being drawn into the conflict. It was necessary for the United
States to give aid in planes, mechanized equipment, arms, ammunition, and essential war materials.[44] The fall of France, an
editorial said, emphasized the necessity for defense, "of such
power that no alien force" could overcome it and the necessity of
drastic action against the powers "within our gates that would
betray us."[45]

Personnel changes at the *Globe-Democrat* during the depression years had included the loss for five years of Yost and the
addition of the publisher's son, E. Lansing Ray, Jr. Yost may
have hastened his death in May, 1941, by returning to the paper
the year before.

To the men of his profession, Casper Yost was known as a
keen, fair-minded judge, who weighed impartially and inter-
preted facts clearly.[46] During his twenty-six years as chief of the
editorial page, he received many awards for his distinguished
work on the paper and for his work with the American Society
of Newspaper Editors. He was given an honorary degree of
Doctor of Laws by Lincoln Memorial University in 1926, by
McKendree College in 1928, and by the University of Missouri
in 1934. In 1940 Culver-Stockton College conferred upon him the
degree of Doctor of Literature, and in 1936 he received the
Sigma Delta Chi national award for scholarship in journalism. In
conferring the University of Missouri Award for Distinguished
Service in Journalism upon Yost in 1932, Dean Walter Williams
said that the editor "perceived a most serious lack in forms of

professional co-operation and labored to remedy it through the formation of the American Society of Newspaper Editors—its first president, author, journalist, gentleman."[47]

A studious little man who weighed scarcely a hundred pounds, Yost added much to the journalistic traditions of St. Louis by his contributions to the development of professional ethics, which he practiced scrupulously in the conduct of his editorial page. His connection with the *Globe-Democrat* could not help adding to the prestige of the paper. Regrettably, he did not value timeliness in editorials and often would allow editorials with a "news peg" to remain on his desk until after the *Post-Dispatch* had published one on the same subject.[48] This was true in the smoke elimination campaign, for example. Yet his editorial series, "The American Way of Life," was so forceful that it was printed in booklet form and widely circulated.

Replacing Yost was Louis LaCoss, who had joined the staff in 1923. Before that he had worked on the *San Diego Sun* and on three Kansas newspapers—the *Walnut Valley Times*, the *Parsons Sun*, and the *Kansas City Star*. From 1915 to 1923, except for a brief period of military service in World War I, he worked for the Associated Press, part of the time in Mexico City. He was chief of the St. Louis office of the Associated Press when he came to the *Globe-Democrat* as a copy editor. Later he became a special writer for the paper and traveled extensively to cover important news events such as national political conventions. *Globe-Democrat* readers looked forward to his stories of out-of-the-way places in Missouri which were printed in the Sunday magazine sections.[49]

Ray had confidence in Yost, but in 1949 he was placing his hopes for the survival of his paper in his son. A graduate of Princeton University, young Ray had toured Europe for a year before coming to work at the *Globe-Democrat*. Ray believed that his son, Lansing, Jr., should know the paper from the ground up so that he could take over the duties of publisher later. Young Ray agreed, and accordingly began by riding the midnight trucks that carried the newspaper into Missouri and Illinois. When he worked as a reporter, the city editor did not spare him.

In 1935 he was a legislative correspondent in Jefferson City, and later he covered the spring training of the St. Louis Cardinals baseball club in Florida.[50] As early as 1938 he was serving as secretary of the Globe-Democrat Publishing Company.

So it was perhaps with quiet confidence that Ray faced the problems of reporting a global war in a newspaper that was making less and less money. Little did he realize the tragedies that the forties held in store for him.

Chapter XVII

The Centenarian

MANAGERIAL problems, so troublesome in the depression years, almost swamped the Globe-Democrat Publishing Company in the nineteen-forties. To be sure, during the war years, the circulation climbed, but as the *Globe-Democrat* approached its hundredth anniversary, the *Post-Dispatch* was far in the lead. In 1944 there was a mere 250 difference in the daily circulation figures of the rivals, but two years later Ray's paper had outstripped the Pulitzer paper by 17,126. In the meantime the circulation of the *Star-Times* had climbed steadily to 192,155. Then in 1951 the *Post-Dispatch* absorbed this journal, and its daily circulation shot up to 400,218, while that of the *Globe-Democrat* reached only 304,623.[1] Never again was Ray able to regain the lead in circulation.

The advertising difficulties during this period were still more acute. By 1945 income from advertising had dropped to only 45 per cent of the total revenue for the year; and in 1946 the *Globe-Democrat* carried only 11,582,081 agate lines of advertising. Compared with 21,076,874 in the *Post-Dispatch* and 10,232,097 in the *Star-Times*,[2] this decline was so great that the K. H. Eggers Report stated:

> The *Post-Dispatch* and the *Star-Times* have shown steady gains and, unless the *Globe-Democrat* is successful in securing additional lucrative advertising contracts, it will show further decline percentagewise in the St. Louis area.

One of the unfavorable factors affecting the *Globe-Democrat* was the encroachment of radio in the advertising field. Up to 1943, for example, newspapers were getting in excess of 50 per cent of the total amount of money spent for advertising. Radio

commercials, however, reduced this proportion.[3] Moreover, the
Globe-Democrat did not own or control a radio station until
1948.[4] As the Eggers Report pointed out, the *Post-Dispatch*
operated Radio Station KSD and the *Star-Times*, Radio Station
KXOX. In order to keep the name of the *Globe-Democrat* "before the ears of the listening public," the newspaper had to pay a
premium for commercial time on various stations, whereas the
names of its competitors were mentioned every time the call
letters of their stations were given.

The Eggers Report may have influenced Ray in his subsequent
investment in a radio station. About 1923 the publisher had
ordered the equipment for a station, but the *Post-Dispatch* had
outmaneuvered him, acquiring the equipment Ray had ordered
and opening Station KSD. Later the *Globe-Democrat* had owned
one-sixteenth interest in Station KMOX.[5] Ray, however, did not
believe that a newspaper man should be in the radio business. He
once expressed his philosophy thus:

> I have never been anything but a newspaper man. My
> whole business interest is in newspaper work, and I try con-
> scientiously to maintain this interest in integrity. I have no
> outside business connections. Of course, I have personal in-
> vestments, but I make it a strict rule, from which I never
> deviate under any circumstances, not to buy stocks or se-
> curities of any company whose influence might transgress
> on my sole and first interest—the *Globe-Democrat*.[6]

This philosophy prompted the publisher eventually to sell the
paper's interest in Station KMOX.[7]

However, Ray's son, who was assistant publisher of the paper
and secretary of the Globe-Democrat Publishing Company when
he died in 1946, was intensely interested in radio, particularly in
high frequency modulation. Through him, Ray had also become
enthusiastic about FM broadcasting[8] and in August, 1946, obtained tentative authority from the Federal Communications
Commission to operate an FM radio station.[9] Douglas Houser, as
first vice-president of the firm, warned Ray that FM would not
prove popular because people would not buy a second radio
merely to be able to listen during thunderstorms.[10] Nevertheless,

at a cost of $1,900,000, Ray erected, in 1948, the lavish Globe-Democrat Tower Building at Twelfth and Cole streets, as something of a memorial to his son.[11] Radio Station KWGD-FM went on the air in 1948. But high frequency radio broadcasting did prove unpopular, and the station went off the air the next year and merged with Station KWK, which leased the Tower Building for twenty years. The *Globe-Democrat* remained, however, a substantial stockholder in that station, which was an outlet for the Mutual Broadcasting Company.[12]

Again labor problems plagued the Globe-Democrat Publishing Company. In December, 1944, the "flyboys," handymen in the pressroom, went on a three-day strike. Pressmen refused to cross the picket lines, and for the first time in more than seventy years the paper missed being printed.[13] The next year newspaper carriers went on a strike that lasted twenty-two days. These carriers, though independent operators and not connected with the *Globe-Democrat,*[14] were permitted to organize under the National Relations Board. Their strike hurt the paper. Under a contract negotiated with the American Newspaper Guild in July, 1946, wages of personnel were more than doubled. For example, the salary of a classified advertising salesman was increased from a base of thirty dollars to a base of sixty-five dollars. The salary of telephone girls shot from twenty-two dollars to forty-five dollars a week. Editorial writers and reporters who had been with the paper for seven years drew a set salary of one hundred dollars a week under the new contract, which also called for a forty-two hour week with overtime, and dismissal pay ranging from one to twenty-eight weeks. According to the Eggers Report "extensive vacations, sick leaves, leaves of absence," and the like had "virtually taken the management of the newspapers out of the hands of the publisher."

Ray also had to contend with newsprint shortage, one of the grave newspaper problems of the post-war era. When price controls and allocations were lifted from this commodity following the war, it was more difficult to buy than ever. Its price soared from sixty-five dollars a ton on April 1, 1945, to ninety-three dollars two years later.[15]

Of course, the Globe-Democrat Publishing Company tried to keep its profits up. The price of the *Globe-Democrat* was raised twice. In 1946 the daily paper was selling for five cents in the St. Louis area, and the Sunday paper for ten cents. By 1952 the price of the Sunday paper had been raised to fifteen cents. Advertising rates were also raised, but still the net profits of the company left much to be desired. In fact, in 1941, a bare ten years before the paper was to mark its hundredth anniversary, the company earned a net profit of only $1,147. This climbed in 1943 to $363,982, but in 1945 it was down again to $216,780,[16] not a very large sum considering what the paper had once made.

Publisher Ray was faced in 1941 with naming a new managing editor. Joseph McAuliffe died in July that year. Once more the *Globe-Democrat* mourned the loss of a noted editor. McAuliffe sometimes had seemed to lack system in his assignments. For example, when Louis LaCoss was in Texas covering the death of Rogers Hornsby's mother during the World Series of 1926, McAuliffe wired him to go immediately to Cleveland without telling the reporter what to cover. It was only by chance that LaCoss discovered a political "scoop."[17] Nevertheless, to newspaper men, McAuliffe was as good an editor as he was a reporter. When he died the *New York Times* commented that his death marked the end of an era of St. Louis journalism. McAuliffe was, the *Times* said, "among several now gone who were known to newspaper men over the country as makers of St. Louis journalism."[18]

Again Ray did not look far to get a replacement. He promoted his assistant managing editor, Lon M. Burrowes, who had come to the *Globe-Democrat* in 1913. Burrowes was the son of a newspaper editor in Sedalia, Missouri, had worked as a reporter on two Sedalia papers and the *St. Louis Times*, and had served as a copy editor on the *Post-Dispatch*. At the *Globe-Democrat* he had started as a reporter. Through the years he had been a rewrite man, copy editor, telegraph editor, and chief of the copy desk.[19] Though quick-tempered at times, Burrowes was noted for his kindnesses to newspaper men in and out of trouble.

And so it was Burrowes and LaCoss, now chief of the editorial page, who took up the burden of reporting World War II and keeping *Globe-Democrat* readers informed of the paper's policies during those trying times. With a penchant for long, penetrating editorials, LaCoss discussed the possibilities of war; with black "streamer" headlines Burrowes told of events leading up to the attack on Pearl Harbor.

On December 1, 1941, LaCoss told his readers that Japan, "for all its gun-muscling, its flaming truculence," feared war "like the bubonic plague." But he warned that the Nipponese had gone too far to retreat without yielding "face" in the Orient. Again, on December 4, he predicted that the Japanese would fight in spite of their precarious economic conditions.

Then after the attack on Pearl Harbor, he wrote:

> For the second time within a quarter of a century, America has found that a power of the might and economic influence achieved by the United States cannot escape involvement in any widespread conflict that may grip nations. Our oceans are no longer any barrier for isolation. We have been destined from the beginning to be forced into this war.[20]

The "war gauntlet" had been flung in our teeth, he said. Now "let the totalitarian prophets of force and slaughter and international rapine learn how democracy can act in militant national harmony when grim issues challenge," and he called for an all-out war effort.[21]

The *Globe-Democrat* also warned that the war would not be short. The job of "ridding the Pacific of brown men" coupled with "the vast potentialities" that loomed in the Atlantic would be "one of the biggest this nation has ever faced." But we would win because of our "assembly lines."[22]

In May, 1945, when victory in Europe seemed only hours away, the *Globe-Democrat* called for "no relaxation" of effort until victory was won on all fronts. LaCoss regretted that the terrible price paid to stop Hitler could not have been foreseen when peaceful nations were "too afraid of the so-called risks inherent in the the use of economic or military force for the protection of peace."[23] He marked time while the world waited for word of the armistice by commending President Truman for advocating immediate action against war criminals and General Eisenhower for his magnificent job in defeating the Germans.[24] When at last the glad news came of this event which marked the "final act in Europe in this most terrible of wars," the editor reminded readers that the war was still going on. Japan was still to be conquered.[25]

The *Globe-Democrat* called the news on August 7, 1945, that an atom bomb had been dropped on Hiroshima thrilling and terrible. The very manner in which the epochal bomb had been dropped could only strike despair into Nipponese hearts and should bring the Pacific war to a sudden end. Prophetically, La-Coss wrote that the "oratorical shibboleth" of predicting that another major war would wipe out civilization was now a horrible truism. "Another war would obliterate our civilization, and Armageddon could no longer be a catchword of hyperbole." But even while waiting for Japan's final capitulation, the far-sighted editor noted that it was "painfully plain that America was not prepared for the conversion to peace" and for the problems that an atomic era would bring.[26]

News coverage of World War II in the *Globe-Democrat* was good, but reporting this world-wide conflict posed different problems from those of the three former wars which the paper had covered so thoroughly. Publisher Ray did not keep a staff of reporters in the field, as did the paper in previous wars.[27] Instead, he used the reports of the Associated Press and of the *New York Times* news service, a practice common among newspapers, since only a few of the largest papers in the nation could afford to have their own men cover the European or the Pacific fighting. Writers of the *Globe-Democrat* who were on military leave occasionally sent in feature articles. For example, Larry Schulenberg, an editorial writer, reported from Iwo Jima after March, 1945. Washington news, however, was once more reported by the paper's own bureau there, and Ray sent a special correspondent, Justin L. Faherty, to San Francisco in April, 1945, to cover the United Nations.

After the war the *Globe-Democrat* continued its special ser-

vices to the St. Louis area. Projects besides the sponsoring of the
Golden Gloves and the Soap Box Derby included the Quizdown
and Spelling Bee, the Christmas Choral Pageant, and the Missouri
Soil Conservation Awards.[28] Alert to community responsibilities
Burrowes devoted much effort to the furtherance of worthy
civic, religious, and charitable causes. He gave especial attention
to such campaigns as a *Globe-Democrat* drive which resulted in
a new master traffic control law devised to revitalize the St. Louis
downtown area. He also encouraged investigations which led to
the exposure of corruption in the national and local office of the
Department of Internal Revenue.[29] His reporters wrote factual
and interpretative articles that revealed the need for better civic
conditions. Front page reports on poor runways at Lambert Air
Field with such caustic comments as "more wind and words than
concrete" stimulated improvements that helped St. Louis become
a prominent air transportation center. Other such articles included the advocacy of a scenic drive from the Chain of Rocks to
Carondolet and a city ordinance for the control of rats.[30]

On the editorial page the fight against Roosevelt, so bitter in
1940, became dogged and relentless in 1944. The *Globe-Democrat* accused the President of being a Communist because of the
company he kept—Sidney Hillman, Phillip Murray, and Earl
Browder, sneered at him for saying jobs would be plentiful after
the war, and criticized him for the secrecy surrounding his
foreign diplomatic meetings. But one of Roosevelt's greatest sins
had been against American business, which he had shackled with
restrictions, regulations, back-breaking taxes, and discriminatory
maneuvers.[31]

Although maintaining that it was an independent newspaper
bound to no party, the *Globe-Democrat* urged a "down-the-line
vote for Republican candidates from President to Mayor." In no
other way could the traditional American way of life be rescued
from those who had violated it for twelve years.[32] Yet not since
the old *Missouri Democrat* had campaigned for Lincoln had the
paper favored other than a Republican president. Now Publisher
Ray was fighting as hard as had McKee, Fishback, and Houser

for a return to "real democracy, a government by and for the people."[33]

As in previous campaign years the *Globe-Democrat* rallied to the support of the President after his election. On November 8, election day, the *Globe-Democrat* predicted that the nation would rally behind whoever was elected president "as surely and as solidly as in the past." On the next day an editorial declared that "all of us" must accept a fourth Roosevelt administration in "a spirit of good sportsmanship." The paper wished the President well and trusted that "the confidence reposed in him by the electorate" would not be violated. "For our country's sake we trust his administration will be as wise as the millions who voted for him have confidence it will be."

When Roosevelt died the *Globe-Democrat* acknowledged his greatness. He was called "one of the most unusual and vivid personalities who ever flashed across the troubled horizons of a world which in his time has suffered from the plague of a corroding depression and from the most devastating war since time began." As no man before him, he had "changed the course of this country's destiny" by altering the social, economic, and political life of the nation. The country was in his eternal debt for his dynamic leadership in the early days of his first administration. Through him had emerged a new United States, "which, approve of him or not, will bear his imprint for ages to come."[34]

As for the new President, the *Globe-Democrat* believed that Harry S. Truman had the necessary qualities of statesmanship "to see us through" the war. He came to office without "elaborate equipment as to special information," but there should be confidence that he would "make a go of it."[35] By the 1948 presidential campaign, however, the paper was doubting Truman's ability. Editorials criticized him relentlessly for trying to undermine this country's foreign policy and accused him of postponing peace.[36] Yet in this campaign Ray seemed to be returning to his middle-of-the-road stand of the early thirties. Editorials favored Republican candidates, but they were neither so numerous nor so acrimonious as in the two preceding elections. Whoever was elected, the paper said, there would be no change in the Marshall plan principle, and the Republicans and the Democrats were substantially in agreement.[37]

The *Globe-Democrat* believed that the President took a "wise and logical" course in ordering the United States sea and air forces to aid the embattled South Koreans and that the American people would support him. LaCoss wrote that the outcome of the invasion would determine the future of the United Nations, and he prayed that God would grant the United States "the perspective, intelligence, and courage to pilot the cause of freedom to peace."[38]

But the paper continued to criticize Truman's foreign policy, even doubting that either the President or Secretary Dean Acheson knew what the policy was. Thus after the fiasco in North Korea it was easy for the *Globe-Democrat* to wage a heated battle against the Democrats in the 1952 presidential campaign and to champion Eisenhower. On October 1 of that year the paper refuted Adlai Stevenson's charge of a "one-party press" by pointing to the press outcry and publicity about Richard Nixon's campaign funds. There could not have been "a more convincing demonstration that we still have in this country an independent press which is unfettered by allegiance to any party." Furthermore, the paper attacked President Truman for stumping the country and speaking in behalf of Stevenson. Truman's "Give 'em Hell" utterances were called beneath the dignity of the President, and he was blamed for the development of the campaign into one of bitterness, vituperation, and clashing personalities.[39]

In the meantime Ray's son had died. During World War II young Lansing had served in the Army Intelligence Corps and had been awarded the Legion of Merit for his work in the Mediterranean area. However, he received a head injury in the course of his service, and in March, 1945, had been sent home to convalesce. Never very strong thereafter, he had been unable to assume the responsibilities of the Globe-Democrat Publishing Company as his father had hoped. In 1946 he died of a cerebral hemorrhage. Thus ended Ray's long dream of turning his paper over to his son.[40]

As the *Globe-Democrat* approached its hundredth anniversary, the Housers lost their long connection with the paper. William C. Houser died in April, 1950. For thirty-nine years he had been a part of the paper, having served, as has been noted, as a classified advertising salesman, cashier, and treasurer. He had been second vice-president since 1935.[41]

In June, 1951, Douglas B. Houser resigned as first vice-president of the company. His retirement, he said, would allow younger men to assume the place in the business that they should. Several weeks later the Globe-Democrat Publishing Company acquired the shares of the firm belonging to him and his wife and to Mrs. Sears Lehman, his sister.[42]

Now Ray was the only descendant of the original owners left to direct the paper. But he gathered around him a number of capable men. He named James C. Burkham, his nephew, as president of the company in 1949. Burkham had learned, along with Lansing, Jr., the business of running the *Globe-Democrat*, and had served in the Army Intelligence Corps in World War II. Ray said that he counted on Burkham to make a "big success in one of the greatest professions in the world, as president of a metropolitan newspaper holding the respect of thousands of readers."[43]

Three new vice-presidents were chosen—C. A. Weis, Louis LaCoss, and Edwin Evers. Weis, who had come to the paper as auditor in 1947, had been a member of the Board of Directors of Station KWK since 1949 and treasurer of the firm since 1950. At the time of his appointment as vice-president in July, 1951, he was also serving as vice-president of the Institute of Newspaper Controllers and Finance Officers.[44]

LaCoss and Evers became vice-presidents in February, 1952. That year the director of the editorial page brought honor to himself and to his paper by winning a Pulitzer Prize for his editorial, "The Low Estate of Public Morals." This was a scathing attack on the state of affairs in Washington during the dying years of the Truman administration. LaCoss became the only *Globe-Democrat* man ever to win the coveted award.[45]

Evers, production manager, had been with the paper more than thirty years. He had started as a galley boy in the composing room and had moved up through the ranks as a printer, make-up foreman, composing room foreman, mechanical superintendent, and production manager. He became nationally recognized for his labor-relations work in the newspaper field, frequently addressing conferences throughout the nation on the subject of human relations with a view to improving understanding between employee and employer.[46]

Ray himself, who retained his three-way position of publisher, editor, and chairman of the Board of Directors, had by this time become nationally known as a scrupulously honest newspaperman. He had been given an honorary Doctorate of Laws degree by Washington University in 1925. The University of Missouri Honor Award had been bestowed on him in 1946 in recognition of his forty-three years of service on his paper, his effective work in behalf of many important social and cultural organizations in St. Louis and Missouri, and his leadership in such organizations as the Associated Press, the Audit Bureau of Circulation, the National Better Business Bureau, and other important groups. In accepting the award Ray said that the editor of a newspaper was nothing more than the presiding officer of a staff of able and conscientious men.[47]

Ray was now sixty-seven years old. His paper would soon mark its hundredth anniversary. Even though he had good men to edit the *Globe-Democrat* he must think ahead, he knew, to the time when he would no longer be able to guide its policies.

Chapter XVIII

The Second Century

SCARCELY had the *Globe-Democrat* finished reporting the election of Dwight D. Eisenhower to the presidency of the United States in 1952 when it paused to note its centennial anniversary. On November 9, in honor of the occasion, it brought out a special 64-page "coloroto" magazine supplement with stories describing the growth of St. Louis and of eleven firms which had their modest beginnings in the year that William McKee had taken over so auspiciously the publication of the old *Missouri Democrat*. Of course, a short history of the paper was included, too. Interestingly enough, the anniversary issue was printed on two huge color presses purchased the year before from the *Star-Times* when it was absorbed by the *Post-Dispatch*. The addition of these gave Ray's plant seven presses with a potential capacity to print per hour 260,000 copies of a 32-page paper. As President Burkham pointed out, this equipment was a far cry from the old Hoe ten-cylinder revolving press that required ten men to operate it.[1] Indeed, Ray could look back with justifiable pride on the contributions of his family newspaper to the progress and development of the St. Louis area.

The first eight years of the *Globe-Democrat's* second century were to prove as exciting and turbulent as were its early years in the previous century. They were years marked with drastic changes and fraught with strife. Yet the paper brought to its readers a brand of journalism reminiscent of the McKee and McCullagh years.

By 1953, Ray, nearing seventy, was in poor health. He was no longer physically able to give the paper the dynamic leadership it needed or to cope with the many problems inherent in such a large organization. Nor had he a son to whom he could relinquish some of his many responsibilities. Consequently, he began seeking a buyer. He wanted, he said, to pick his successor—someone who would permit the *Globe-Democrat* to remain "complete master of its destiny, someone who would carry on the policies of his family."[2]

Two years later, in 1955, Ray found such a man in Samuel Irving Newhouse, a multiple newspaper owner.[3] Among newspapermen, Newhouse had the reputation of allowing local editors a very considerable autonomy,[4] and Ray believed that a Newhouse paper would be for "the best interests of the *Globe-Democrat*, of my beloved city, and of the community at large."[5] And so to him Ray sold the paper for $6,250,000.

The sale included 23 per cent of the stock of KWK, Incorporated. With this, however, Newhouse assumed a $1,500,000 debt on the television station.[6] The new owner agreed also to continue Ray's policy of retiring employees with pensions paid out of current earnings and to forfeit a million dollars to the Ray estate if he sold the paper within five years.[7]

Newhouse made only a few changes in the top officers of the company. Ray stayed with the paper as editor, publisher, and chairman of the Board of Directors. As such, he continued to set the political and editorial policies of the paper. C. Arthur Weis moved up from vice-president and treasurer to president of the Globe-Democrat Publishing Company, while James Burkham stepped down from president to vice-president and assistant editor. Later Burkham went into the newspaper business for himself.

The new owner also moved two *Globe-Democrat* men into positions with his other papers: Justin L. Faherty, who had become Ray's assistant in 1950, became director of news, features, and special services for the Newhouse newspapers; and Aaron G. Benesch, former chief of the *Globe-Democrat's* Washington Bureau, who had become managing editor of the paper when Burrowes died in August, 1953, went back to Washington as the representative for Newhouse newspapers in the press gallery of Congress.[8] Both contributed articles to the *Globe-Democrat*.

After the sale of the paper, Ray's health continued to fail. Five months later, on August 30, 1955, his seventy-first birthday, E. Lansing Ray died at his summer home in Rye Beach, New Hampshire. And so was broken the last link between the *Globe-Democrat* and its original owners.

Missourians mourned for the man who for nearly a half century had dominated the *Globe-Democrat*. The Missouri House and Senate passed resolutions of tribute to his memory, and the *Globe-Democrat's* annual Christmas Choral Pageant in 1955 was conducted as a memorial to him. Then, in recognition of his service to the paper, a plaque was placed in the lobby of the *Globe-Democrat* building.[9]

After Ray's death Newhouse brought in Richard H. Amberg to become publisher. At the time of his appointment Amberg was publisher of the *Syracuse Post-Standard*, another Newhouse paper. A graduate of Harvard, he previously had served as general manager of *Newsday*, a Long Island, New York, newspaper; as administrative assistant on the *New York Herald-Tribune*; and as editor and publisher of the *Blizzard*, Oil City, Pennsylvania.[10] His years of experience had given birth to a journalistic philosophy that was to revitalize the *Globe-Democrat*.

The new publisher told his staff that the paper was to be a fighter for the right. It would take sides on every issue; it would never run away from battle. "We will try," he said, "to make a newspaper in the best interests of the community. We will be FOR St. Louis."

A good newspaper, Amberg believed, should emphasize "constructive news, news analysis, and news treatment."[11] To help make this philosophy an actuality in the *Globe-Democrat*, a new position was created—that of executive editor in charge of the news department—and Charles E. Pierson was brought to the paper in 1956 to fill this post. Pierson had started his career in 1928 with the *Pittsburgh Press*. From there he went to the *Toledo Blade*, and by 1933 he was serving as news editor of the *Cincinnati Post*. Later he returned to the *Pittsburgh Press* as managing editor.

Thus Amberg and Pierson took up the task of rebuilding the
Globe-Democrat into the forceful journalistic leader that the
new publisher envisioned. They were to find their path a rocky,
but rewarding one.

Chapter XIX

New Policies, New Trends, New Troubles

THREE of the great newspapers in the Midwest are like baseball teams, Publisher Amberg liked to point out. The *Chicago Tribune* played a fine game in right field, he said. The *Post-Dispatch* played a good game in left field, "albeit occasionally over the foul line"; but the proper place for the *Globe-Democrat* should be as "a good hard-hitting center fielder."[1]

This analogy points up the publisher's general philosophy which has guided the paper since Ray's death—to battle for St. Louis, to give emphasis to crusades on the local and state-wide level, and, as has been stated, to place great "emphasis on constructive news, news analysis, and news treatment."[2]

Amberg did not wait long to apply this journalistic philosophy to the *Globe-Democrat*. When he came to St. Louis the paper had eight right-wing conservative columnists. "Even if I agreed with them philosophically, which I did not," the publisher said, "I did not think this was good newspapering."[3] To give *Globe-Democrat* readers a more "complete spectrum of columnar opinion," he dropped all of the columnists except George Sokolsky and David Lawrence and added Holmes Alexander, Roscoe Drummond, Sylvia Porter, and Inez Robb. Later he added Victor Riesel and Robert Ruark.

The new tenor of the paper was reflected especially in the editorial page, where the *Globe-Democrat* once more began taking positions on controversial questions, often in advance of its competitor. No longer did its editorial writers wait for the *Post-Dispatch* to take a stand.[4] Editorials became more forceful, Amberg himself often writing the lead editorial.

236

He was not afraid to speak out and often initiated constructive programs. For example, he was disturbed because Missouri was one of the eight states which drew no interest on its idle funds in various banks. Amberg approached Governor Phil M. Donnelly on the matter.[5] The Governor then submitted such a proposal to the legislature. The *Globe-Democrat* published a series of news articles and editorials on the subject. Shortly afterward the legislature approved the idea, and a constitutional amendment allowing the funds to draw interest was passed. In the first eighteen months after the law went into effect, the state collected $2,247,-779 in interest.[6] Then, indeed, the paper could point with justifiable pride to the success of its campaign.

Other evidence of the paper's aggressive editorial policy was seen in its support of political candidates. Although in 1956 the *Globe-Democrat* supported Dwight D. Eisenhower for re-election to the presidency of the United States, it supported a Republican for governor and a Democrat for senator in Missouri, and a Democrat for governor and a Republican for senator in Illinois.

An even more graphic example of the paper's bipartisanship appeared in an editorial, "Best Men for Their Jobs," printed on October 28, 1958. Here the paper endorsed and supported candidates for the Missouri State Senate and House, the St. Louis County Council, and the Circuit Court. Of the nine men mentioned, five were Republicans, three were Democrats, and the political affiliation of one was not mentioned. As late as August, 1960, Amberg explained the paper's political policy: "We now support whatever candidate regardless of party we believe best qualified."[7] What a far cry this was from August, 1860, when McKee pledged his paper to the Republican party!

Nor did the *Globe-Democrat* fail to pledge itself to support certain state and municipal reforms, many of which were decidedly controversial. On January 1, 1959, it announced editorially that it favored and would fight for raising the driving age from sixteen to eighteen; enacting a point system for the suspension of drivers' licenses; raising taxes on gasoline, liquor, and cigarettes; placing a withholding tax on state incomes; en-

238   ST. LOUIS GLOBE-DEMOCRAT

acting a search and seizure law for the State Highway Patrol; and passing a branch banking law. Some of these measures were enacted into laws by the 1959 Missouri Legislature.

The paper also boosted its local coverage and evinced a vigorous, effective leadership in community, state, and national affairs by giving big play to public projects. So effectual had this work become that on October 21, 1958, the *Globe-Democrat* was given the tenth annual Inland Press Association award for outstanding community service. Presented by the University of Missouri School of Journalism, the honor was bestowed on the 106-year-old paper for a wide variety of community projects.[8]

Chief among these were the editorials and articles promoting the passage of a bill allowing idle funds of Missouri to draw interest; a series of news stories and editorials which resulted in better airline service for St. Louis; a front-page editorial and rotogravure section, which brought contributions of $102,000 for the purchase of a heart-lung machine for the St. Louis Children's Hospital; and a series of articles which showed how other cities solved problems in attracting new industries.

Fifteen other projects helped the *Globe-Democrat* win the award. These included a series of articles in 1958 on railroad problems which caused Senator Smathers of Florida to say the paper had more to do than any other force with the sympathetic approach which Congress and the White House took on this issue. The paper was cited particularly for stimulating interest in community welfare through its annual awards to the Woman of Achievement, to the Man of the Year, and to state officials for Meritorious Public Service. Honorable mention also went to the *Globe-Democrat* for its outstanding coverage of city, state, and federal affairs affecting its readers.

By this time almost every issue gave evidence that the paper was the crusading *Globe-Democrat* of old. For example, on October 16, 1958, a story told about action being taken to oust city aldermen who did not live in the districts which they represented—action that resulted from earlier stories revealing unsightly conditions in these districts. Also in this issue, Louis M. Kohlmeier, one of the paper's top writers, discussed branch banking; Ted Schafers, another fine reporter, wrote of the "speed traps" in Illinois; and Ray J. Noonan told of the effect of coming elections on the fluoridation of St. Louis County's water supply.

Then in January, 1959, the *Globe-Democrat* "broke" a story that it had been sitting on for three weeks. The paper had received information that gambling was going on in a "confectionery" and that police officers were frequenting the store. After notifying the Board of Police Commissioners, the *Globe-Democrat* cooperated with police inspectors in an investigation that led to the suspension of two police officers. Part of the evidence used was four hundred pictures taken by Bob Briggs, a *Globe-Democrat* photographer who set up his camera with a telephoto lens in a rented room across the street from the store. The three-week surveillance necessary to gather evidence was a secret known only to the editors and to a few top police officers. To decrease the possibility of a "tip-off," conferences with the police were held in the home of City Editor George Killenberg. When the story was released, the *Globe-Democrat* "bannered" it and printed pictures of police officers who had visited the store.[9]

Another portion of the *Globe-Democrat* that began showing great improvement was the women's section. Publisher Amberg had noted when he came to St. Louis that too many of his papers were being bought by men going away from home in the mornings instead of being delivered to the homes where the women would have an opportunity to read them. It was the publisher's philosophy that a paper should have great appeal for women, and he believed that the direction of flow of the *Globe-Democrat* could be reversed by improving the women's pages.[10]

To accomplish this, a competent women's editor was employed; new features and articles appealing to women were added.[11] Then the *Globe-Democrat* began sponsoring two big fashion shows each year "to raise the level of fashion consciousness" among St. Louis women.[12] It also sponsored the "Modern Living Show" each September. This display of home furnishings and equipment was soon drawing more than 200,000 people. Still another service to women was the yearly giving of a Woman of Achievement award to a St. Louis woman. By 1960 there was little doubt that the women's pages in the *Globe-Democrat* had gained the same excellence that its sports and financial sections had always had. Furthermore, the direction of flow had so changed that the home-delivered circulation in the St. Louis metropolitan area alone had increased 60,000 in five years.[13]

Such news coverage had brought the paper by early 1959 to a point where it could challenge the *Post-Dispatch* for leadership. It was gradually creeping up on its rival in circulation and advertising. In March, 1955, when Newhouse bought the paper, its daily circulation trailed that of the *Post-Dispatch* by nearly 100,-000. The same was true of its Sunday circulation.[14] But in September, 1958, Amberg could boast that his total five-day circulation had gained 44,000, while that of the *Post-Dispatch* had lost 17,000. A difference of only 57,672 separated the total circulation figures of the two papers.[15]

Publisher Amberg could also boast of advertising gains. In 1958 the *Globe-Democrat* was said to have gained more new advertising linage than any other paper in the country's biggest markets. From January 1, 1956, through November 30, 1958, advertising had increased by 2,703,505 lines while the *Post-Dispatch* had lost 1,547,288.[16] Although the paper was still far from overtaking its rival, it was beginning to challenge. When Amberg inserted a series of page advertisements in *Editor and Publisher*, telling of gains made by the *Globe-Democrat*, the *Post-Dispatch* found it expedient to defend its position of leader in circulation and advertising in the same medium.[17]

But on February 21, 1959, catastrophe struck. The paper's 332 employee members of the American Newspaper Guild walked out. The *Globe-Democrat* had to cease publication, and its 665 other employees were idled.

The Guild wanted a funded pension plan "comparable" to that of the Pulitzer Publishing Company and presented its side of the issue in an advertisement in the *Post-Dispatch* on February 22. The union declared that it was striking against a newspaper for the first time in twenty-five years and that the strike was against S. I. Newhouse, "New York owner of a chain of newspapers." It had presented its first pension proposal in November, 1957, it said, had acceded to a request for delay in March, 1958, and had submitted its present proposal on November 17, 1958. Since then, it had sought in vain for serious negotiations. Publisher Amberg, the union stated, had not entered the controversy until February 19, when he had asked for another delay until next year's negotiations. He had made no counter proposals, and now the union's patience was exhausted.

Amberg, in an advertisement in the same issue of the *Post-Dispatch*, explained the position of the *Globe-Democrat* management. Repeatedly in the past, he said, the Guild had praised the company's policy, set up by Ray, of paying pensions to retired employees out of current earnings. In 1958, for example, seventy-one employees had been paid in excess of $100,000. In addition, the company had continued the full payments on their life and health insurance. The publisher explained that eleven other unions with whom the company had contracts, some of which dated back almost a century, had cooperated with management in a "healthy system of give and take." Only the Guild, with pay scales already the highest in the nation, had refused to make any concessions. Management had agreed, he said, to deposit a sum into a jointly administered bank account and to negotiate in the remaining ten months of the contract with the Guild (due to expire on December 31, 1959) the beginning of a funded pension plan. But to start such a system immediately would cost $1,130,000 alone for those employees already retired, and approximately $550,000 per year for twenty years to fund a plan even roughly comparable to that of the Pulitzer system. Amberg said that he refused to agree "at gun point" to such "exorbitant" demands. There was not that much money available, and he predicted that publication would probably not be resumed soon.

Angry words followed angry words. Amberg called the Guild's revised proposals "sucker bait," a tantalizingly low first cost, but not big enough to carry the plan. The Guild, in turn, charged management with "little evidence of sincerity." A few idled employees took work elsewhere; others eked out an existence on strike benefits of up to eighty dollars.[18]

The next dramatic development came a week after the walkout with the announcement that the *Post-Dispatch* had bought the building and printing equipment of the *Globe-Democrat* and would print the Newhouse paper under contract after the strike was settled. Ownership of the two papers and direction of their news, editorial, advertising, and circulation policies would remain separate. The *Globe-Democrat* would seek new office space, and its Sunday edition would be converted into a weekend package with the paper's local magazine, *This Week*, and *American Weekly*, issued on Saturday forenoon for ten cents. The purchase price was not disclosed, but the building had been assessed at $741,000, its land at $129,000, and local realtors estimated the market value at $2,000,000. The contract printing arrangement was unusual in certain aspects, but it followed a national trend, dictated by rising costs, of using one set of presses to print morning and afternoon papers. This plan was already in effect in Chicago, Chattanooga, and Birmingham. In the latter city, another Newhouse paper printed the *Post-Herald* for Scripps-Howard. But there the two organizations had a common sales and distribution organization, only the editorial departments being separate.[19]

According to Publisher Amberg, the new arrangement was made necessary by the demands of the Guild. He explained that even the Guild's third and least expensive proposal would cost his newspaper approximately $550,000 a year for twenty years. The *Globe-Democrat*, he said, had never made as much as $550,000 profit a year since the boom days of the war, and he saw no prospects for making that much.[20] Newhouse said flatly that the deal was forced on his organization because of the Guild's insistence on a funded pension plan. "We had no choice. They had a gun at our heads."[21]

Immediately the Guild denied responsibility for forcing the sale. The *Globe-Democrat*, a union executive said, was trying to make a "convenient scapegoat" out of his organization, and he declared that the sale had been planned in advance.[22]

With the sale came another issue. Management asked that it be given freedom to discharge personnel not needed under the changed production system, but the Guild refused to accept this proposal because it considered job security was at stake.[23] As the weeks wore on, negotiations remained deadlocked.

Rumors were circulated throughout the state that Newhouse would sell the *Globe-Democrat*. Management denied this. "I can assure you," Amberg said, "that the *Globe-Democrat* will continue in the future, as it has in the past, as an independent newspaper, and as a mighty force for the good in St. Louis, in Missouri, and in America."[24] But the rumors persisted, and an angry dispute arose over whether the newspaper threatened to suspend publication if the union did not agree to management demands. Both sides once more resorted to advertisements in the *Post-Dispatch* to explain their stands. Publisher Amberg appealed to his employees to end the strike "tomorrow with justice and honor to all concerned." Apparently, he said, the only major issue now was the Guild's insistence that the company pay people for whom there would be no work when the new production system went into effect. He asked only for rights which, he said, were in Guild contracts throughout the country and which had given Guildsmen security on countless other newspapers.[25]

But the Guild rejected the *Globe-Democrat's* latest proposals. Amberg, a Guild spokesman said, was under the illusion that the editorial employees, to whom the company had promised freedom from firings, would abandon the other departments. Such evaluations were "insulting to the integrity and courage" of the news staff.[26]

In the meantime, more than 300,000 Missourians missed their morning *Globe-Democrats*, and they complained. On March 20, Governor James Blair offered to send in state mediators. His offer was made as he spoke on the "Missouri Forum," a KOMU-TV panel program. Next, State Senators Michael Kinney and C. R. Hawkins wanted to institute an official investigation of the strike by a legislative committee. Amberg welcomed the move, but the Guild branded it as intervention by a friend of management, notably Senator Kinney, who the year before had received the *Globe-Democrat's* "Outstanding Legislator" award. However, the strike was settled before a hearing could be held.

The Guild sought to supply the demand for a morning paper and even filed articles of incorporation for such a publication. But the paper was never started, as several community and union groups offered mediation services with the hope that the *Globe-Democrat* would resume publication. Among these were Harold Gibbons, right-hand man to James Hoffa, Teamster Union president, and Archbishop Joseph E. Ritter, whose appeal, it was said, brought about the talks that resulted in eventual agreement.[27]

Tentative agreement on guaranteed pensions, not on the funded pensions sought by the union, and relaxation of a job security clause, insisted on by management, was reached on May 9; but further negotiations were required on technical points. In addition, Amberg had to meet with the eleven other mechanical unions which would no longer be under contract to arrange accrued benefits and severance pay.[28]

Meanwhile, Amberg negotiated a ten-year lease with the International Shoe Company for the Terminal Railroad Building, which was located only a block and a half from the old *Globe-Democrat* Building. It was to be equipped with tubes and a conveyor system to link it with the printing plant in the building which the *Post-Dispatch* had bought, and was to house the *Globe-Democrat's* editorial and business offices. The publisher also announced that the paper would be on a seven-day basis when publication was resumed, with news sections being inserted in the Sunday package.[29]

It took time to iron out these difficulties, so that it was not until June 1 that the *Globe-Democrat*, after a 99-day shutdown, could scream in its headlines, "We're Back!" In an editorial, which was also used as a double-page paid advertisement in *Editor and Publisher*, June 6, 1959, Publisher Amberg reviewed and discussed the strike. He said that only 80 of the 332 union members were present at the meeting at which authority to strike had been given. He declared that, in the end, the new plan was "no better in any single respect than past practices" and that in at least three important matters it provided less benefits. He branded as untrue and cruelly harmful the talk to the effect that the paper would be sold. To help scotch these rumors, Newhouse had insisted upon putting into the new contract a penalty clause which would double the severance pay if he should sell. Amberg foresaw "a greater, stronger, more effective *Globe-Democrat.*"

The Guild attempted to refute many of these statements in a double-page advertisement in the June 20 issue of *Editor and Publisher.* There Guild executives denied many of Amberg's claims and said that the publisher was "flatly mis-stating the results" when he wrote that the Guild had made no gains in the strike. But the Guild agreed that rumors of the sale of the paper proved cruelly harmful. A representative of the Newhouse organization, according to the Guild statement, had lent credence to these rumors when he had threatened to close the paper entirely if the Guild did not surrender to company demands.

Nevertheless, Amberg's statement that nobody ever won a strike that lasted as long as this one was painfully true. Lost during the ninety-nine days were an estimated $5,000,000 in revenue to the *Globe-Democrat,* an estimated $600,000 in workers' pay, and incalculable long-range losses in subscribers and advertisers.[30] In March alone the *Post-Dispatch* increased its advertising volume by a million lines, its daily circulation by 60,000, and its Sunday circulation by 150,000.[31]

In spite of losses in circulation and advertising, the first week of publication after the strike found the *Globe-Democrat* well on the way to quick recovery. The daily run was over 330,000, with a 56-page paper being issued on Monday and a 48-page thereafter. The first Sunday package contained a 68-page main news section and three issues of supplements, some of them dating back to February and March. An agency for the national advertisement of a product that had been put on the market only two months before saved its schedule for the *Globe-Democrat.* Other national accounts also indicated makeup schedules of linage. Publisher Amberg declared hopefully that he anticipated pre-strike normalcy within two weeks.[32]

Unfortunately, before the two weeks were up, another strike caused both papers to cease publication. On June 10, forty-four stereotypers at the *Post-Dispatch* walked out. Such a strike was the calculated risk that Newhouse had taken when he contracted for the printing of his paper. However, since the *Post-Dispatch* was also closed, as well as the Kansas City newspapers which were tied up by a strike two weeks later, the *Globe-Democrat* could not lose more subscribers and advertising to its competitors. And when this strike was terminated two weeks later, the *Globe-Democrat* took up where it had left off, operating under Amberg's concept that responsibility for community leadership was just as important as the sound reporting of national and international affairs. As the hot summer wore on, it became evident to *Globe-Democrat* readers that the paper had survived another crisis.[33]

Chapter XX

In Retrospect

WHEN the *Globe-Democrat* moved into its sixth new home on August 1, 1959, it could look back on 107 years of progress. Generally it had been a "typical" paper. It prospered in good times and sometimes floundered, along with other papers, in periods of financial panic. Its progress paralleled the development of modern journalism and the growth of St. Louis. As a party paper, it was either vituperatively partisan or conservatively slanted, according to the trends of the times. In broad, thorough, and objective news coverage, the *Globe-Democrat* was in the vanguard. Under McCullagh, it was one of the last of the personal journals. During the era of "yellow journalism," it was "yellower" than most. In the pre-World War I days, it was essentially isolationist like most of its Midwest contemporaries. Always Republican, the *Globe-Democrat*, along with many metropolitan papers, yielded slow and grudging ground to Franklin Roosevelt's reform programs. With World War II and the formation of the United Nations, the paper abandoned isolationism and took a one-world view. All in all, the *Globe-Democrat* had been a representative and normal paper—not a world savior with panaceas for mankind's ills, but a sound business run aggressively and successfully.

And the *Globe-Democrat* had not been an unsignificant newspaper. Its continuous flow of dedicated editors and publishers had set the paper well above the average. Benton, Blair, Brown, Foy, Hume, and Grosvenor—all fought vigorously and effectively for theories which they expounded in the *Globe-Democrat* pages. Publisher-owner McKee risked life and limb in his twenty-seven-year crusade that carried the paper politically from Free-Soilism to Republicanism and even beyond, for a brief period, to that outer fringe of lunacy, Radicalism. McKee, more than any other one man, made the *Globe-Democrat* a powerful weapon for human rights. For this reason, his culpability in the Whisky Ring graft should be regarded as a temporary aberration, with his guilt mitigated by that odd climate of public opinion in the corrupt Grant era. He and his family paid in full for this one mistake.

Two great editors, McCullagh and King, pushed the paper into the front ranks of metropolitan journalism. McCullagh, with his great sense of news, created daily a paper that was rarely equalled in his time for reader interest. The talented, incisive editor pioneered in the use of short, pithy sentences and paragraphs and in effective interviewing. King, a great organizer as well as a fine writer, departmentalized the news which McCullagh had so diversified. The last of the one-man editors, he it was who imposed the system and organization demanded by the complexities of the newspaper business at the turn of the century.

Almost unseen in the shadows of these two great editors hid the dim figure of "Pay-any-price-for-news" Houser, probably the most underrated of all contributors to the *Globe-Democrat's* success. For sixty-three years, he was the financial troubleshooter and oiler of the business machinery. Under his direction the upward climb of the paper was as steady as that of the prosperous expanding American economy.

Nor should Yost be forgotten. Little Casper, though tagged "Arsenic-and-old-lace" by his contemporaries, might better be called the father of the modern concept of the responsibility of the press—a concept often lost today in the more dramatic scuffles about freedom of the press. Probably nobody has stated so well as Yost the obligations that the power of the press imposes on itself. And, of course, Yost instigated, if indeed he did not actually write, the famous "Code of Newspaper Ethics" set up by the American Society of Newspaper Editors.

For more than a half-century, most of the time at the helm, E. Lansing Ray lived the *Globe-Democrat*. He struggled valiantly to maintain the paper's high standard, and in general he succeeded. His problems, while not so dramatic as those of his ancestor McKee, were probably more complex and less easy to solve. His were not the problems of a lusty young paper fighting to get a start in a booming frontier city. His were the problems of a paper grown a little ill with old age, struggling to keep abreast of a dynamic society. In a period when his paper represented for the most part a minority viewpoint, he fought for what he believed was for the good of St. Louis and the country. As in McKee's time, the paper was both loved and hated. Yet the *Globe-Democrat* remained above average, and Ray, his life overshadowed by personal tragedies, was beloved by the community which he had served so well for so long.

All in all, the *Globe-Democrat's* history has been a colorful one. While longevity, as McCullagh once pointed out about "Old 1808," is no sure and final guarantee of worth, there is a certain dignity in traditions. And of these, the *Globe-Democrat* has its share. The paper has many and varied claims to distinction—a century in the same family; chief Abolition paper in a Border State; survivor of Civil War mobbings; friend and champion of Abraham Lincoln; proving ground for such noted writers as James Redpath, Henry Morton Stanley, and Theodore Dreiser; survivor of that giant skeleton-in-the-closet, the Whisky Ring frauds; backer and friend of Lindbergh; promoter of transportation by water, land, and air; crusader for smoke elimination; publicizer of the strange story of Patience Worth.

With the advent of the Newhouse ownership came a rebirth. Publisher Amberg and Editor Pierson breathed new life into the *Globe-Democrat*, and it became the lusty, crusading paper of old—a paper not afraid of a fight, not afraid of change. Once more it was pioneering. Though not the first metropolitan paper to go to contract printing, it was a leader in this trend. And from its new home it continued its revitalized service to its community, its state, and its nation.

Footnotes

CHAPTER I

1. Jonas Viles, "Sections and Sectionalism in a Border State," *The Mississippi Valley Historical Review*, XXI (June, 1934), 12-13.
2. *Weekly Globe-Democrat*, December 25, 1879.
3. Walter B. Stevens (ed.), *The Brown-Reynolds Duel, A Complete Documentary Chronicle of the Last Bloodshed Under the Code Between St. Louisans* (St. Louis: The Franklin Club, 1911), p. 29. For a list of the equipment belonging to the *Democrat*, see City of St. Louis, General Records, Book P-6, p. 257.
4. The earliest known extant copies of the *Democrat* are in the Library of Congress. These include: October 13, 1852 (Wednesday), Vol. 1, no. 90; October 17, 1852 (Sunday), Vol. 1, no. 94; October 29, 1852 (Friday), Vol. 1, no. 104; and October 31, 1852 (Sunday), Vol. 1, no. 105. From this, it is judged that the paper was issued six days a week and that the first issue was July 1, 1852.
5. *Daily Missouri Democrat*, August 7, 1852, quoted in the *St. Louis Intelligencer*, August 9, 1852.
6. Walter B. Stevens, *St. Louis, the Fourth City* (St. Louis: The S. J. Clark Publishing Company, 1909), I, 212.
7. From a biographical sketch of Frank P. Blair in the Frank P. Blair papers, Missouri Historical Society, St. Louis; John F. Hume, *The Abolitionists, Together with Personal Memories of the Struggle for Human Rights*, 1830-1864 (New York: G. P. Putnam's Sons, 1905), p. 189.
8. Thomas J. Scharf, *History of Saint Louis City and County* (Philadelphia: Louis H. Everts and Company, 1883), I, 927-928.
9. Winston Churchill, *The Crisis* (New York: Grosset and Dunlap, 1901). In this novel set in St. Louis in the Civil War and pre-Civil War eras, Virginia Carvel, the heroine, and her pro-South friends called the *Democrat* "dirty," "abhorred," and "hated"; but they read it.
10. *St. Louis Intelligencer*, August 9, 10, 1852; *Missouri Republican*, July 17-August 7, 1852.
11. Stevens, *The Brown-Reynolds Duel*, p. 29. Blair and Pickering had a previous encounter in 1849.
12. *St. Louis Globe-Democrat*, December 29, 1879.
13. *Boonville Weekly Advertiser*, January 28, 1876.
14. Scharf, *History of St. Louis*, I, 928.

15. Cited in *St. Louis Intelligencer*, August 10, 1852; *Missouri Democrat*, October 13, 1852.
16. City of St. Louis, General Records, Book P-6, p. 257.
17. C. I. Filley to William McKee, St. Louis, January 27, 1877, printed in *St. Louis Daily Times*, January 28, 1877. Chauncey I. Filley's Political Scrapbook, State Historical Society, Columbia, Missouri.
18. *St. Louis Intelligencer*, December 21, 1852.
19. *Daily Missouri Democrat*, January-February, 1854.
20. *Ibid.*, November 1-8, 1853.
21. *Ibid.*, May 21, 1853.
22. William Vincent Byars (ed.), "Issues of the Civil War under the Pierce Administration as Illustrated in Hostile Correspondence and Duel between B. Gratz Brown and Thomas C. Reynolds" (unpublished manuscript, Missouri Historical Society, St. Louis), p. 118.
23. *Daily Missouri Democrat*, May 21, 1853.
24. *Ibid.*, May 11, 1853.
25. Alfred McClung Lee, *The Daily Newspaper in America: The Evolution of a Social Instrument* (New York: The Macmillan Company, 1937), pp. 103, 703.
26. Scharf, *History of St. Louis*, I, 930; Stevens, *The Fourth City*, I, 213.
27. Daniel M. Grissom, "Personal Recollections of Distinguished Missourians," *Missouri Historical Review*, XXIX (April, 1924), 423-425.
28. P. Orman Ray, "B. Gratz Brown," *Dictionary of American Biography* (New York: Charles Scribner's Sons, 1933), III, 105-107.
29. B. Gratz Brown to Orlando Brown, St. Louis, March 10, 1850, Brown papers, Filson Club, Louisville, Kentucky.
30. *St. Louis Intelligencer*, August 10, 1852; Walter B. Stevens, *Missouri the Center State, 1821-1915* (St. Louis: The S. J. Clark Publishing Company, 1915), I, 227.
31. *Weekly Globe-Democrat*, December 25, 1879.

CHAPTER II

1. U. B. Phillips, "The Southern Whigs, 1834-54," *Essays in American History Dedicated to Frederick Jackson Turner* (New York: Henry Holt, 1910), p. 228.
2. Galusha Anderson, *The Story of a Border City During the Civil War* (Boston: Little, Brown and Company, 1908), pp. 28-31, 182-187.
3. Cited in William E. Smith, *The Francis Preston Blair Family in Party Politics* (New York: The Macmillan Company, 1933), I, 400.
4. *Daily Missouri Democrat*, August 12, 1854.
5. *Ibid.*, November 30, December 4, 12, 1855.
6. *Ibid.*, November 1, 1853; February 4, 1854.
7. *Ibid.*, February 4 and 13, 1854.
8. *Ibid.*, July 11, 1854.
9. *Ibid.*, October 31, 1853.
10. *Ibid.*, February 4, 9, 13, 1854.
11. *Ibid.*, April 13, 1854.

12. Frank Luther Mott, *American Journalism, A History of Newspapers in the United States through 260 Years, 1690-1950*, (New York: The Macmillan Company, 1950), p. 295.

13. *Daily Missouri Democrat*, February 24, May 11, September 11, 1855.

14. B. Gratz Brown to Orlando Brown, House of Representatives, February 9, 1855, Brown papers, Filson Club, Louisville, Kentucky.

15. For a complete account of the Brown-Reynolds duel, see Stevens, *The Brown-Reynolds Duel*.

16. *Daily Missouri Democrat*, March 17, April 21, 1854.

17. *Ibid.*, March 15, 17, 1855.

18. *Ibid.*, July 25, 28, 31, August 4, 1856.

19. Stevens, *The Brown-Reynolds Duel*, p. 80.

20. *Daily Missouri Democrat*, July 29, 1856.

21. Stevens, *The Brown-Reynolds Duel*, pp. 139-140; Isaac H. Sturgeon to Miss Lois Dalton, May 27, 1906, Missouri Historical Society, St. Louis, Missouri. The duel was arranged at the Sturgeon home.

22. *Daily Missouri Democrat*, August 9, 12, 1854.

23. *Ibid.*, June 7, July 20, 23, August 2, 15, 1855.

24. Stevens, *The Fourth City*, I, 222; Charles F. Horner, *The Life of James Redpath and the Development of the Modern Lyceum* (New York: Barse and Hopkins, 1926), pp. 23, 53.

25. Alvin F. Harlow, "James Redpath," *Dictionary of American Biography*, XV, 443-444.

26. *Daily Missouri Democrat*, July 23, August 8, 9, 23, 24, 1855. Redpath told some of his experiences in Missouri and Kansas in his own book, *The Roving Reporter: or Talks with Slaves in the Southern States* (New York: A. B. Burdick, 1859), pp. 189-198, 269-349.

27. Charles Robinson, *The Kansas Conflict* (New York: Harper and Brothers, 1892), p. 487.

28. Harlow, "James Redpath," *Dictionary of American Biography*, XV, 443-444.

29. *Ibid.*, Stevens, *The Fourth City*, I, 222.

30. *Daily Missouri Democrat*, April 1, 28, May 21, 1855.

31. *Ibid.*, July 22, November 13, 23, 1855; March 3, 1857.

32. Robert J. Rombauer, *The Union Cause in St. Louis in 1861* (St. Louis: Nixon-Jones Printing Company, 1909), p. 150.

33. Smith, *The Francis Preston Blair Family*, I, 325.

34. *Daily Missouri Democrat*, January 8, February 18, March 7, 18, April 24, May 20, 1856.

35. *Ibid.*, April 8, 1856.

36. *Jefferson City Examiner*, March 8, 1856.

37. *Daily Missouri Democrat*, March 4, 1856.

38. Cited in Smith, *The Francis Preston Blair Family*, I, 345.

39. *Daily Missouri Democrat*, August 14, 1856.

40. *Ibid.*, August 3, 1856.

41. *Ibid.*, August 5, 1856.

42. John H. Ulbricht, "Frank P. Blair and Missouri Politics" (unpublished Master's thesis, University of Missouri, 1936), p. 149.

43. Cited in Smith, *The Francis P. Blair Family*, I, 400. Benton said in a letter dated February 23, 1857, that Blair and Brown should have made known their intentions before the election that he might not have been deceived. He reiterated his policy, that he was against legislated emancipation. Clipping of letter in Benton Papers, Missouri Historical Society, St. Louis, Missouri.
44. McKee and Fishback were first listed as proprietors on the masthead of the *Democrat*, January 23, 1857.
45. William Hyde and Howard L. Conard (eds.), *Encyclopaedia of St. Louis* (New York: The Southern History Company, 1899), II, 784-785; Richard Edwards and M. Hopewell, *Edwards' Great West* (St. Louis: *Edwards Monthly, A Journal of Progress*, 1860), p. 175; Scharf, *History of St. Louis*, I, 926-927.
46. *Daily Missouri Democrat*, January 28, 1857.
47. *Ibid.,* February 13, March 24, 1857.
48. *Ibid.,* April 2, 4, 6, 1857.
49. *Ibid.,* April 7, 14, 15, 1857.
50. *Ibid.,* January 12, February 18, 22, March 20, 22, 31, 1858.
51. *Ibid.,* January 13, 1858.
52. *Ibid.,* January 18, March 16, 1858.
53. *Ibid.,* January 20, February 19, April 4, May 26, June 11, 1858.
54. *Ibid.,* July 21, 1858.
55. *Ibid.,* August 3-27, September 10-17, December 21, 1858.
56. Scharf, *History of St. Louis*, I, 626.
57. F. P. Blair, Jr., to M. Blair, cited in Smith, *The Francis Preston Blair Family*, I, 400. Although Smith dates this letter June 3, 1859, Brown's letter of resignation appeared in the *Democrat* on April 11, 1859.

CHAPTER III

1. Anderson, *Story of a Border City*, pp. 2-3.
2. *Ibid.,* pp. 8-9; Daniel J. Kenny, *American Newspaper Directory*, 1861.
3. *Daily Missouri Democrat*, January 1, 1855, August 27, 1860.
4. *Ibid.,* June 15, 1858.
5. *Ibid.,* August 24, 1858.
6. *Ibid.,* August 24, 1860.
7. *Ibid.,* January 24, 1854.
8. *Ibid.,* June 15, 1858.
9. Walter B. Stevens, "Joseph B. McCullagh," *Missouri Historical Review*, XXV (October, 1930), 5-6.
10. *Ibid.,* p. 4; *St. Louis Post-Dispatch*, December 31, 1896.
11. *Daily Missouri Democrat*, June 26, July 21, 1854.
12. *Ibid.,* March 16, 1859.
13. *Ibid.,* July 1, 1858.
14. *Ibid.,* October 28, 1858.
15. *Ibid.,* February 11, 1859.
16. *Ibid.,* August 14, 1860.
17. *Ibid.,* March 16, 1859.
18. *Ibid.,* October 15, 1859.

19. *Ibid.*, April 8, 1853.
20. *Ibid.*, June 15, 1860.
21. *Ibid.*, August 24, 1860.
22. *Ibid.*, January 17, 1857.
23. *Ibid.*, July 21, 1854.
24. *Ibid.*, March 28, 1857.
25. *Liberty Tribune*, March 25, 1859.
26. *Daily Missouri Democrat*, November 7, 1853; March 30, 31, 1854.
27. *Ibid.*, November 4, 1853.
28. *Ibid.*, January 20, 1857.
29. *Ibid.*, April 6, 1853.
30. *Ibid.*, March 3, 1854.
31. *Ibid.*, January 6, 8, 1855; November 12, December 15, 1860.
32. *Ibid.*, December 8, 1857.
33. *Ibid.*, July 18, 1860.
34. *Ibid.*, October 9, 1858.
35. *Ibid.*, January 12, 1854.
36. McKee and Fishback Business Bill, Missouri Historical Society, St. Louis, Missouri. The notations on this bill, upon which D. M. Houser as book-keeper had signed a receipt, indicated that the firm had trouble collecting.
37. *Daily Missouri Democrat*, June 26, 1854.
38. *Ibid.*, November 12, 1853.
39. *Ibid.*, February 15, 1854.

CHAPTER IV

1. *Kennedy's St. Louis Directory*, 1859. Foy was listed as associate editor of the *Democrat*, but confirmation of information for the book was probably made in 1858.
2. Minnie Organ, "History of the County Press of Missouri," *Missouri Historical Review*, IV (July, 1910), 262.
3. *Ibid.*, p. 263.
4. Walter B. Stevens, "Lincoln and Missouri," *Missouri Historical Review*, X (January, 1916), 66.
5. Rombauer, *The Union Cause in St. Louis in 1860*, p. 130.
6. *Daily Missouri Democrat*, April 20, 1859.
7. *Ibid.*, May 2, 1859.
8. *Ibid.*, May 6, 1859.
9. *Ibid.*, October 21, 25, 1859.
10. *Ibid.*, May 3, 9, 21, 1859.
11. *Ibid.*, July 29, August 3, November 1, 1859.
12. *Ibid.*, November 16, 1859.
13. *Ibid.*
14. *Ibid.*, March 10, 12, 1860.
15. Stevens, "Joseph B. McCullagh," *Missouri Historical Review*, XXV (October, 1930), 4.
16. *Daily Missouri Democrat*, May 10, 1860. Villard later said that he had written special assignments for B. Gratz Brown while he was at Pike's Peak in 1859-1860 and that he reported notable political meetings of 1860 for the

Missouri Democrat. Memoirs of Henry Villard, Journalist and Financier, 1835-1900 (Westminster: Archibald Constable and Company, 1904), I, 127-138.

17. *Daily Missouri Democrat,* May 19, June 19, 1870. After May 19, all issues of the paper carried the National Republican slate.
18. *Ibid.,* May 19, 1860.
19. *Ibid.,* April 18, 1860.
20. *Ibid.,* May 4, 1860.
21. *Ibid.,* June 15, 23, 1860.
22. *Ibid.,* August 14, October 24, 1860.
23. *Ibid.* July 18, 1860; *supra,* p. 36.
24. *Ibid.*
25. *Ibid.,* August 24, 28, 1860.
26. *Ibid.,* March 12, June 19, 1860.
27. *Ibid.,* November 3, 6, 1860.
28. *Edwards' St. Louis City Directory,* 1860.
29. *Daily Missouri Democrat,* November 6, 1860.
30. *Ibid.,* November 6, 1860. Although Lincoln did not carry the state of Missouri, getting only 17,028 votes, he did carry St. Louis. The completed returns for St. Louis were Lincoln, 9,946; Bell, 4,931; Douglas, 9,275; and Breckenridge, 609.
31. *Ibid.,* November 17, 23; December 15, 27, 1860; and January 29, 1861.
32. *Ibid.,* January 5, 1861.
33. *Ibid.,* January 21, 1861.
34. *Ibid.*
35. *Ibid.,* March 1, 1861. "G. W. F." was probably George W. Fishback, part owner of the *Democrat.*
36. *Ibid.,* March 1-5, 1861.
37. A reference to this appointment was made in "Memorandum Concerning Patronage in St. Louis," April 16, 1863. *The Collected Works of Abraham Lincoln,* ed. Roy P. Basler, *et al.* (New Brunswick: Rutgers University Press, 1958), VI, 173.
38. After the *Democrat* split with Blair, Foy and Blair founded the *St. Louis Union* as a national Union organ in opposition to the *Democrat.* Scharf, *The History of St. Louis,* I, 600. Foy was also an editorial writer for the *Post-Dispatch.*
39. Scharf, *The History of St. Louis,* I, 925. Little is known of Lewis. Probably he was the author of several lengthy articles printed in the *Democrat* from 1859 to 1861 and signed "A. H."
40. Royal Cortissoz, *The Life of Whitelaw Reid* (New York: Charles Scribner's Sons, 1921), I, 104, 137.
41. John F. Hume, *The Abolitionists* (New York: G. P. Putnam's Sons, 1905), pp. 154-158. Hume wrote that the young hero in Winston Churchill's *The Crisis, supra,* had experiences similar to his own, in that he was a lawyer from New England who settled in St. Louis shortly before the Civil War and contributed articles on antislavery to the *Democrat.* Friends of the cause donated money for the publishing of a collection of Hume's articles in a pamphlet which was distributed throughout Missouri. *Ibid.,* p. 157.

42. *Daily Missouri Democrat,* April 2, 1861.
43. *Ibid.,* February 21, 1861.
44. *Ibid.,* February 8, 23, 1861. Rombauer said that this was a deliberate exaggeration to deter an attack. Rombauer, *The Union Cause in St. Louis,* p. 154.
45. *Ibid.,* May 3, 1861. Governor Jackson's order was printed verbatim and run on the front page.
46. *The Missouri Republican,* May 11, 1861. This paper had a more objective account of the event than did the *Democrat* of May 13. The War Department Records include the following communication: P. S. Sanderson to J. T. Sanderson, Washington, D. C., May 11, 1861, "The following has just been received from St. Louis: 'General Frost's brigade Missouri Militia surrendered unconditionally at the demand of the Federal troops. . . . Twenty persons, including two women and several children, killed and many wounded. Great excitement and Republican newspapers threatened by mob.'" *The War of Rebellion, Official Records,* (Washington: Government Printing Office, 1893), Series II, Vol. VI, pt. II, 107. A good bystander's account can be found in Anderson, *The Story of a Border City During the Civil War,* pp. 88-105.
47. "Account of Protection of *Democrat* from a Mob of Rebels," by W. J. Fry, May 18, 1861, Newspaper Collection, Missouri Historical Society, St. Louis, Missouri.
48. *Daily Missouri Democrat,* May 14, 18, 1861.
49. *Ibid.,* July 26, August 31, 1861.
50. *Ibid.,* August 31, September 3, 1961.
51. F. P. Blair, Jr., "Address to His Constituents," dated October 8, 1862, cited in Smith, *The Blair Family in Politics,* II, 215.
52. *Daily Missouri Democrat,* September 17, 24, 1861.
53. Hume, *The Abolitionists,* pp. 157, 159.
54. *Daily Missouri Democrat,* February 10, 18, 1862.
55. *Ibid.,* June 25, July 11, 19, 1862. No person could vote or hold office who did not take an oath that he would protect and defend the government and that he would not give aid and comfort to the enemies or that he had not taken arms against the United States since December 7, 1861.
56. *Ibid.,* September 3, 24, 1863.
57. *Ibid.,* July 1, 1865.
58. *Ibid.,* April 4, 1865.
59. *Ibid.,* November 2, 17, 1864.
60. *Ibid.,* July 9, 23, 1863.
61. *Ibid.,* January 12, 13, 1865.
62. *Ibid.,* February 9, 24, March 7, 1865.
63. *Jefferson City Times,* March 4, 1865.
64. *Daily Missouri Democrat,* April 10-28, 1865.
65. *Ibid.,* April 17, 19, 20, 1865.
66. *Ibid.,* July 1, 1865.

CHAPTER V

1. A wag, commenting on the evening editions, said that they were issued to contradict the lies printed in the morning papers. Anderson, *The Story of a Border City During the Civil War*, pp. 144-145.
2. *Daily Missouri Democrat*, May 10, 1864; April 17, January 20, 1865.
3. C. I. Filley to Brother Jay, St. Louis, January 28, 1861, Filley Family Papers, Missouri Historical Society, St. Louis, Missouri.
4. *Ibid.*, April 16, 28, 1862.
5. *Daily Missouri Democrat*, September 23, 1861.
6. *Ibid.*, November 3, 1863.
7. *Ibid.*, March 24, 1862; August 3, 1863.
8. *Ibid.*, March 4, 1861; July 12, 1862; October 3, 1863; November 9, 1864.
9. *Ibid.*, September 24, 1861.
10. *Ibid.*
11. *Ibid.*, October 14, 1863.
12. Cutler J. Andrews, *The North Reports the Civil War* (Boston: Little, Brown and Company, 1958), p. 657; Scharf, *A History of St. Louis*, I, 936.
13. *St. Louis Post-Dispatch*, December 31, 1896.
14. Andrews, *The North Reports the Civil War*, pp. 751-758.
15. *Daily Missouri Democrat*, February 5, 1861.
16. *Ibid.*, February 11, 1861.
17. *Ibid.*, April 13, 1861.
18. *Ibid.*, April 15, 1861.
19. *Ibid.*, June 17-August 5, 1861.
20. Andrews, *The North Reports the Civil War*, p. 121.
21. *Daily Missouri Democrat*, July 19, 1861.
22. *Ibid.*, June 18, 1861.
23. *Ibid.*, August 5-22, 1861.
24. *Ibid.*, June 18, 1861.
25. *Ibid.*, July 23, 1861.
26. *Ibid.*, June 24, 1861.
27. *Ibid.*, July 26, 1861.
28. *Ibid.*, August 17, 20, 1861.
29. *Supra*, p. 48.
30. *Ibid.*, September 27, 1861.
31. *Ibid.*, October 9, 1861.
32. *Ibid.*, November 6, 1861.
33. *Ibid.*, March 3, 1862.
34. For a good discussion of guerrilla fighting in Missouri, see Richard Smith Brownlee, *Gray Ghosts of the Confederacy* (Baton Rouge: Louisiana University Press, 1959).
35. *Liberty Tribune*, November 1, 1861.
36. *Daily Missouri Democrat*, September 21, 1861.
37. *Ibid.*, March 24, 1862.
38. *Ibid.*, June 14, 1862.
39. *Ibid.*, September 4, 1863.
40. *Ibid.*, May 27, 1862; April 28, September 4, 1863.

41. *Ibid.*, September 16, 1861.
42. *Ibid.*, October 17, 1861, April 20, 1862.
43. *Ibid.*, January 6, 1861.
44. *Ibid.*, January 21, 1862.
45. *Ibid.*, February 28, May 21, 1862.
46. *Ibid.*, March 26, 1862.
47. *Tri-Weekly Missouri Democrat*, March 11, 1863.
48. J. M. Schofield to Lincoln, St. Louis, July 14, 1863, *War of the Rebellion, Official Records*, Series I, XXII, pt. II, 373-374; see also William H. Herndon and Jesse William Weik, *The Life of Lincoln* (Chicago: D. Appleton and Company, 1890), III, 462.
49. Henry T. Blow to Lincoln, St. Louis, July 13, 1863, and A. Lincoln to J. O. Broadhead, Washington, July 15, 1863, *War of the Rebellion, Official Records*, Series I, XXII, pt. II, pp. 366, 375.
50. Lincoln to Schofield, Washington, July 13, 1863, and Lincoln to Blow, Washington, July 13, 1863, *ibid.*, p. 366.
51. *Daily Missouri Democrat*, July 15, 1863.
52. *Ibid.*, July 22, 1863. For Schofield's compliance, see Lincoln to Schofield, Washington, July 20, 1863, *War of the Rebellion, Official Records*, Series I, XXII, pt. II, 383.
53. *Daily Missouri Democrat*, August 16, 30, September 2, November 29, December 6, 1861.
54. Scharf, *History of St. Louis*, I, 694.
55. *Daily Missouri Democrat*, April 2, 18, May 31, 1861.
56. *Ibid.*, September 3, December 22, 1861.
57. *Ibid.*, March 3, 1862.
58. *Ibid.*, October 10, 1861.
59. Scharf, *History of St. Louis*, I, 537.
60. *Daily Missouri Democrat*, September 24, 1861.
61. *Ibid.*, December 12, 20, 1861.
62. *Ibid.*, February 1, 4, 14, 1862. In *The Crisis*, Winston Churchill, the American novelist, has a description of one of these auctions which closely parallels newspaper accounts.
63. *Ibid.*, February 1, 1862.
64. *Ibid.*, August 28, 1862.
65. *Ibid.*, October 2, 20, 1863.
66. City of St. Louis, General Records, Book 258, p. 305.
67. C. I. Filley, *Some Republican History of Missouri* (St. Louis: Gast Banknote and Lithograph Company, 1898), p. 81.
68. Hume, *The Abolitionists*, pp. 157-159.
69. F. P. Blair, Jr., "Address to His Constituents," October 8, 1862, cited in Smith, *The Blair Family in Politics*, II, 215.
70. *Daily Missouri Democrat*, January 12, 16, 1862.
71. *Ibid.*
72. *Ibid.*, July 8, 1864.
73. *Ibid.*, May 8, 1865.
74. Andrews, *The North Reports the Civil War*, pp. 657, 660.
75. *Daily Missouri Democrat*, December 19, 21, 26, 1864.

76. *Ibid.*, May 28, 1862.
77. Stevens, *The Fourth City*, I, 1061; *Edwards' St. Louis Directory*, 1864.
78. City of St. Louis, General Records, Book 255, p. 207.

CHAPTER VI

1. Smith, *The Francis Preston Blair Family*, I, 417.
2. *Ibid.;* "Agreement Regarding the *Missouri Democrat*, July 3, 1857," *Collected Works of Abraham Lincoln*, II, 410.
3. Hay and Nicolay later collaborated in writing *Abraham Lincoln, A History* (New York: The Century Company, 1890), 10 vols.
4. *Collected Works of Abraham Lincoln*, II, 537. In 1858, Blair was serving in Congress, having been elected in 1856. But he lost in his campaign for re-election.
5. Walter B. Stevens, "Lincoln and Missouri," *Missouri Historical Review*, X (January, 1916), 67.
6. *Ibid.*, p. 68.
7. *Ibid.;* Daily Missouri Democrat, August 30, September 24, 1858.
8. *Daily Missouri Democrat*, September 3, 1857; January 8, 1861.
9. Stevens, "Lincoln and Missouri," pp. 68-69.
10. "Endorsement on Margin of *Missouri Democrat*, May 17, 1860," *Collected Works of Abraham Lincoln*, IV, 50, 462; William H. Herndon and Jesse William Weik, *The Life of Lincoln* (Chicago: D. Appleton and Company, 1890), III, 462. Lincoln intended that Davis should not promise any office, but he did.
11. A. Lincoln to Edward Bates, Springfield, Illinois, December 18, 1860, *Collected Works of Abraham Lincoln*, IV, 83.
12. Draft of letter, Winfield Scott to Captain Nathaniel Lyon, War Department, April 30, 1860, Abraham Lincoln Papers, Missouri Historical Society, St. Louis, Missouri.
13. *Daily Missouri Democrat*, January 8, 1861.
14. *Ibid.*, March 5, 1861.
15. *Ibid.*, March 5, 8, 1861.
16. *Ibid.*, August 31, 1861; Robert C. Harper, *Lincoln and the Press* (New York: McGraw-Hill Book Company, 1951), p. 139; A. Lincoln to John C. Fremont, September 11, 1861, *Collected Works of Abraham Lincoln*, IV, 517-518.
17. *Daily Missouri Democrat*, September 18, 1861.
18. *Ibid.*, March 13, 1862.
19. *Ibid.*, January 30, 1863.
20. *Ibid.*, March 6, 1863.
21. *Tri-Weekly Missouri Democrat*, February 9, 20, 1863.
22. *Weekly Missouri Democrat*, September 2, 1862.
23. *Ibid.*, September 2, 1863.
24. *Ibid.*
25. Truman Woodruff to Lincoln, St. Louis, April 9, 1863, *Collected Works of Abraham Lincoln*, VI, 178.
26. *Weekly Globe-Democrat*, December 29, 1879.

27. "Memorandum Concerning Patronage in Missouri," *Collected Works of Abraham Lincoln*, VI, 178.
28. *Supra*, p. 60
29. A. Lincoln to Honorable H. T. Blow, War Department, Washington, July 13, 1863; A. Lincoln to Major General John M. Schofield, Executive Mansion, Washington, July 20, 1863, *War of Rebellion, Official Records*, Series I, XXII, pt. II, 366, 383.
30. H. T. Blow to Abraham Lincoln, St. Louis, July 13, 1863, *ibid.*, p. 366.
31. This figure was a greatly exaggerated combination of the subscriptions to the daily, weekly, and tri-weekly editions. No exact figures are available, but the combined subscriptions probably did not total 30,000.
32. *Tri-Weekly Missouri Democrat*, July 13, 1863.
33. *Ibid.; Supra*, p. 60.
34. *Ibid.*, September 21, 23, 1863; *Daily Missouri Democrat*, September 24, 1863.
35. *Supra*, p. 49.
36. *Tri-Weekly Missouri Democrat*, October 3, 1863. Other newspapers whose officials signed the petition: *Neue Zeit* and *Westliche Post*, St. Louis; *Chillicothe Constitution; Missouri State Times; St. Charles Democrat; Springfield Missourian; Weekly Union of States*, Bethany; *Atchison County Journal; Rolla Express.*
37. *Ibid.*, October 23, 1863.
38. *Ibid.*, *Daily Missouri Democrat*, October 23, November 30, 1863.
39. *Ibid.*, February 3, 8, 11, 1864.
40. *Ibid.*, February 15, 22, 1864.
41. *Tri-Weekly Missouri Democrat*, September 14, 1863; January 14, February 24, March 7, 1864; Hume, *The Abolitionists*, p. 180.
42. "Autobiography of Charles D. Drake" (unpublished manuscript, State Historical Society of Missouri, Columbia, Missouri), p. 940; *Daily Missouri Democrat*, January 15, February 24, 1864.
43. Hume, *The Abolitionists*, p. 180.
44. *Daily Missouri Democrat*, March 7, 1864.
45. *Ibid.*, March 17, 1864; *Tri-Weekly Missouri Democrat*, February 29, 1864.
46. Thomas E. Barclay, "The Liberal Republican Movement in Missouri," *Missouri Historical Review*, XX (October, 1925), 271.
47. *Tri-Weekly Missouri Democrat*, April 11, 1864.
48. *Daily Missouri Democrat*, April 11, May 2, 6, 1864.
49. *Ibid.*, June 1, 10, 1864.
50. *Ibid.*, June 10, 13, 1864.
51. Hume, *The Abolitionists*, p. 180.
52. *Daily Missouri Democrat*, November 14, 1864.
53. Lincoln to Secretaries of St. Marie Brass Band and St. Cecelia Society (forgery), November 16, 1860, *ibid.; Collected Works of Abraham Lincoln*, VIII, 464. References to other possible forgeries can be found in Clinton B. Fisk to Major General Dodge, Macon, January 5, 1865, *War of Rebellion, Official Records*, Series I, XXII, pt. II, 383.
54. Henry T. Blow to Lincoln, St. Louis, December 20, 1864, and Lincoln to Joseph Holt, Washington, December 20, 1864, AGO Special Orders, No.

475, December 30, 1864, *Collected Works of Abraham Lincoln*, VIII, 187-188.
55. *Tri-Weekly Missouri Democrat*, April 17, 1865.
56. *Ibid.*, April 17, 19, 21, 1865.
57. *Daily Missouri Democrat*, April 17—May 8, 1865.
58. *Tri-Weekly Missouri Democrat*, April 17, 1865.
59. Rombauer, *The Union Cause in St. Louis in 1861*, p. 130.

CHAPTER VII

1. *Daily Missouri Democrat*, August 7, 1865.
2. *Ibid.*, November 13-December 18, 1865.
3. "Autobiography of Charles D. Drake," p. 778.
4. For a sound evaluation of Drake, see David DeArmond March, "The Life and Times of Charles D. Drake" (unpublished doctoral dissertation, University of Missouri, Columbia, 1949).
5. *Daily Missouri Democrat*, April 21, 1865.
6. *Ibid.*, June 23, 1866.
7. Walter Williams, "William Mason Grosvenor," *Dictionary of American Biography*, ed. Allen Johnson and Dumas Malone, VIII, 26; G. W. Curtis to Grosvenor, May 19 and June 27, 1866, and Horace White to Grosvenor, August 1, 1866, Grosvenor Papers, cited in Thomas C. Barclay, "The Liberal Republican Movement in Missouri," *Missouri Historical Review*, XX (January, 1926), 277.
8. Williams, *ibid.*, p. 26; *Ste. Genevieve Representative* in Grosvenor papers, cited in Barclay, *ibid.*, p. 278.
9. George William Curtis to W. McKee and G. W. Fishback, June 26, 1866, Barclay, *ibid.*
10. Cited in Barclay, *ibid.*, p. 278.
11. *Daily Missouri Democrat*, November 23, 25, 1866.
12. *Ibid.*, April 27, July 17, 1868.
13. *Ibid.*, November 28, December 1, 1868.
14. Barclay, "The Liberal Republican Movement," p. 271.
15. *Daily Missouri Democrat*, January 3, 1866; February 21, December 20, 1867; April 10, May 18, 1868.
16. Schurz to Theodore Petrassche, St. Louis, June 27, 1867, *Intimate Letters of Carl Schurz, 1841-1869* trans. Joseph Schafer (Madison: Historical Society of Wisconsin, 1928), pp. 398-400.
17. Oswald Garrison Villard, "Carl Schurz," *Dictionary of American Biography*, XVI, 466-476.
18. Schurz to his wife, St. Louis, September 21, 1867, *Intimate Letters of Carl Schurz*, pp. 398-400.
19. *Daily Missouri Democrat*, September 21, 1867.
20. William Hyde, "Newspapers and Newspaper People of Three Decades," *Missouri Historical Society Publications* (St. Louis: Missouri Historical Society, 1896), I, No. 12, pp. 14-15.
21. Schurz to his wife, St. Louis, November 28, 1868, *Intimate Letters of Carl Schurz*, pp. 453-454; *The Reminiscences of Carl Schurz* (New York: The McClure Company, 1908), III, 294-295.

22. *Daily Missouri Democrat,* November 28, December 1, 14, 1868.
23. *Boonville Weekly Advertiser,* January 28, 1876.
24. *The Reminiscences of Carl Schurz,* III, 295.
25. *Ibid.,* p. 296.
26. Schurz to his wife, November 16, 1868, *Intimate Letters of Carl Schurz,* pp. 451-453.
27. *The Reminiscences of Carl Schurz,* **III, 296.**
28. *Daily Missouri Democrat,* January 14, 1869.
29. *Ibid.,* January 11-20, 1869.
30. "Autobiography of Charles D. Drake," pp. 1217-1220.
31. *Daily Missouri Democrat,* January 4, 15, 16, 1869.
32. *Ibid.,* January 15, 1869.
33. *Ibid.,* January 20, 1869.
34. Statement of Grosvenor in *New York Herald,* n. d., Grosvenor papers, cited in Barclay, "The Liberal Republican Movement in Missouri," *Missouri Historical Review,* XX (April, 1926), 437.
35. *Daily Missouri Democrat,* December 17, June 16, July 15, 1869; January 5, 1870.
36. *Ibid.,* January 26, 1870. The *Democrat* was running a section called "Voice of the Press," which was made up of political utterances of various Missouri newspapers.
37. *Ibid.,* June 15, 1870.
38. Scharf, *History of St. Louis,* I, 929; C. I. Filley to William McKee, January 15, 1877, cited in Filley, *Some Republican History of Missouri,* p. 116.
39. C. I. Filley to William McKee, *ibid.*
40. *Daily Missouri Democrat,* September 3, 1870; *The Reminiscences of Carl Schurz,* III, 321-323.
41. *Daily Missouri Democrat,* September 3-7, 1870.
42. Grosvenor to Schurz, February 16, 1871, Schurz papers, cited by Barclay, "The Liberal Republican Movement in Missouri," *Missouri Historical Review,* XXI (October, 1926), 71.
43. Grosvenor to editors of the *New York Evening Post, ibid.,* p. 72.
44. *Daily Missouri Democrat,* September 28-October 15, 1870.
45. For a discussion of McKee's implications in the whisky frauds, see Chapter X. McCullagh will also be discussed in later chapters.

CHAPTER VIII

1. Mott, *American Journalism,* pp. 384, 388; Allan Nevins, *The Emergence of Modern America, 1865-1878* (New York: The Macmillan Company, 1927), p. 240.
2. *Daily Missouri Democrat,* January 24, 1871.
3. *Ibid.*
4. John Clark Crighton, *Missouri and the World War, 1914-1917: A Study in Public Opinion* (Columbia: University of Missouri, 1947), pp. 22-23.
5. *Daily Missouri Democrat,* April 10, 1868.
6. *The Autobiography of Sir Henry Morton Stanley,* ed. Dorothy Stanley (Boston: Houghton Mifflin Co., 1909), pp. 223-228.

7. *Ibid.*, p. 223; Constance Lindsay Skinner, "Henry Morton Stanley," *Dictionary of American Biography*, XVII, 509-513.
8. *Ibid.*
9. *Daily Missouri Democrat*, August 1-November 28, 1867. The *Democrat* published more than thirty letters from Stanley during this period.
10. Skinner, "Henry Morton Stanley," p. 511. One historian has said that Stanley left the *Democrat* in December, 1867. Ian Anstruther, *Dr. Livingstone, I Presume?* (New York: E. P. Dutton and Company, 1956), p. 34.
11. *Daily Missouri Democrat*, June 19, July 7, 1866; April 18, 1868; August 11, 1870; April 25, 1871.
12. *Ibid.*, June 19, August 16, 1869; March 9, 1871.
13. The Whisky Ring trials of 1869 are not to be confused with the Whisky Ring exposé of 1875 in which McKee was involved.
14. *Daily Missouri Democrat*, May 6, 1869.
15. *Ibid.*, August 14, 29, October 9, 1866.
16. *Ibid.*, June 21, December 27, 1865.
17. *Ibid.*, February 20, July 22, 1868.
18. *Missouri Democrat Extra*, Ulysses S. Grant papers, Missouri Historical Society, St. Louis.
19. *Daily Missouri Democrat*, January 1, 1867; April 7, 1868; July 7, 1866; October 20, 1870.
20. *Ibid.*, January 1, 1869.
21. *St. Louis Reference Record*, comp. and ed. William A. Kelsoe (St. Louis: Von Hoffman Press, n. d.), p. 42; Stevens, *The Fourth City*, I, 241-242.
22. *Daily Missouri Democrat*, August 26, 31, September 5, 19, 27, 1867.
23. *Liberty Tribune* (Liberty, Missouri), May 10, 1867.
24. *Daily Missouri Democrat*, July 28, 1866.
25. *Liberty Tribune*, May 10, 1867.
26. *The People's Tribune* (Jefferson City), August 1, 1866.
27. *Liberty Tribune*, May 29, 1867.
28. *Ibid.*, September 6, 1867.
29. *Daily Missouri Democrat*, August 9, 1867.
30. *Ibid.*
31. *Ibid.*
32. *Ibid.*, July 22, 1870.
33. *Ibid.*, May 6, 1869.
34. *Edward's City Directory*, 1867, 1868, 1869, 1872.
35. *St. Louis Globe-Democrat*, October 10, 1915.
36. *Ibid.*, December 29, 1879.
37. Walter Williams, "Joseph Burbridge McCullagh," *Dictionary of American Biography*, XII, 5.

CHAPTER IX

1. Scharf, *History of St. Louis*, I, 926; Stevens, *The Fourth City*, I, 228.
2. Scharf, *ibid.*, I, 936. Fishback sold the *Dispatch* when he bought the *Democrat*.
3. Nevins, *The Emergence of Modern America*, p. 60.

4. *Encyclopaedia of the History of St. Louis*, III, 1634; Scharf, *History of St. Louis*, I, 926; City of St. Louis, General Records, Book 453, p. 52.
5. *Missouri Republican*, March 23, 1872.
6. *Ibid.*
7. City of St. Louis, General Records, Book 453, p. 52.
8. *Missouri Republican*, March 23, 1872.
9. Walter B. Stevens, "Joseph B. McCullagh," *Missouri Historical Review*, XXVI (April, 1932), pp. 256-257.
10. City of St. Louis, General Records, Book 448, p. 324.
11. *Ibid.*, Book 446, p. 338.
12. *The Missouri Democrat*, March 25, 1872. Fishback dropped the word "daily" from the title of the paper the day he bought it.
13. Testimony of Daniel B. Houser in McKee's Case, *St. Louis Globe-Democrat*, January 28, 1876.
14. *Ibid.*, December 29, 1879.
15. *St. Louis Daily Globe*, July 18, 1872.
16. *Ibid.*
17. Testimony of John H. Concannon in McKee's Case, *St. Louis Globe-Democrat*, January 26, 1876.
18. The column disappeared from the paper about the time Davis died in 1873.
19. Stevens, "Joseph B. McCullagh," p. 256.
20. *The Missouri Republican*, January 20-31, 1876.
21. Stevens, "Joseph B. McCullagh," pp. 256-258.
22. Testimony of McCullagh in McKee's Case, *St. Louis Globe-Democrat*, January 28, 1876.
23. Stevens, "Joseph B. McCullagh," p. 259.
24. *St. Louis Democrat*, November 14, 1873. Fishback had changed the name of his journal on January 1, 1873.
25. *St. Louis Daily Globe*, November 2, 1873.
26. *Encyclopaedia of the History of Missouri*, ed. H. L. Conard (New York: The Southern History Company, 1901), IV, 250.
27. Stevens, "Joseph B. McCullagh," p. 158.
28. *St. Louis Post-Dispatch*, December 20, 1879.
29. *St. Louis Dispatch*, January 7, 1874.
30. *Ibid.*; Don C. Seitz, *Joseph Pulitzer: His Life and Letters* (New York: Simon and Schuster, 1924), p. 46.
31. *St. Louis Dispatch*, January 7, 1874. The price was given as $47,500 by Victor Rosewater, *History of Co-operative News-Gathering in the United States* (New York: D. Appleton and Company, 1930), p. 181.
32. *St. Louis Dispatch*, January 7, 1874. Missouri Staats-Zeitung Company was the name of the firm according to *Gould's St. Louis Directory*, 1874 and 1875.
33. *Ibid.*
34. *St. Louis Democrat*, January 8, 1874.
35. *Ibid.*
36. Nevins, *The Emergence of Modern America*, pp. 290-299.
37. Averages were computed from the following issues of both papers: October 1, 12, 22; November 3, 14, 24, 1873.

38. *St. Louis Daily Globe,* November 16; December 1, 10, 1873.
39. *Ibid.,* November 27, December 2, 1873.
40. *Ibid.,* November 4, 1873.
41. Stevens, "Joseph B. McCullagh," pp. 258-260.
42. *Ibid.*
43. *Ibid.*
44. John McDonald, *Secrets of the Great Whiskey Ring; and Eighteen Months in the Penitentiary* (St. Louis: W. S. Bryan, 1880), pp. 126-127.
45. *Ibid.*
46. Stevens, "Joseph B. McCullagh," p. 261.
47. *Ibid.*
48. *Encyclopaedia of the History of St. Louis,* III, 1634; Scharf, *History of St. Louis,* I, 927; Stevens, *The Fourth City,* I, 227; *Jefferson City People's Tribune,* May 19, 1875.
49. Stevens, "Joseph B. McCullagh," p. 259.
50. *St. Louis Globe-Democrat,* May 20, 1875.
51. *Ibid.,* May 20, 1876; February 24, 1878.
52. *A History of the City of St. Louis and Vicinity,* comp. John Devoy (St. Louis: John Devoy, 1898), p. 263; Scharf, *History of St. Louis,* I, 930; *St. Louis Post-Dispatch,* December 20, 1879.
53. *Ibid.*

CHAPTER X

1. Scharf, *History of St. Louis,* II, 1044.
2. McDonald, *The Secrets of the Whiskey Ring,* p. 20.
3. McKee, Fishback & Co. to Gen. Grant, President of the United States, St. Louis, September 5, 1869, *ibid.,* 22.
4. *Ibid.*
5. *Ibid.,* pp. 28-29.
6. *Ibid.,* p. 33.
7. *Ibid.,* pp. 19-36.
8. John A. Joyce to McDonald, St. Louis, October 15, 1870, *ibid.,* pp. 34-35.
9. *Ibid.,* pp. 40-41.
10. *Ibid.,* pp. 51-52.
11. *Ibid.,* p. 59.
12. *Ibid.,* p. 29.
13. *Ibid.,* p. 107.
14. Statement of Grosvenor, *ibid.,* p. 43; Chauncey I. Filley, Political Scrapbook, State Historical Society, Columbia, Missouri.
15. *St. Louis Weekly Globe-Democrat,* December 25, 1879; *St. Louis Post Dispatch,* December 20, 1879.
16. United States Congress, House of Representatives, *Testimony before Select Committee concerning the Whiskey Frauds,* 44th Cong., 1st sess., Misc. Doc. 186. (Washington, D. C.: Government Printing Office, 1876), p. 31; *St. Louis Globe-Democrat,* January 26, 1876.
17. Statement of Grosvenor, cited in McDonald, *Secrets of the Whiskey Ring,* p. 43.

18. Cited in H. V. Boynton, "The Whiskey Ring," *North American Review*, CXIII (October, 1876), 282.

19. Nevins, *The Emergence of Modern America*, p. 178.

20. McDonald, *Secrets of the Whiskey Ring*, p. 126.

21. Interview with Avery by Gibson, Washington correspondent for the *New York Sun*, cited in *ibid.*, p. 297; *St. Louis Reference Record*, p. 99.

22. Boynton, "The Whiskey Ring," p. 290.

23. Walter Williams, "William Mason Grosvenor," *Dictionary of American Biography*, VIII, 26.

24. Colony was later retained as a special investigator for the Internal Revenue Service, *St. Louis Reference Record*, p. 99.

25. *St. Louis Globe-Democrat*, January 27, 1876.

26. *Ibid.*, January 28, 1876.

27. *Ibid.*

28. *Ibid.*

29. *Boonville Weekly Advertiser*, November 12, 1875.

30. *Missouri Republican*, January 28, 1876.

31. *St. Louis Globe-Democrat*, January 30, 1876; *St. Louis Daily Times*, January 22, 1876.

32. *Ibid.*; see also *Boonville Weekly Advertiser*, January 28, 1876.

33. *St. Louis Dispatch*, January 29, 1876.

34. *Missouri Republican*, January 24, 1876.

35. *St. Louis Dispatch*, January 18, 1876.

36. *St. Louis Globe-Democrat*, January 28, 1876.

37. *Ibid.*, January 26, 1876.

38. *Ibid.*, January 29, 1876.

39. *St. Louis Daily Times*, January 22, 1876.

40. *St. Louis Dispatch*, February 1, 1876.

41. *St. Louis Globe-Democrat*, April 28, 1876.

42. *St. Louis Dispatch*, February 1, 1876.

43. *Missouri Republican*, February 1, 1876.

44. *St. Louis Globe-Democrat*, April 27, 1876.

45. *Ibid.*

46. *St. Louis Daily Times*, April 15, 1876.

47. *St. Louis Reference Record*, p. 136.

48. Quoted in *Weekly Globe-Democrat*, December 25, 1879.

49. *St. Louis Globe-Democrat*, February 24, 1878.

50. *Ibid.*, May 13, 1876.

51. *Ibid.*, January 31, 1876.

52. *Weekly Globe-Democrat*, December 25, 1879.

53. *Ibid.*; *St. Louis Post-Dispatch*, December 20, 1879.

54. *Ibid.*

55. *Weekly Globe-Democrat*, December 25, 1879.

56. *Ibid.*

57. *Missouri Republican*, December 21, 1879.

58. *St. Louis Post-Dispatch*, December 20, 1879.

Footnotes 267

CHAPTER XI

1. Quoted in the *St. Louis Republic*, January 1, 1897.
2. Stevens, "Joseph B. McCullagh," *Missouri Historical Review*, XXVI (April, 1932), 258.
3. Arthur Meier Schlesinger, *The Rise of the City, 1878-1898* (New York: Macmillan Company, 1936), p. 185.
4. *Ibid.*, p. 200.
5. *St. Louis Globe-Democrat*, January 6, 1878.
6. *Ibid.*, December 24, 1877-February 24, 1878.
7. *Ibid.*, February 24, 1878.
8. *Ibid.*, July 16, 1879.
9. *Ibid.*, July 17, 1879.
10. *Ibid.*, July 26, August 26, 1879.
11. *Ibid.*
12. Walter B. Stevens, "New Journalism in Missouri," *Missouri Historical Review*, XVIII (October, 1923), 63.
13. McCullagh to W. B. Stevens, St. Louis, March 19, 1891, Newspaper Collection, Missouri Historical Society, St. Louis.
14. McCullagh to W. B. Stevens, St. Louis, November 18, 1891, *ibid.*; Stevens, "New Journalism," *Missouri Historical Review*, XVIII (January, 1924), 553.
15. McCullagh to W. B. Stevens, St. Louis, November 25, 27, December 3, 1891, Newspaper Collection, Missouri Historical Society, St. Louis.
16. McCullagh to W. B. Stevens, St. Louis, n.d., *ibid.*
17. Stevens, "Joseph B. McCullagh," *Missouri Historical Review*, XXVII (October, 1932), 60-62; *St. Louis Globe-Democrat*, March 11, November 23, 1885.
18. Stevens, *ibid.*, XXVI (April, 1932), 260; Stevens, "New Journalism," *ibid.*, XVIII (January, 1924), 199-203; *St. Louis Globe-Democrat*, November 9, 1952.
19. U. S. Census Office, *The Eleventh Census, 1890* (Washington, D. C. Government Printing Office), Part I, p. 434.
20. *St. Louis Globe-Democrat*, January 10, 11, 1878.
21. Ida M. Tarbell, *The Nationalizing of Business, 1878-1898*. (New York: Macmillan Company, 1936), p. 18; *St. Louis Globe-Democrat*, November 9, 1952; August 2, 1959.
22. Stevens, "New Journalism," *Missouri Historical Review*, XVIII (July, 1924), 559-561.
23. *St. Louis Globe-Democrat*, March 6, 11, 1885.
24. Stevens, "New Journalism," *Missouri Historical Review*, XVIII (January, 1924), 204; *ibid.*, (July, 1924), 553-561; Stevens, "Joseph B. McCullagh," *ibid.*, XVIII (January, 1934), 125-127; *St. Louis Globe-Democrat*, July 1-14, 1894.
25. *The Beginning and the Growth of a Great Newspaper*, comp. Paul G. Heneke (Pamphlet, St. Louis: The Globe Printing Company, 1954), p. viii; *St. Louis Globe-Democrat*, May 2, 1884.
26. Theodore Dreiser, *A Book About Myself* (New York: Boni and Liveright, 1922), p. 97.
27. McCullagh to Stevens, St. Louis, November 20, 1890, Newspaper Collection, Missouri Historical Society, St. Louis.

28. McCullagh to Stevens, St. Louis, January 28, 1891, *ibid.*
29. Dreiser, *A Book About Myself*, p. 168.
30. McCullagh to Stevens, January 10, 1893, August 13, 1894, March 19, 1891, Newspaper Collection, Missouri Historical Society, St. Louis.
31. *St. Louis Reference Record*, pp. 44-46. Kelsoe, editor and compiler of this book, was one of the *Globe-Democrat* competitors who was "scooped" because he could not cross the river.
32. Orrick Johns, *Time of Our Lives: The Story of My Father and Myself* (New York: Stackpole Sons, 1937), p. 53.
33. *St. Louis Globe-Democrat*, March 8, 1885; December 23, 1887.
34. Schlesinger, *The Rise of the City*, p. 162.
35. Stevens, *The Fourth City*, I, 227-228.
36. Silas Bent, *Ballyhoo: The Voice of the Press* (New York: Boni and Liveright, 1921), pp. 42-43.
37. *St. Louis Globe-Democrat*, March 8, 1885.
38. Stevens, "New Journalism," *Missouri Historical Review*, XIX (April, 1925), 428.
39. *St. Louis Globe-Democrat*, March 8, 1885.
40. *Ibid.*, December 31, 1883.
41. Schlesinger, *The Rise of the City*, p. 112.
42. *St. Louis Globe-Democrat*, April 15, 1855; June 6, 1882.
43. *St. Louis Globe-Democrat*, March 9, 1885.
44. McCullagh to Stevens, St. Louis, August 13, 1894, and March 27, 1893, Newspaper Collection, Missouri Historical Society, St. Louis.
45. *St. Louis Republic*, January 1, 1897.
46. Clipping of cartoon, Newspaper Collection, Missouri Historical Society, St. Louis.
47. McCullagh to Stevens, July 10, 1890, November 20, 1887, January 9, 1891, *ibid.*
48. *St. Louis Republic*, January 1, 1897; *New York Times*, January 1, 1897; *Encyclopaedia of the History of Missouri*, ed. H. L. Conard (New York: The Southern Literary Company, 1901), IV, 249-251; Walter Williams, "Joseph Burbridge McCullagh," *Dictionary of American Biography*, XII, 5.
49. Stevens, "Joseph B. McCullagh," *Missouri Historical Review*, XXVII, (April, 1933), 257-259.
50. *Ibid.*; Stevens, "New Journalism," *ibid.*, XIX (April, 1925), 430-435.
51. Stevens, "New Journalism," *ibid.*, p. 434; *St. Louis Globe-Democrat*, March 8, 28, 1885.
52. *Ibid.*, October 18-24, 1886.
53. *Ibid.*, March 8, 1885; December 23, 1887; April 30, 1892.
54. *Ibid.*, December 3, 10, 17, 1887; January 12, 1892.
55. *St. Louis Republic*, January 2, 1897.
56. *Ibid.*; Stevens, "Joseph B. McCullagh," *Missouri Historical Review*, XXVII (April, 1933), 257-259.
57. *St. Louis Globe-Democrat*, July 11, 1879.
58. McCullagh to Stevens, St. Louis, January 5, 1888, Newspaper Collection, Missouri Historical Society, St. Louis.

59. Chauncey I. Filley to Miss Stella Dunn, St. Louis, March 30, 1919, Filley Family Papers, Missouri Historical Society, St. Louis.
60. Stevens, "Joseph B. McCullagh," *Missouri Historical Review,* XXVII (October, 1932), 260.
61. *Ibid.,* p. 264.
62. *St. Louis Republic,* January 2, 1897.
63. Stevens, "New Journalism," *Missouri Historical Review,* XVII (April, 1924), 404-407.
64. *St. Louis Globe-Democrat,* July 31-August 31, 1879.
65. Stevens, "Joseph B. McCullagh," *Missouri Historical Review,* XXVI (October, 1931), 50-53.
66. Stevens, "Joseph B. McCullagh," *Missouri Historical Review,* XXVII (January, 1933), 152-153; Stevens, "New Journalism," *ibid.,* XIX (April, 1925), 430-435.
67. *St. Louis Globe-Democrat,* June 11-August 7, 1880; July 3, 1881.
68. *Ibid.,* May 25-June 8; October 29, 1884.
69. *Ibid.,* July 22, 1884.
70. *Ibid.,* July 26, 31, 1884.
71. *Ibid.,* March 8, 1885.
72. *Ibid.,* January 13, 18, February 2, 9, March 21, 22, 1885.
73. *Ibid.,* August 23, 24, September 17, 28, 1888; May 13, 1892.
74. *Ibid.,* August 23, September 17, 29, 1888.
75. *Ibid.,* November 5, 6, 1892.
76. *Ibid.,* January 7, 1893.
77. Walter B. Stevens, "The Political Turmoil in Missouri," *Missouri Historical Review,* XXXI (October, 1936), 8-9.
78. James C. Espy's interview with Colonel Joseph Burbridge McCullagh, typed copy with attached explanations by the author, Newspaper Collection, Missouri Historical Society, St. Louis.
79. Dreiser, *A Book About Myself,* pp. 92, 98, 116.
80. *Ibid.;* Stevens, *The Fourth City,* I, 294.
81. *St. Louis Reference Record,* pp. 14, 44-56, 115; Stevens, "New Journalism," *Missouri Historical Review,* XIX (January, 1925), 328.
82. A two-page partial manuscript, believed to be in McCullagh's handwriting, Newspaper Collection, Missouri Historical Society, St. Louis; postscript to a letter, signed H. A. D., n. d., *ibid.*
83. Stevens, "New Journalism, *Missouri Historical Review,* XVII (April, 1924), 408.
84. *St. Louis Post-Dispatch,* December 31, 1896.
85. McCullagh to Stevens, St. Louis, March 12, 1886, Newspaper Collection, Missouri Historical Society, St. Louis.
86. McCullagh to Stevens, St. Louis, March 11, 1891, *ibid.*
87. *St. Louis Post-Dispatch,* December 31, 1896.
88. *Ibid.*
89. *New York Times,* January 1, 1897.
90. *St. Louis Republic,* January 1, 1897.
91. Stevens, "Joseph B. McCullagh," *Missouri Historical Review,* XXVI (April, 1932), 60-62.

92. *St. Louis Republic*, January 1, 1897; *St. Louis Post-Dispatch*, December 31, 1896; Dreiser, *A Book About Myself*, p. 168.
93. Eugene Field, *A Little Book of Western Verse* (New York: Charles Scribner's Sons, 1899), pp. 36-39. McCullagh was one of the hundred people who subscribed ten dollars to the first edition of Field's first book of poetry. Charles H. Dennis, *Eugene Field's Creative Years* (New York: Doubleday, Page and Company, 1924), pp. 182-184.
94. *St. Louis Reference Record*, p. 174; Stevens, "New Journalism," *Missouri Historical Review*, XIX (October, 1924), 110-113; Stevens, *ibid.*, (July, 1925), 686-688.
95. *St. Louis Republic*, January 1, 1897; *St. Louis Globe-Democrat*, April 19, August 14, 1892; *The Beginning and Growth of a Great Newspaper*, p. iv.
96. *St. Louis Republic*, January 1, 1897; *St. Louis Post-Dispatch*, December 31, 1896.
97. *St. Louis Republic*, January 1, 1897.
98. *Ibid.;* Stevens, *The Fourth City*, I, 230.
99. *New York Times*, July 10, 1941.

CHAPTER XII

1. Statement of Daniel M. Houser, *St. Louis Republic*, January 1, 1897.
2. Henry Watterson, "The Personal Equation in Journalism," *Atlantic Monthly*, CVI (July, 1910), 40.
3. "D. M. Houser," *Encyclopaedia of the History of Missouri*, III, 307-308.
4. Schlesinger, *The Rise of the City*, p. 186.
5. *St. Louis Globe-Democrat*, April 1, 10, 1892.
6. *Ibid.*, May 4, 1884; March 8, 1885; April 1, 10, 1892.
7. *Ibid.*, February 14, 1915.
8. *Ibid.*, October 9, 12, 1898; August 7, 1907.
9. *Ibid.*, September 11, 1910; February 14, December 12, 26, 1915.
10. *N. W. Ayer and Sons American Newspaper Annual and Directory*, 1891, 1896.
11. Mott, *American Journalism*, p. 498.
12. *St. Louis Globe-Democrat*, November 1, 1884, January 2, 1886; October 9, 1892.
13. Stevens, "New Journalism," *Missouri Historical Review*, XVII (October, 1923), 322.
14. *St. Louis Globe-Democrat*, December 12, 1883.
15. *Ibid.*, November 1, 1884; November 3, 1885; October 9, 1892.
16. *St. Louis Reference Record*, p. 276.
17. *History of St. Louis*, ed. Devoy, p. 263; *What Makes the Globe-Democrat a Great Paper* (St. Louis: The Globe Printing Company, n. d.), p. 3.
18. Stevens, *The Fourth City*, I, 234.
19. *History of St. Louis*, ed. Devoy, p. 263; *What Makes the Globe-Democrat a Great Paper*, p. 3.
20. "D. M. Houser," *Encyclopaedia of the History of Missouri*, III, 308.
21. Stevens, "New Journalism," *Missouri Historical Review*, XVII (April, 1923), 323.

22. *Ibid.,* (July, 1923), 475. Two letters from John Knapp to George Knapp from London, dated July 15 and August 17, 1872, in the Newspaper Collection, Missouri Historical Society, St. Louis, speak of this.
23. Stevens, "New Journalism," *Missouri Historical Review,* XVII (April, 1923), 323; Stevens, *The Fourth City,* I, 247.
24. Stevens, "New Journalism," *ibid.,* p. 323.
25. *N. W. Ayer and Sons American Newspaper Annual and Directory,* 1886.
26. *Ibid.,* 1903.
27. *St. Louis Globe-Democrat,* February 14, 1915.
28. Stevens, "New Journalism," *Missouri Historical Review,* XIX (January, 1925), 331.
29. *Ibid.,* pp. 331-332.
30. *Ibid.,* p. 332.
31. *Ibid.,* p. 333.
32. Stevens, *The Fourth City,* I, 235.
33. Stevens, "New Journalism," *"Missouri Historical Review,* XVIII (April, 1924), 411-414.
34. *St. Louis Reference Record,* p. 174.
35. Mott, *American Journalism,* p. 433; Stevens, "New Journalism," *Missouri Historical Review,* XIX (July, 1925), 676; Scharf, *History of St. Louis,* I, 937.
36. Stevens, *ibid.,* p. 677.
37. *N. W. Ayer and Sons American Newspaper Annual and Directory,* 1900. The *Post-Dispatch* had a circulation of 81,832; the *Globe-Democrat,* 79,172. These were the publishers' sworn estimates.
38. *Ibid.,* 1915.
39. *St. Louis Reference Record,* p. 174.
40. *N. W. Ayer and Sons American Newspaper Annual and Directory,* 1899. The circulation of the Sunday *Globe-Democrat* was 102,602 in 1898, but the next year it dropped to 87,096. That was the first year that the Sunday *Post-Dispatch* reached 100,000.
41. *Ibid.,* 1916. The *Post-Dispatch* had a circulation of 333,207 to the *Globe-Democrat's* 173,197.
42. Interview with Douglas B. Houser, September 3, 1958.
43. Stevens, "New Journalism," *Missouri Historical Review,* XVII (April, 1923), 324-326.
44. *Boonville Weekly Advertiser,* May 19, 1905.
45. *St. Louis Globe-Democrat,* May 7, 1905. The will was quoted in its entirety.
46. Interview with Douglas B. Houser, September 3, 1958.
47. *Ibid.*
48. *St. Louis Globe-Democrat,* October 10, 1915. D. M. Houser to D. R. Francis, St. Louis, April 29, 1914, Francis papers, Missouri Historical Society, St. Louis.
49. *St. Louis Post-Dispatch,* October 10, 1915.
50. *St. Louis Globe-Democrat,* October 10, 1915.
51. "D. M. Houser," *Encyclopaedia of the History of Missouri,* III, 307-308.

52. Stevens, "Joseph B. McCullagh," *Missouri Historical Review*, XXVIII (April, 1934), 208.
53. Interview with Douglas B. Houser, September 2, 1958.

CHAPTER XIII

1. *St. Louis Post-Dispatch*, December 31, 1896.
2. *St. Louis Republic*, January 1, 1897.
3. Walter Williams, "Captain Henry King," *Dictionary of American Biography*, X, 390; *New York Times*, March 16, 1915; *St. Louis Globe-Democrat*, March 16, 1915.
4. Stevens, "New Journalism," *Missouri Historical Review*, XIX (April, 1925), 427.
5. *St. Louis Globe-Democrat*, March 16, 1915.
6. Captain Henry King, "Commencement Day Address at Kansas State University," June 6, 1906, quoted in *History of Kansas Newspapers* (Topeka: Kansas State Historical Society and Department of Archives, 1916), p. 16.
7. *St. Louis Globe-Democrat*, March 16, 1915.
8. *Ibid.*, May 20, 1904.
9. Cited in Stevens, *The Fourth City*, I, 250.
10. *Ibid.*, p. 234; "Historical Notes and Comments," *Missouri Historical Review*, XXXVII (October, 1942), 108; *St. Louis Reference Record*, p. 275.
11. *Ibid.*; see also Leon William Lindsay, "A Biography of David R. McAnally, Jr.," (unpublished Master's thesis, University of Missouri, Columbia).
12. Cited in *St. Louis Globe-Democrat*, March 16, 1915, and in Stevens, *The Fourth City*, I, 234.
13. Cited in *St. Louis Globe-Democrat*, November 9, 1952.
14. Delos F. Wilcox, "The American Newspapers: A Study in Social Psychology," *Annals of the American Academy of Political and Social Science*, XVI (July, 1900), 71-72.
15. *St. Louis Globe-Democrat*, February 18, 1896; October 7, 1899.
16. *Ibid.*, March 16-23, 1897.
17. *Ibid.*, March 16-18, 1897.
18. The *Post-Dispatch*, December 31, 1896, had used large black headlines across three columns to tell of McCullagh's death.
19. See Mott, *American Journalism*, p. 539.
20. *St. Louis Reference Record*, pp. 121, 275.
21. *St. Louis Globe-Democrat*, July-August, 1904.
22. *St. Louis Reference Record*, p. 274.
23. *Ibid.*, p. 86; *Who Was Who in America, 1897-1942* (Chicago: A. N. Marquis Company, 1942), I.
24. *Ibid.*; Casper Yost File, *Globe-Democrat* Reference Library.
25. *St. Louis Globe-Democrat*, November 9, 1952; *Encyclopedia of St. Louis*, p. 1630.
26. *St. Louis Reference Record*, p. 273; *St. Louis Globe-Democrat*, 1904-1915.
27. *Ibid.*, August 11, 1907; February 14, 1915.
28. *Ibid.*, January 30, 1898; October 8, 1899; February 12, 1905; August 11, 1907; February 14, June 8, 1915.

29. *Ibid.*, November 10, 24, 1907.
30. These books include *The Making of a Successful Husband*: *Letters of a Happily Married Man to His Son* (New York: G. W. Dillingham Company, 1907), and *The Making of a Successful Wife*: *Letters of a Father to His Daughter* (New York: G. W. Dillingham Company, 1907).
31. New York: Henry Holt and Company, 1916.
32. See Marcus M. Wilkerson, *Public Opinion and the Spanish-American War*: *A Study in War Propaganda* (Baton Rouge: Louisiana State University Press, 1932).
33. *St. Louis Globe-Democrat*, March 8-14, 1897.
34. *Ibid.*, February 16, 17, 1898.
35. *Ibid.*, February 17, 1898–August 13, 1898; *St. Louis Reference Record*, pp. 77-78. Some stories from Cuba were signed by Charles M. Pepper.
36. *Ibid.*, March 15, 1915.
37. *St. Louis Reference Record*, p. 82.
38. Stevens, *The Fourth City*, I, 1130.
39. David R. Francis, *The Universal Exposition of 1904* (St. Louis: Louisiana Purchase Exposition Co., 1913), p. 76.
40. David R. Francis to Captain King, St. Louis, June 15, 1903, Francis Papers, Missouri Historical Society, St. Louis.
41. *St. Louis Globe-Democrat*, July 1–December 1, 1904.
42. David R. Francis to Captain King, St. Louis, June 15, 1903, Francis Papers, Missouri Historical Society, St. Louis; Stevens, *The Fourth City*, I, 1101-1102.
43. *St. Louis Globe-Democrat*, October 7, 1958; *St. Louis Reference Record*, pp. 274-275.
44. Wilcox, "American Newspapers," p. 56; Alfred McClung Lee, *The Daily Newspaper in America*: *The Evolution of a Social Instrument* (New York: The Macmillan Company, 1937), p. 645.
45. See Louis G. Geiger, "The Public Career of Joseph W. Folk," (unpublished doctoral dissertation, University of Missouri, 1948).
46. *St. Louis Globe-Democrat*, February 29, March 10, 18, September 20, 1904.
47. *Missouri State Tribune*, Jefferson City, December 8, 1899; August 21, 1901.
48. Chauncey I. Filley to Miss Stella Dunn, St. Louis, March 30, 1919, Filley Family Papers, Missouri Historical Society, St. Louis.
49. Cook V. Globe Printing Company, *Southwestern Reporter*, 127:332.
50. *St. Louis Globe-Democrat*, December 6, 1897.
51. C. I. Filley's Political Scrapbook, State Historical Society of Missouri, Columbia.
52. *St. Louis Globe-Democrat*, October 4, 10, 1900.
53. *Ibid.*, October 12, 1904.
54. *Ibid.*, October 5, 1908.
55. *Ibid.*, October 10, 1908.
56. *Ibid.*, October 6, 11, 1912.
57. *Ibid.*, March 16, 1915.
58. *Ibid.*; Williams, "Captain Henry King," p. 390.
59. *New York Times*, March 16, 1915; *St. Louis Republic*, March 16, 1915.
60. Williams, "Captain Henry King," p. 390.

CHAPTER XIV

1. Interview with Douglas B. Houser, September 2, 1958; James W. Markham, *Bovard of the Dispatch* (Baton Rouge: Louisiana State Press, 1954), pp. 82-83.
2. E. Lansing Ray File, *Globe-Democrat* Reference Library.
3. Joseph J. McAuliffe File, *Globe-Democrat* Reference Library. McAuliffe came from a family of reporters. Florence D. White, his cousin, became an executive of the *New York World;* and his brother, Dan J. McAuliffe, once served as managing editor of the *Republic.*
4. *Ibid.*, McAuliffe wrote for *Leslie's Monthly Magazine* an article on Ed Butler, a central figure in many of the Folk exposures. See "From Blacksmith to Boss," LVIII (October, 1904), 635-636.
5. *Ibid.*
6. *New York Times*, May 2, 1941; Joseph J. McAuliffe File, *Globe-Democrat* Reference Library.
7. *St. Louis Globe-Democrat*, June 18, 1916.
8. *Ibid.*, August 3, 7, September 27, 1914.
9. *Ibid.*, August 17, September 7, 1914.
10. *Ibid.*, June 29, August 18, September 30, 1914.
11. *Ibid.*, August 22, September 20, October 2, 1914; February 28, 1910.
12. Crighton, *Missouri and the World War*, p. 26.
13. *St. Louis Globe-Democrat*, January 24, May 22, 1915.
14. *Ibid.*, December 30, 31, 1914; January 12, February 3, 6, March 19, September 15, 21, 25, 1915.
15. *Ibid.*, April 10, 1915.
16. *Ibid.*, May 11, 1915.
17. *Ibid.*, April 20, 1916.
18. *Ibid.*, April 21, 1916.
19. *Ibid.*, April 26, 1916.
20. *Ibid.*, February 22, June 23, 1916.
21. Crighton, *Missouri and the World War*, p. 129.
22. *St. Louis Globe-Democrat*, December 29, 1914; May 28, 1915; December 9, 1916.
23. *Ibid.*, May 13, June 6, 8, 1916.
24. *Ibid.*, October 4, 24, 25, 1916.
25. *Ibid.*, January 23, 26, 1917.
26. *Ibid.*, February 5-19, 1917.
27. *Ibid.*, March 2, 4, 20, 22, 1917.
28. Casper S. Yost File, *Globe-Democrat* Reference Library; *New York Times*, May 31, 1941.
29. E. Lansing Ray Diary, University of Missouri, Columbia.
30. *Ibid.*
31. *Ibid.*
32. *Ibid.*
33. *Ibid.*

34. "Special Soldiers, Sailors and Marine Edition," *Globe-Democrat*, January 1, 1919. The *Globe-Democrat* also used this small format for several house organs from 1918-1923. *Teamwork* was an illustrated magazine for advertisers, and *Handclasp* was a publication for the mechanical employees. A few copies of each of these publications are in the Missouri Historical Society's Newspaper Collection, St. Louis.
35. Interview with Douglas B. Houser, September 2, 1958; Douglas B. Houser file, *Globe-Democrat* Reference Library.
36. William C. Houser File, *Globe-Democrat* Reference Library.
37. *N. W. Ayer and Sons American Newspaper Annual and Directory*, 1920.
38. *Jefferson City Democrat-Tribune*, December 3, 1919.
39. Francis J. Wade to Mrs. Genevieve Knapp, St. Louis, October 10, 1919, Newspaper Collection, Missouri Historical Society, St. Louis; Stevens, "New Journalism," *Missouri Historical Review*, XIX (January, 1925), 333.
40. This price was carried on the company's balance sheet as "*St. Louis Republic* Purchase," an intangible asset.
41. *Globe-Democrat* Reference Library.
42. "*Republic* Sale," *Editor and Publisher*, LII (December 11, 1919, 28; *Jefferson City Democrat-Tribune*, December 3, 1919.
43. *Ibid.*
44. E. Lansing Ray File, *Globe-Democrat* Reference Library.
45. Full page advertisement of *Globe-Democrat* in *Editor and Publisher*, LII (December 11, 1919), 28.

CHAPTER XV

1. Preston William Slosson, *The Great Crusade and After, 1914-1928* (New York: The Macmillan Company, 1931), pp. 140-141; *St. Louis Chamber of Commerce News*, January 21, November 12, 1929.
2. Slosson, *ibid.*, p. 97.
3. "*Republic* Sale," *Editor and Publisher*, LII (December 11, 1919), 28.
4. *St. Louis Globe-Democrat*, May 7, 1905; *St. Louis Post-Dispatch*, March 24, 1955; Interview with Douglas B. Houser, September 2, 1958.
5. Minutes of the Meeting of Stockholders, March 8, 1922; November 26, 1922; April 10, 1925; April 30, 1925, *Globe-Democrat* official files; State of Missouri, Office of Secretary of State, Corporation Book 76, p. 45; Book 80, p. 10; Book 18, p. 398; Book 83, p. 369; Book 85, p. 186. In 1922, the company had assets worth $2,521,122 and liabilities of $1,652,525.
6. *St. Louis Globe-Democrat*, November 9, 1952.
7. *New York Times*, May 31, 1941; Casper S. Yost, *The Principles of Journalism* (New York: D. Appleton and Company, 1924), pp. 7, 115.
8. *Ibid.*, p. 8.
9. *St. Louis Globe-Democrat*, October 6, 20, 1920.
10. *Ibid.*, October 13, 1928.
11. *Ibid.*, October 28, 1924.
12. *Ibid.*, September 18, 1927; September 28, October 13, 1928.
13. Charles A. Lindbergh, *The Spirit of St. Louis* (New York: Charles Scribner's Sons, 1953), p. 34.

14. Joseph J. McAuliffe File, *Globe-Democrat* Reference Library.
15. Lindbergh, *The Spirit of St. Louis*, p. 155.
16. *Ibid.*, p. 165.
17. *St. Louis Globe-Democrat*, October-November, 1929.
18. The parade of the Veiled Prophet had been, since 1878, a leading social event in St. Louis. See *Globe-Democrat*, October 7, 1958, for a complete history of this event.
19. *Ibid.*, November 8, 1931.
20. K. H. Eggers Report, October 1, 1947, *Globe-Democrat* official files.
21. *N. W. Ayer and Sons Newspaper Annual and Directory*, 1927.
22. Interview with Douglas B. Houser, September 2, 1958.
23. K. H. Eggers Report.
24. *Ibid.*; *St. Louis Globe-Democrat*, November 7, 1931.
25. "Page and Paper Sizes and Other Mechanical Data of 8,000 Dailies," *Editor and Publisher*, LXIII (October 25, 1930), 23.
26. *St. Louis Globe-Democrat*, November 8-20, 1931.

CHAPTER XVI

1. K. H. Eggers Report. Made in 1947, this report was an examination of the Globe-Democrat Publishing Company for the purpose of ascertaining the value of its shares in order to settle the estate of Mrs. E. Lansing Ray, who died in 1946. K. H. Eggers was the vice-president of the St. Louis Union Trust Company.
2. *St. Louis Globe-Democrat*, October 15-23, 1932.
3. Mott, *American Journalism*, p. 675; K. H. Eggers Report.
4. *Ibid.*; *N. W. Ayer and Sons Directory of Newspapers and Periodicals*, 1936, 1941.
5. *Ibid.* The *St. Louis Star* and the *St. Louis Times* were merged in 1932.
6. K. H. Eggers Report.
7. Dixon Wecter, *The Age of the Great Depression, 1929-1941* (New York: The Macmillan Company, 1948), p. 88.
8. K. H. Eggers Report.
9. Interview with Douglas B. Houser, September 2, 1958; interview with Louis LaCoss, October 16, 1958.
10. *St. Louis Globe-Democrat*, October 1-3, 1932; July 15-October 6, 1933.
11. *New York Times*, May 31, 1941.
12. *St. Louis Globe-Democrat*, November-December, 1931.
13. *Ibid.*, November 1, 1932.
14. *Ibid.*, June 16, 1933.
15. *Ibid.*, May 9, 1934.
16. *Ibid.*, March 1, 1935.
17. *Ibid.*, June 14, 1933; May 23, 1934; November 21, 1936.
18. *Ibid.*, October 27, November 21, 1936.
19. *Ibid.*, March 21, June 28, 1933.
20. *Ibid.*, October 5, 9, 1932.
21. *Ibid.*, October 8, 1932.
22. *Ibid.*, October 13, 1932.

23. *Ibid.,* October 1, 25, 1932.
24. *Ibid.,* May 1, 1934.
25. *Ibid.,* November 9, 1932.
26. *Ibid.,* March 5, 1933.
27. *Ibid.,* March 6, 18, June 1, 1933.
28. *Ibid.,* June 26, 1933.
29. *Ibid.,* May 8., 1934.
30. *Ibid.,* October 2, 27, 1936.
31. *Ibid.,* October 1, 2, 1936.
32. *Ibid.,* October 21, 1936.
33. This explanation headed each editorial.
34. This phrase was used to describe Yost on a menu of a banquet in New York, at which the editor was a guest. Interview with Louis LaCoss, November 16, 1958.
35. *St. Louis Globe-Democrat,* October 17, 20, 1940.
36. *Ibid.,* November 6, 1940.
37. *Ibid.,* November 7, 1940.
38. *Ibid.,* October 3, 1932; March 21, 23, June 13, 1933.
39. *Ibid.,* March 6, 1935.
40. *Ibid.,* March 16, 17, 1939.
41. *Ibid.,* September 3, 1939.
42. *Ibid.*
43. *Ibid.,* May 11, 1940.
44. *Ibid.,* June 7, 8, 1940.
45. *Ibid.,* June 14, 1940.
46. *New York Times,* May 31, 1941; *St. Louis Globe-Democrat,* November 8, 1931.
47. *Ibid.,* May 6, 1932.
48. Interview with Louis LaCoss, October 16, 1958.
49. *Ibid.; St. Louis Globe-Democrat,* November 9, 1952.
50. *Ibid.,* June 8, 1946.

CHAPTER XVII

1. K. H. Eggers Report; *N. W. Ayer and Sons Directory of Newspapers and Periodicals,* 1952.
2. *Ibid.*
3. *Ibid.*
4. Interview with H. O. Wilkat, general auditor of the *Globe-Democrat,* July 6, 1958.
5. Interview with Douglas B. Houser, September 2, 1958.
6. *St. Louis Globe-Democrat,* November 9, 1952.
7. Interview with Douglas B. Houser, September 2, 1958; interview with Louis LaCoss, editorial page editor of the *Globe-Democrat,* October 16, 1958.
8. *Ibid.*
9. KWGD File, *Globe-Democrat* Reference Library.
10. Interview with Douglas B. Houser, September 2, 1958.
11. *Ibid.;* interview with Louis LaCoss, October 16, 1958.

12. KWGD and KWK files, *Globe-Democrat* Reference Library.
13. Interview with G. D. Bauman, personnel manager of the *Globe-Democrat*, October 16, 1958. "Flyboys" do not rank as high as apprentices.
14. Carriers were not permitted to organize under the Taft-Hartley law, according to Bauman.
15. K. H. Eggers Report.
16. *Ibid.*
17. Interview with Louis LaCoss, October 16, 1958.
18. *New York Times*, July 10, 1941.
19. *St. Louis Globe-Democrat*, August 8, 1953.
20. *Ibid.*, December 8, 1941.
21. *Ibid.*, December 9, 1941.
22. *Ibid.*, December 10, 11, 1941.
23. *Ibid.*, May 1, 2, 1945.
24. *Ibid.*, May 3, 5, 1945.
25. *Ibid.*, May 5, 8, 9, 1945.
26. *Ibid.*, August 10-15, 1945
27. Interview with Louis LaCoss, October 16, 1958. Neither was there a staff of reporters in the field during the Korean conflict.
28. *St. Louis Globe-Democrat*, November 9, 1952.
29. *Ibid.*, November 9, 1952; August 8, 1953.
30. *Ibid.*, June, 1948; November 9, 1952.
31. *Ibid.*, October 5, 6, 21, 30, 1944.
32. *Ibid.*, October 16, 1944.
33. *Ibid.*, November 5, 1944.
34. *Ibid.*, April 13, 1945.
35. *Ibid.*
36. *Ibid.*, October 11, 1948. See also issues of October 12, 17, 24.
37. *Ibid.*, November 1, 1948.
38. *Ibid.*, June 26, 27, 28, 29, 30, 1950.
39. *Ibid.*, October 3, 1952.
40. *Ibid.*, June 8, 1946.
41. *Ibid.*, April 23, 1950.
42. *Ibid.*, June 19, 1951.
43. *Ibid.*, January 20, 1950; November 9, 1952.
44. *Ibid.*, July 20, 1951.
45. *Ibid.*, November 9, 1952.
46. *Ibid.*, February 22, 1952.
47. Interview with Louis LaCoss, October 16, 1958; *New York Times*, August 31, 1955; *The University of Missouri Bulletin*, vol. 47, no. 21, Journalism Series 106.

CHAPTER XVIII

1. "New Presses Installed," *Overset*, I (January, 1952), 1-2; "Message of James C. Burkham, President, *Globe-Democrat*," *ibid.*, p. 5.
2. "Statement of E. Lansing Ray," released by Managing Editor Aaron G. Benesch, at 4:35 p.m., March 23, 1955, quoted in *St. Louis Post-Dispatch*, March 24, 1955.

3. Newhouse owned ten papers in New York, New Jersey, Pennsylvania, and Oregon and radio and television stations in New York, Pennsylvania, and Oregon. *Ibid.; New York Times*, March 24, 1955.
4. *Ibid.*
5. "Statement of E. Lansing Ray," *St. Louis Post-Dispatch*, March 24, 1925.
6. *New York Times*, March 24, 1955. Ray was said to have owned over 65 per cent of the stock of the Globe-Democrat Publishing Company.
7. "Statement of Publisher Richard H. Amberg" in advertisement in *St. Louis Post-Dispatch*, February 22, 1959; "*St. Louis Globe-Democrat* Goes to Contract Printing," *Editor and Publisher*, XCII (February 28, 1959), 13.
8. "The Empire Builder," p. 56.
9. *St. Louis Globe-Democrat*, December 22, 1955; March 13, June 6, 1956.
10. *Ibid.*, September 8, 1955.
11. Richard H. Amberg to Jim Allee Hart, St. Louis, August 8, 1960.

CHAPTER XIX

1. Richard H. Amberg to Jim Allee Hart, St. Louis, August 8, 1960.
2. *Ibid.*
3. *Ibid.*
4. *Ibid.;* interview with Louis LaCoss, October 16, 1958.
5. *Ibid.*
6. *St. Louis Globe-Democrat*, October 21, 1958.
7. Richard H. Amberg to Jim Allee Hart, St. Louis, August 8, 1960.
8. *St. Louis Globe-Democrat*, October 21, 1958.
9. *Ibid.*, January 6-9, 1959; "Peeping Lens Shows Cops in Gambling Spot," *Editor and Publisher*, XCII (January 17, 1959), 58.
10. Richard H. Amberg to Jim Allee Hart, St. Louis, August 8, 1960.
11. *Ibid.*
12. *Ibid.*
13. *Ibid.*
14. *N. W. Ayer and Sons Directory of Newspapers and Periodicals*, 1956.
15. Advertisement of *St. Louis Globe-Democrat, Editor and Publisher*, XCII (January 17, 1959), 5.
16. *Ibid.*
17. See issues of December 27, 1958, January 24 and February 7, 1959.
18. "Seeds in St. Louis," *Time*, LXXIII (June 1, 1959), 66.
19. *St. Louis Post-Dispatch*, February 28, 1959; "Alliance of Necessity," *Time*, LXXIII (March 9, 1959), 70; "*St. Louis Globe-Democrat* Goes to Contract Printing," *Editor and Publisher*, XCII (March 9, 1959), 13.
20. *Ibid.*
21. *Ibid.*
22. *Ibid.*
23. *Ibid.*
24. *Ibid.*
25. *St. Louis Post-Dispatch*, March 22, 1959.
26. *Ibid.*

27. "Senators to Probe St. Louis Strike," *Editor and Publisher*, XCII (April 25, 1959), 121; *St. Louis Post-Dispatch*, April 17, 1959; "Pact Near in Newhouse Negotiations," *Editor and Publisher*, XCII (May 16, 1959), 16.
28. *Ibid.; St. Louis Post-Dispatch*, May 9, 12, 1959.
29. "June 1 Target Date for *Globe-Democrat*," *Editor and Publisher*, XCII (May 5, 1959), 10; "*St. Louis Globe-Democrat* Set to Roll Again June 1," *ibid.*, (May 30, 1959), 9.
30. "Seeds in St. Louis," *Time*, LXIII (June 1, 1959), 66.
31. "Pulitzer Urges End of Rival's Shutdown," *Editor and Publisher*, XCII (April 18, 1959), 16.
32. "We're Back! *Globe* Tells St. Louis," *ibid.*, (June 6, 1959), 12.
33. One year after the crippling strike was settled, the *Globe-Democrat* had made phenomenal progress in recouping its losses in advertising and circulation. By July, 1960, Publisher Amberg could point to an increase of 2.2 per cent in total display advertising and to .4 per cent in total advertising as compared to the paper's percentage of the field for the previous year. The lower percentage in total advertising was due to the paper's large losses in classified advertising.

Its circulation increases were far better, particularly in view of the *Post-Dispatch*'s increase in circulation of 65,500 during the strike. For the three-month period following the strike, the *Globe-Democrat*'s circulation dropped to 309,943 from its pre-strike circulation of 334,240. This loss included the 40,000 daily circulation which the paper voluntarily gave up through the racks because of the tremendously high cost that would have been involved, as well as its losses to the *Post-Dispatch*. However, during January-March, 1960, it had climbed to 340,914, an all-time high for the paper. On this extraordinary circulation increase, Publisher Amberg commented: "I honestly believe this is a record unequalled in American journalism."

Bibliography

A. MANUSCRIPTS, DOCUMENTS, AND PRIVATE PAPERS

Thomas H. Benton Papers. Missouri Historical Society, St. Louis, Missouri.

Frank P. Blair Papers. Missouri Historical Society, St. Louis, Missouri.

James O. Broadhead Papers. Missouri Historical Society, St. Louis, Missouri.

B. Gratz Brown Papers (Transportation). Missouri Historical Society, St. Louis, Missouri.

Orlando Brown Papers. Filson Club, Louisville, Kentucky.

K. H. Eggers Report, October 1, 1947. *Globe-Democrat* Official Records, St. Louis, Missouri.

David R. Francis Papers. Missouri Historical Society, St. Louis, Missouri.

Filley Family Papers. Missouri Historical Society, St. Louis, Missouri.

Chauncey I. Filley's Political Scrapbook. State Historical Society, Columbia, Missouri.

Ulysses S. Grant Papers. Missouri Historical Society, St. Louis, Missouri.

KWGD File. *Globe-Democrat* Reference Library, St. Louis, Missouri.

KWKD File. *Globe-Democrat* Reference Library, St. Louis, Missouri.

Abraham Lincoln Papers. Missouri Historical Society, St. Louis, Missouri.

Joseph J. McAuliffe File. *Globe-Democrat* Reference Library, St. Louis, Missouri.

McKee and Fishback Business Papers, 1859. Missouri Historical Society, St. Louis, Missouri.

Minutes of the Meeting of Stockholders, March 8, 1922; November 26, 1922; April 10, 1925; April 30, 1925. *Globe-Democrat* Official Records, St. Louis, Missouri.

Missouri, State. Office of the Secretary of State, Jefferson City. Corporation Book 18, p. 398; Corporation Book 76, p. 45; Corporation Book 80, p. 398; Corporation Book 83, p. 369; Corporation Book 84, p. 213; Corporation Book 85, p. 186.

Newspaper Collection. Missouri Historical Society, St. Louis, Missouri.

E. Lansing Ray Diary. University of Missouri Library, Columbia, Missouri.

E. Lansing Ray File, *Globe-Democrat* Reference Library, St. Louis, Missouri.

St. Louis, City. General Records. Book P-6, p. 256; Book 80, p. 10; Book 258, p. 306; Book 266, p. 207; Book 446, p. 338; Book 448, p. 324; Book 453, p. 52.

Casper Yost File. *Globe-Democrat* Reference Library, St. Louis, Missouri.

B. BOOKS

Anderson, Galusha, *The Story of a Border City During the Civil War*. Boston: Little, Brown and Company, 1908.

Andrews, J. Cutler. *The North Reports the Civil War*. Pittsburgh: University of Pittsburgh Press, 1955.

Angle, Paul M. *New Letters and Papers of Lincoln*. Boston: Houghton Mifflin Company, 1930.

Anstruther, Ian. *Dr. Livingston, I Presume?* New York: E. P. Dutton and Company, 1956.

Basler, Roy P. *et al.* (ed.). *Collected Works of Abraham Lincoln*, 8 vols. New Brunswick, New Jersey: Rutgers University Press, 1953.

Bent, Silas. *Ballyhoo: The Voice of the Press*. New York: Boni and Liveright, 1927.

Churchill, Winston. *The Crisis*. New York: Grosset and Dunlap, 1901.

Cortissoz, Royal. *The Life of Whitelaw Reid*. New York: Charles Scribner's Sons, 1921.

Crighton, John Clark. *Missouri and the World War, 1914-1917: A Study in Public Opinion*. The University of Missouri Studies, Vol. XXI, no. 3, Columbia: University of Missouri, 1947.

Dennis, Charles H. *Eugene Field's Creative Years*. New York: Doubleday, Page and Company, 1924.

Devoy, John (comp.). *A History of St. Louis and Vicinity*. St. Louis: John Devoy, 1898.

Dreiser, Theodore. *A Book About Myself*. New York: Boni and Liveright, 1922.

Edwards, Richard and M. Hopewell. *Edwards' Great West*. St. Louis: *Edwards' Monthly, A Journal of Progress*, 1860.

Field, Eugene. *A Little Book of Western Verse*. New York: Charles Scribner's Sons, 1899.

Filley, C. I. *Some More Republican History of Missouri, 1856-1902*. St. Louis: Chutman Printing Company, 1902.

——————. *Some Republican History of Missouri*. St. Louis: Gast Bank Note and Lithograph Company, 1898.

Francis, David R. *The Universal Exposition of 1904*. St. Louis: Louisiana Purchase Exposition Company, 1913.

Grosvenor, William. *Does Protection Protect? An Examination of the Effect of Different Forms of Tariff upon American Industry*. New York: D. Appleton and Company, 1871.

Harper, Robert C. *Lincoln and the Press*. New York: McGraw-Hill Book Company, 1951.

Herndon, William H. and Jesse William Weik. *The Life of Lincoln*. 3 vols. Chicago: D. Appleton and Company, 1890.

History of the War in Front Pages: Actual Reproductions of Newspaper Front Pages Selected from the St. Louis Globe-Democrat, Concerning Major Events of World War II. St. Louis: St. Louis Globe-Democrat, n.d.

Horner, Charles E. *The Life of James Redpath and Development of the Modern Lyceum*. New York: Borse and Hopkins, 1926.

Hume, John F. *The Abolitionists, Together with Personal Memories of the Struggle for Human Rights, 1830-64.* New York: G. P. Putnam's Sons, 1905.

Johns, Orrick. *Time of Our Lives: The Story of My Father and Myself.* New York: Stackpole Sons, 1937.

Kelsoe, W. A. (ed.). *St. Louis Reference Book.* St. Louis: Von Hoffman Press, n.d.

Lee, Alfred McClung. *The Daily Newspaper in America: The Evolution of a Social Instrument.* New York: The Macmillan Company, 1937.

Leftwich, W. M. *Martyrdom in Missouri.* 2 vols. St. Louis: S. W. Book and Publishing Company, 1870.

Lindbergh, Charles A. *The Spirit of St. Louis.* New York: Charles Scribner's Sons, 1953.

————. *We.* New York: G. P. Putnam's Sons, 1927.

McDonald, John. *Secrets of the Whiskey Ring; and Eighteen Months in the Penitentiary.* St. Louis: W. S. Bryan, 1880.

Mangold, George B. *The Challenge of St. Louis.* New York: Missionary Education Movement of St. Louis, 1917.

Markham, James W. *Bovard of the Post-Dispatch.* Baton Rouge: Louisiana State University Press, 1954.

Memoirs of Henry Villard, Journalist and Financier, 1835-1900. 2 vols. Westminster: Archibald Constable and Company, 1904.

Mott, Frank Luther. *American Journalism: A History of Newspapers in the United States through 260 Years, 1690-1950,* revised. New York: The Macmillan Company, 1950.

Nevins, Allan. *The Emergence of Modern America, 1865-1878.* (*A History of American Life,* Vol. VIII.) New York; The Macmillan Company, 1927.

Pochman, Henry A. *New England Transcendentalism and St. Louis Hegelianism.* Philadelphia: Carl Schurz Memorial Foundation, Inc., 1948.

Redpath, James. *The Roving Reporter: or Talks with Slaves in the Southern States.* New York: A. B. Burdick, 1859.

Regier, C. C. *The Era of Muckrakers.* Chapel Hill: The University of North Carolina Press, 1932.

Robinson, Charles. *The Kansas Conflict.* New York: Harper and Brothers, 1892.

Rombauer, Robert J. *The Union Cause in St. Louis in 1861.* St. Louis: Nixon Jones Printing Company, 1909.

Rosewater, Victor. *History of Co-operative News-Gathering in the United States.* New York: D. Appleton and Company, 1930.

Schafer, Joseph. (trans.). *Intimate Letters of Carl Schurz, 1841-1869.* Madison: State Historical Society of Wisconsin, 1928.

Scharf, Thomas J. *History of Saint Louis City and County.* 2 vols. Philadelphia: Louis H. Everts and Company, 1883.

Schlesinger, Arthur Meier. *The Rise of the City, 1878-1898.* (*A History of American Life,* Vol. X.) New York: Macmillan Company, 1933.

Seitz, Don C. *Joseph Pulitzer, His Life and Letters.* New York: Simon and Schuster, 1924.

Shoemaker, Floyd C. *Missouri and Missourians.* 5 vols. Chicago: The Lewis Publishing Company, 1943.

Slosson, Preston William. *The Great Crusade and After, 1914-1928.* (*A History of American Life*, Vol. XII.) New York: The Macmillan Company, 1931.

Smith, William E. *The Francis Preston Blair Family in Politics.* 2 vols. New York: The Macmillan Company, 1933.

Snider, Denton J. *The St. Louis Movement in Philosophy, Literature, Education, Psychology with Chapters of Autobiography.* St. Louis: Sigma Publishing Company, 1920.

Stanley, Dorothy (ed.). *The Autobiography of Sir Henry Morton Stanley.* Boston: Houghton Mifflin Company, 1909.

Stevens, Walter B. *St. Louis, the Fourth City, 1784-1909.* 2 vols. St. Louis: The S. J. Clark Publishing Company, 1909.

——————. *Centennial History of Missouri* (*the Center State*), *One Hundred Years in the Union, 1820-1921.* St. Louis: The S. J. Clark Publishing Company, 1909.

——————. *The Blair-Reynolds Duel, A Complete Documentary Chronicle of the Last Bloodshed under the Code Between St. Louisans.* St. Louis: The Franklin Club, 1911.

——————. *Missouri, the Center State, 1821-1915.* St. Louis: The S. J. Clark Publishing Company, 1915.

Switzler, William F. *Switzler's Illustrated History of Missouri from 1841-1877.* St. Louis: C. R. Barnes, 1879.

Tarbell, Ida M. *The Nationalizing of Business, 1878-1898.* (*A History of American Life*, Vol. IX.) New York: The Macmillan Company, 1936.

The Reminiscences of Carl Schurz, 1841-1869. 3 vols. New York: The McClure Company, 1908.

Violette, Eugene Morrow. *A History of Missouri.* Boston: D. C. Heath and Company, 1918.

Wasserman, Jacob. *Bula Matari: Stanley, Conqueror of a Nation.* New York: Boni and Liveright, 1933.

Wecter, Dixon. *The Age of the Great Depression, 1929-1941.* (*A History of American Life*, Vol. XIII.). New York: The Macmillan Company, 1948.

Wilkerson, Marcus M. *Public Opinion and the Spanish American War: A Study in War Propaganda.* University Studies, Number 8. Baton Rouge: Louisiana State University Press, 1932.

Yost, Casper S. *Patience Worth, A Psychic Mystery.* New York: Henry Holt and Company, 1916.

——————. *The Making of a Successful Husband: Letters of a Happily Married Man to His Son.* New York: D. W. Dillingham Company, 1907.

——————. *The Making of a Successful Wife: Letters of a Father to His Daughter.* New York: D. W. Dillingham Company, 1907.

——————. *The Principles of Journalism.* New York: D. Appleton and Company, 1924.

——————. *The Quest of God, A Journalist's View of the Basis of Religious Faith.* New York: Fleming H. Revell Company, 1929.

C. PERIODICALS

"Advertisement of *St. Louis Globe-Democrat*," *Editor and Publisher*, XCII (January 17, 1959), 5.

"Alliance of Necessity," *Time*, LXXIII (March 9, 1959), 70.

"Amberg Scotches Rumor About *Globe-Democrat*," *Editor and Publisher*, XCII (March 28, 1959), 110.

Barclay, Thomas C. "The Liberal Republican Movement in Missouri," *Missouri Historical Review*, XX (October, 1925), 3-78; XXI (January, 1926), 232-262; XXI (April, 1926), 406-437; XXI (July, 1926), 515-563; XXI (October, 1926), 59-108.

Boynton, H. V. "The Whiskey Ring," *North American Review*, CXXIII (October, 1876), 282-315.

Grissom, David M. "Personal Recollections of Distinguished Missourians," *Missouri Historical Review*, XIX (April, 1925), 423-426.

Grover, George. "Civil War in Missouri," *Missouri Historical Review*, VIII (October, 1913), 1-28.

Guese, Lucius E. "St. Louis and the Great Whiskey Ring," *Missouri Historical Review*, XXXVI (January, 1942), 160-189.

"Historical Notes and Comments," *Missouri Historical Review*, XXXVII (October, 1942), 107-108.

"June 1 Target Date for *Globe-Democrat*," *Editor and Publisher*, XCII (May 5, 1959), 10.

Laughlin, Scera Bright. "Missouri Politics During the Civil War," *Missouri Historical Review*, XXIII (April, 1929), 400-426; XXIII (July, 1929), 583-618; XXIV (October, 1929), 87-113; XXIV (January, 1930), 261-284.

"List of Old-Timers," *Overset*, I (January, 1952), 5.

McAuliffe, Joseph J. "From Blacksmith to Boss," *Leslie's Monthly Magazine*, LVIII (October, 1904), 635-639.

"Message of James C. Burkham, President," *Overset*, I (January, 1952), 2.

"New Presses Installed," *Overset*, I (January, 1952), 1.

"Newspapers Break Lineage Records in 1925," *Editor and Publisher*, LVIII (January 9, 1926), 5.

Organ, Minnie. "History of the County Press in Missouri," *Missouri Historical Review*, IV (January, 1910), 111-133; IV (April, 1910), 149-166; IV (July, 1910), 252-308.

"Pact Near in Newhouse Negotiations," *Editor and Publisher*, XCII (May 16, 1959), 16.

"Page and Paper Sizes and Other Mechanical Data of 2,000 Dailies," *Editor and Publisher*, LXIII (October 25, 1930), 23.

"Peeking Lens Shows Cops in Gambling Spot," *Editor and Publisher*, XCII (January 17, 1959), 58.

"Pulitzer Urges End of Rival's Shutdown," *Editor and Publisher*, XCII (April 18, 1959), 16.

"*Republic* Sale," *Editor and Publisher*, LII (December 11, 1919), 28.

"*St. Louis Globe-Democrat* Closes in Pension Dispute," *Editor and Publisher*, XCII (February 28, 1959), 52.

"*St. Louis Globe-Democrat* Goes to Contract Printing," *Editor and Publisher,* XCII (February 28, 1959), 13.

"*St. Louis Globe-Democrat* Set to Roll Again July 21," *Editor and Publisher,* XCII (May 5, 1959), 10.

"Seeds in St. Louis," *Time,* LXIII (June 1, 1959), 66.

"Senators to Probe in St. Louis Strike," *Editor and Publisher,* XCII (April 24, 1959), 121.

Smith, George Winston. "New England Business Interests in Missouri During the Civil War," *Missouri Historical Review,* XLI (October, 1946), 1-18.

Stevens, Walter B. "Joseph B. McCullagh," *Missouri Historical Review,* XXV October, 1930), 3-9; XXV (January, 1931), 245-253; XXV (April, 1931), 425-431; XXV (July, 1931), 576-584; XXVI (October, 1931), 40-53; XXVI (January, 1932), 153-162; XXVI (April, 1932), 256-266; XXVI (July, 1932), 375-386; XXVII (October, 1932), 50-62; XXVII (January, 1933), 151-156; XXVII (April, 1933), 257-261; XXVII (July, 1933), 337-343; XXVIII (October, 1933), 38-42; XXVIII (January, 1934), 125-129; XXVIII (April, 1934), 206-210.

—————————. "Lincoln and Missouri," *Missouri Historical Review,* X (January, 1916), 63-119; XVIII (April, 1924), 382-391.

—————————. "The New Journalism in Missouri," *Missouri Historical Review,* XVII (April, 1923), 321-331; XVII (July, 1923), 470-478; XVIII (October, 1923), 55-63; XVIII (January, 1924), 197-211; XVIII (April, 1924), 404-414; XVIII (July, 1924), 553-561; XIX (October, 1924), 105-113; XIX (January, 1925), 325-337; XIX (April, 1925), 427-437; XIX (July, 1925), 675-688.

—————————. "The Political Turmoil of 1874 in Missouri," *Missouri Historical Review,* XXXI (October, 1936), 3-9.

—————————. "The Tragedy of the *St. Louis Republic*," *Missouri Historical Review,* XXII (January, 1928), 139-149.

"The Empire Builder," *Time,* LXII (August 11, 1958), 56.

Viles, Jonas. "Sections and Sectionalism in a Border State," *The Mississippi Valley Historical Review,* XXI (June, 1934), 3-22.

Watterson, Henry W. "The Personal Equation in Journalism," *Atlantic Monthly,* CVI (July, 1910), 40-47.

"We're Back! *Globe* Tells St. Louis," *Editor and Publisher,* XCII (June 6, 1959), 12.

Wilcox, Delos F. "The American Newspaper, A Study in Social Psychology," *Annals of the American Academy of Political and Social Science,* XVI (July, 1900), 56-92.

D. PUBLICATIONS OF THE GOVERNMENT, LEARNED SOCIETIES, AND OTHER ORGANIZATIONS

Abstract of the Twelfth Census of the United States, 1900, ed. William R. Merrian, Director of the United States Census Office. Washington: Government Printing Office, 1902.

History of Kansas Newspapers. Kansas State Historical Society and Department of Archives. Topeka: Kansas State Printing Company, 1916.

Johnson, Charles P. "Personal Recollection of Some of Missouri's Eminent Statesmen and Lawyers," *Proceedings of State Historical Society of Missouri,* 1903.

Problems of Journalism: Proceedings of the Second Annual Meeting of the American Society of Newspaper Editors. Atlantic City, April 25-26, 1924.

Southwestern Reporter. Vol. 127. St. Paul: West Publishing Company, 1910.

Testimony Before Select Committee Concerning the Whiskey Frauds (44th Cong., 1st sess.; H. R. Misc. Doc. 186). Washington, D. C.: Government Printing Office, 1876.

U. S. Census Office. *The Eleventh Census, 1890.* Pt. I. Washington, D. C.: Government Printing Office, 1890.

War of Rebellion, Official Records. Series I, Vol. 22; Series II, Vol. 6. Washington, D. C.: Government Printing Office, 1894.

E. UNPUBLISHED MATERIALS

"Autobiography of Charles D. Drake." Unpublished manuscript, State Historical Society of Missouri, Columbia.

Byars, William Vincent (ed.). "Issues of Civil War under Pierce Administration as Illustrated in Hostile Correspondence and Duel Between B. Gratz Brown and Thomas C. Reynolds." Unpublished manuscript, Missouri Historical Society, St. Louis.

Geiger, Louis M. "The Public Career of Joseph W. Folk." Unpublished doctoral dissertation, University of Missouri, Columbia, 1948.

Hammond, T. B. "The Development of Journalism in Missouri." Unpublished Master's thesis, University of Missouri, Columbia, 1922.

Hartt, Marie. "A Comparative History of the Development of Society News in the *Kansas City Star* and the *St. Louis Globe-Democrat,* 1876-1934." Unpublished Master's thesis, University of Missouri, Columbia, 1935.

Johnson, Edwin Hennessy. "What Constitutes Libel in Missouri." Unpublished Master's thesis, University of Missouri, Columbia, 1938.

Lindsay, William Leon. "A Biography of David R. McAnally, Jr." Unpublished Master's thesis, University of Missouri, Columbia, 1956.

March, David DeArmond. "The Life and Times of Charles Daniel Drake." Unpublished doctoral dissertation, University of Missouri, Columbia, 1949.

Nowels, Ida Mae. "A Study of the Radical Party Movement in Missouri, 1860-1870." Unpublished Master's thesis, University of Missouri, Columbia, 1939.

Padgitt, James Harry. "The History and Development of the Sports Pages as Typified by the *St. Louis Globe-Democrat,* 1876-1938." Unpublished Master's thesis, University of Missouri, Columbia, 1939.

Patterson, Norma Lois. "B. Gratz Brown, The Rise of a Radical, 1850-63." Unpublished doctoral dissertation, University of Missouri, Columbia, 1953.

Tasher, Lucy L. "The *Missouri Democrat* and the Civil War." Unpublished doctoral dissertation, University of Chicago, Chicago, 1936.

Ulbricht, John Harold. "Frank P. Blair, Jr., and Missouri Politics." Unpublished Master's thesis, University of Missouri, Columbia, 1936.

F. NEWSPAPERS

Boonville Weekly Advertiser, November 12, 1875; January 28, 1876; January 2, 1877; December 26, 1879; May 19, 1905. State Historical Society of Missouri, Columbia.

Jefferson City Daily Democrat, March 21, 1911. State Historical Society of Missouri, Columbia.

Jefferson City Democrat Tribune, November 20, 1916; December 3, 1919. State Historical Society of Missouri, Columbia.

Jefferson City Examiner, March 8, 1856. State Historical Society of Missouri, Columbia.

Jefferson City Missouri State Tribune, December 8, 1899; May 4, 1900; August 21, 1901. State Historical Society of Missouri, Columbia.

Jefferson City People's Tribune, August 1, 1866; May 19, 1875. State Historical Society of Missouri, Columbia.

Jefferson City State Times, October 5, 1866. State Historical Society of Missouri, Columbia.

Jefferson City Times, March 4, 1865. State Historical Society of Missouri, Columbia.

Liberty Tribune (Liberty, Missouri), December 18, 1857; March 25, 1859; November 1, 1861; May 10, 29, 1867. State Historical Society of Missouri, Columbia.

Missouri Republican (St. Louis), July 17, August 7, 1852; May 11, 1861; January 21-31, 1876; February 1, 1876; December 21, 1879. State Historical Society of Missouri, Columbia.

Missouri State Tribune (St. Louis), December 8, 1899; May 4, 1900; August 21, 1901. State Historical Society of Missouri, Columbia.

New York Times, January 1, 1897; March 16, 1915; May 2, 31, July 10, 1941; March 24, August 31, December 31, 1955.

St. Louis Chamber of Commerce News, November 12, 1928–December 31, 1929. St. Louis Public Library.

St. Louis Dispatch, November 4, 1873; January 7, 1874; January 18–February 1, 1876. State Historical Society of Missouri, Columbia.

St. Louis Globe, July 18, 1872–May 19, 1875. State Historical Society of Missouri, Columbia.

St. Louis Globe-Democrat, May 20, 1875–August 2, 1959. State Historical Society of Missouri, Columbia.

St. Louis Intelligencer, August 10, 17, September 28, December 21, 28, 1852; June 3, 1853. State Historical Society of Missouri, Columbia.

St. Louis Post-Dispatch, December 20, 1879; December 31, 1896; October 10, 1915; March 24, 1955; February 22, May 23, 28, 1959. State Historical Society of Missouri, Columbia.

St. Louis Republic, January 1, 2, 1897; March 16, 1915. State Historical Society of Missouri, Columbia.

St. Louis Times, January 22, April 15, December 16, 1876. State Historical Society of Missouri, Columbia.

The Daily Missouri Democrat (St. Louis), October 13, 17, 29, 31, 1852. The Library of Congress, Washington, D. C.

The Daily Missouri Democrat (St. Louis), April 5, 1853—May 19, 1875. State Historical Society of Missouri, Columbia.

Weekly Globe-Democrat, December 25, 1879. State Historical Society of Missouri, Columbia.

G. INTERVIEWS AND LETTERS

Interview with G. D. Bauman, personnel director of the *Globe-Democrat*, October 16, 1958.

Interview with Douglas B. Houser, former vice-president of the *Globe-Democrat*, September 2, 1958.

Interview with Louis LaCoss, editor-emeritus of the editorial page of the *Globe-Democrat*, October 18, 1958.

Interviews with Herman Wilkat, auditor of the *Globe-Democrat*, July 17, 1958, and September 3, 1958.

Letters from Richard H. Amberg, publisher of the *Globe-Democrat*, August 17, 1957, and August 8, 1960.

Letter from G. D. Bauman, personnel director of the *Globe-Democrat*, August 6, 1958.

Letters from Douglas B. Houser, former vice-president of the *Globe-Democrat*, August 17, 1958, and August 28, 1958.

Letter from Louis LaCoss, editor-emeritus of the editorial page of the *Globe-Democrat*, October 10, 1958.

Letter from John H. Thaxter, acting chief, Serial Division, Library of Congress, July 25, 1958.

H. REFERENCE WORKS

Dictionary of American Biography, ed. Allen Johnson and Dumas Malone. 18 vols. New York: Charles Scribner's Sons, 1933.

Editor and Publisher International Yearbook, 1858.

Encyclopaedia of the City of St. Louis. 2 vols. New York: The Southern History Company, 1899.

Encyclopaedia of the History of Missouri. 6 vols. New York: The Southern History Company, 1901.

Gould's St. Louis Directory, 1874-1880.

Hubbard's Newspaper and Bank Directory. Vols. I and III. New Haven: Tuttle, Morehouse, and Taylor, 1882-1884.

Kennedy, J. G. C. *Catalog of Newspapers and Periodicals*, 1852.

Kennedy's St. Louis Directory, 1857.

Kenny, D. J. *American Newspaper Directory*, 1861.

Morrison's St. Louis Directory, 1852.

N. W. Ayer and Sons American Newspaper Annual and Directory, 1880-1929.

N. W. Ayer and Sons Directory of Newspapers and Periodicals, 1930-1958.

Pettengill's Newspaper Directory, 1877-1879.

St. Louis Directory, 1854-1856.

St. Louis Business Directory, 1853-1854.

Who Was Who in America, 1897-1942. Vol. I. Chicago: A. N. Marquis Company, 1942.

I. MISCELLANEOUS

Phillips, Ulrich B. "The Southern Whig, 1834-1854," *Essays in American History Dedicated to Frederick Jackson Turner*. New York: Henry Holt, 1910.

Grosvenor, William Mason. *Address of the Radicals of St. Louis to the People of Missouri by Grosvenor, Emil Preetorius, Clinton B. Fish, et al.* St. Louis: Missouri Democrat Book and Job Office, 1868. Pamphlet.

Hencke, Paul G. (comp.) *The Beginnings and the Growth of a Great Newspaper, the St. Louis Globe-Democrat.* Pamphlet. April 16, 1954.

Hyde, William. "Newspapers and Newspaper People of Three Decades," *Missouri Historical Society Collections*, Vol. I, No. 12, 1896.

St. Louis As It Is Today. St. Louis Chamber of Commerce. Pamphlet, 1938.

St. Louis Facts—A Municipal Record. St. Louis Chamber of Commerce. Pamphlet, 1924.

The University of Missouri Bulletin, Journalism Series, Vol. 33, No. 66.

The University of Missouri Bulletin, Journalism Series, Vol. 53, No. 129.

The University of Missouri Bulletin, Journalism Series, Vol. 47, No. 106.

What Makes the Globe-Democrat a Great Newspaper. Pamphlet, n.d.

Index